THE

SEVEN LAMPS

OF

ARCHITECTURE

THE SEVEN LAMPS OF ARCHITECTURE

JOHN RUSKIN

Including illustrations drawn and etched by the author

FARRAR, STRAUS AND GIROUX

NEW YORK

Tenth printing, 1986

Manufactured in the U.S.A.

CONTENTS.

SEVEN LAMPS OF ARCHITECTURE

LIST OF ILLUSTRATIONS.

PLATE 1.

I. ORNAMENTS FROM ROUEN, ST. LO, AND VENICE

II. Part of the Cathedral of St. Lo, Normandy

PLATE III.

III. Traceries from Caen, Bayeux, Rouen and Beavais

PLATE IV.

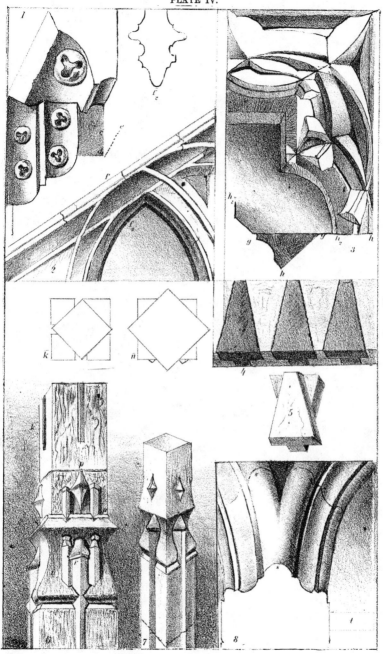

IV. INTERSECTIONAL MOULDINGS

PLATE V.

V. CAPITAL FROM THE LOWER ARCADE OF THE DOGE'S
PALACE, VENICE

VI. Arch from the Facade of the Church of San
Michele at Lucca

PLATE VII.

VII. Pierced Ornaments from Lisieux, Bayeux, Verona, and Padua

PLATE VIII.

VIII. WINDOW FROM THE CA' FOSCARI, VENICE

PLATE IX.

IX. Tracery from the Campanile of Giotto, at Florence

PLATE X.

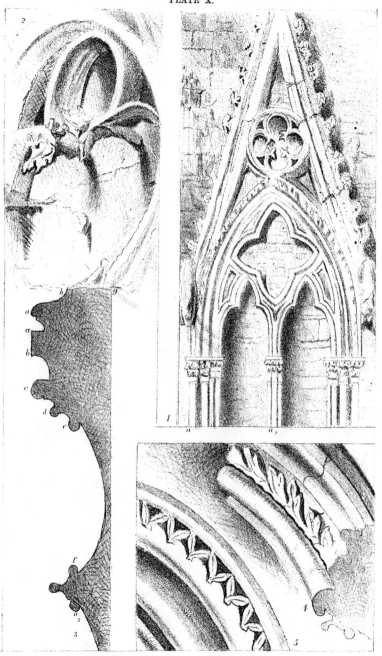

X. Traceries and Mouldings from Rouen and Salisbury.

PLATE XI.

XI. Balcony in the Campo, St. Benedetto, Venice

PLATE XII.

XII. FRAGMENTS FROM ABBEVILLE, LUCCA, VENICE AND PISA

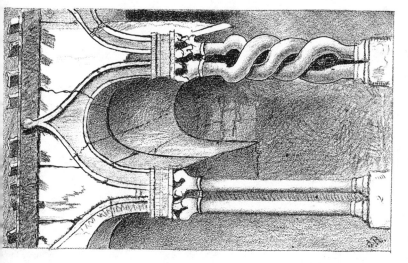

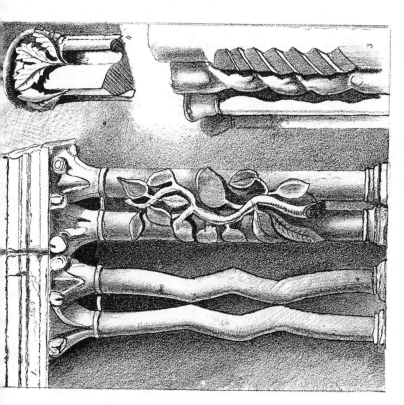

XIII. Portions of an Arcade on the South Side of the
Cathedral of Ferrara

PLATE XIV.

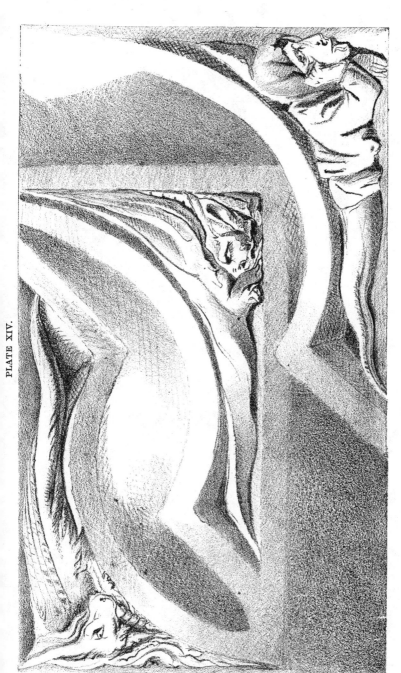

XIV. Sculptures from the Cathedral of Rouen

PREFACE.

THE memoranda which form the basis of the following Essay have been thrown together during the preparation of one of the sections of the third volume of "Modern Painters." * I once thought of giving them a more expanded form; but their utility, such as it may be, would probably be diminished by farther delay in their publication, more than it would be increased by greater care in their arrangement. Obtained in every case by personal observation, there may be among them some details valuable even to the experienced architect; but with respect to the opinions founded upon them I must be prepared to bear the charge of impertinence which can hardly but attach to the writer who assumes a dogmatical tone in speaking of an art he has never practised. There are, however, cases in which men feel too keenly to be silent, and perhaps too strongly to be wrong; I have been forced into this impertinence; and have suffered too much from the destruction or neglect of the architecture I best loved, and from the erection of that which I cannot love, to reason cautiously re-

---

* The inordinate delay in the appearance of that supplementary volume has, indeed, been chiefly owing to the necessity under which the writer felt himself, of obtaining as many memoranda as possible of mediæval buildings in Italy and Normandy, now in process of destruction, before that destruction should be consummated by the Restorer or Revolutionist. His whole time has been lately occupied in taking drawings from one side of buildings, of which masons were knocking down the other; nor can he yet pledge himself to any time for the publication of the conclusion of "Modern Painters;" he can only promise that its delay shall not be owing to any indolence on his part.

specting the modesty of my opposition to the principles which have induced the scorn of the one, or directed the design of the other. And I have been the less careful to modify the confidence of my statements of principles, because in the midst of the opposition and uncertainty of our architectural systems, it seems to me that there is something grateful in any *positive* opinion, though in many points wrong, as even weeds are useful that grow on a bank of sand.

Every apology is, however, due to the reader, for the hasty and imperfect execution of the plates. Having much more serious work in hand, and desiring merely to render them illustrative of my meaning, I have sometimes very completely failed even of that humble aim ; and the text, being generally written before the illustration was completed, sometimes naïvely describes as sublime or beautiful, features which the plate represents by a blot. I shall be grateful if the reader will in such cases refer the expressions of praise to the Architecture, and not to the illustration.

So far, however, as their coarseness and rudeness admit, the plates are valuable ; being either copies of memoranda made upon the spot, or (Plates IX. and XI.) enlarged and adapted from Daguerreotypes, taken under my own superintendence. Unfortunately, the great distance from the ground of the window which is the subject of Plate IX. renders even the Daguerreotype indistinct ; and I cannot answer for the accuracy of any of the mosaic details, more especially of those which surround the window, and which I rather imagine, in the original, to be sculptured in relief. The general proportions are, however, studiously preserved ; the spirals of the shafts are counted, and the effect of the whole is as near that of the thing itself, as is necessary for the purposes of illustration for which the plate is given. For the accuracy of the rest I can answer, even to the cracks in the stones, and the number of them ; and though the looseness of the drawing, and the picturesque character which is necessarily given by an endeavor to draw old buildings as they actually appear, may perhaps diminish their credit for architectural veracity, they will do so unjustly.

The system of lettering adopted in the few instances in which sections have been given, appears somewhat obscure in the references, but it is convenient upon the whole. The line which marks the direction of any section is noted, if the section be symmetrical, by a single letter; and the section itself by the same letter with a line over it, *a.*—*ā*. But if the section be unsymmetrical, its direction is noted by two letters, *a. a. a₂* at its extremities; and the actual section by the same letters with lines over them, *ā. ā. ā₂*, at the corresponding extremities.

The reader will perhaps be surprised by the small number of buildings to which reference has been made. But it is to be remembered that the following chapters pretend only to be a statement of principles, illustrated each by one or two examples, not an essay on European architecture; and those examples I have generally taken either from the buildings which I love best, or from the schools of architecture which, it appeared to me, have been less carefully described than they deserved. I could as fully, though not with the accuracy and certainty derived from personal observation, have illustrated the principles subsequently advanced, from the architecture of Egypt, India, or Spain, as from that to which the reader will find his attention chiefly directed, the Italian Romanesque and Gothic. But my affections, as well as my experience, led me to that line of richly varied and magnificently intellectual schools, which reaches, like a high watershed of Christian architecture, from the Adriatic to the Northumbrian seas, bordered by the impure schools of Spain on the one hand, and of Germany on the other: and as culminating points and centres of this chain, I have considered, first, the cities of the Val d'Arno, as representing the Italian Romanesque and pure Italian Gothic; Venice and Verona as representing the Italian Gothic colored by Byzantine elements; and Rouen, with the associated Norman cities, Caen, Bayeux, and Coutances, as representing the entire range of Northern architecture from the Romanesque to Flamboyant.

I could have wished to have given more examples from our early English Gothic; but I have always found it impossible to work in the cold interiors of our cathedrals, while the daily services, lamps, and fumigation of those upon the Continent, render them perfectly safe. In the course of last summer I undertook a pilgrimage to the English Shrines, and began with Salisbury, where the consequence of a few days' work was a state of weakened health, which I may be permitted to name among the causes of the slightness and imperfection of the present Essay.

INTRODUCTORY.

SOME years ago, in conversation with an artist whose works, perhaps, alone, in the present day, unite perfection of drawing with resplendence of color, the writer made some inquiry respecting the general means by which this latter quality was most easily to be attained. The reply was as concise as it was comprehensive—" Know what you have to do, and do it " —comprehensive, not only as regarded the branch of art to which it temporarily applied, but as expressing the great principle of success in every direction of human effort ; for I believe that failure is less frequently attributable to either insufficiency of means or impatience of labor, than to a confused understanding of the thing actually to be done ; and therefore, while it is properly a subject of ridicule, and sometimes of blame, that men propose to themselves a perfection of any kind, which reason, temperately consulted, might have shown to be impossible with the means at their command, it is a more dangerous error to permit the consideration of means to interfere with our conception, or, as is not impossible, even hinder our acknowledgment of goodness and perfection in themselves. And this is the more cautiously to be remembered ; because, while a man's sense and conscience, aided by Revelation, are always enough, if earnestly directed, to enable him to discover what is right, neither his sense, nor conscience, nor feeling, are ever enough, because they are not intended, to determine for him what is possible. He knows neither his own strength nor that of his fellows, neither the exact dependence to be placed on his allies nor resistance to be expected from his opponents. These are questions respecting which passion may warp his conclusions, and ignorance must limit

them ; but it is his own fault if either interfere with the apprehension of duty, or the acknowledgment of right. And, as
far as I have taken cognizance of the causes of the many failures to which the efforts of intelligent men are liable, more
especially in matters political, they seem to me more largely
to spring from this single error than from all others, that the
inquiry into the doubtful, and in some sort inexplicable, relations of capability, chance, resistance, and inconvenience, in-
variably precedes, even if it do not altogether supersede, the
determination of what is absolutely desirable and just. Nor
is it any wonder that sometimes the too cold calculation of
our powers should reconcile us too easily to our shortcomings,
and even lead us into the fatal error of supposing that our
conjectural utmost is in itself well, or, in other words, that
the necessity of offences renders them inoffensive.

What is true of human polity seems to me not less so of the
distinctively political art of Architecture. I have long felt convinced of the necessity, in order to its progress, of some determined effort to extricate from the confused mass of partial
traditions and dogmata with which it has become encumbered
during imperfect or restricted practice, those large principles
of right which are applicable to every stage and style of it.
Uniting the technical and imaginative elements as essentially
as humanity does soul and body, it shows the same infirmly
balanced liability to the prevalence of the lower part over the
higher, to the interference of the constructive, with the purity
and simplicity of the reflective, element. This tendency, like
every other form of materialism, is increasing with the advance
of the age ; and the only laws which resist it, based upon
partial precedents, and already regarded with disrespect as
decrepit, if not with defiance as tyrannical, are evidently in-
applicable to the new forms and functions of the art, which
the necessities of the day demand. How many these necessities
may become, cannot be conjectured ; they rise, strange and
impatient, out of every modern shadow of change. How far
it may be possible to meet them without a sacrifice of the essential characters of architectural art, cannot be determined
by specific calculation or observance. There is no law, no

principle, based on past practice, which may not be overthrown in a moment, by the arising of a new condition, or the invention of a new material ; and the most rational, if not the only, mode of averting the danger of an utter dissolution of all that is systematic and consistent in our practice, or of ancient authority in our judgment, is to cease for a little while, our endeavors to deal with the multiplying host of particular abuses, restraints, or requirements ; and endeavor to determine, as the guides of every effort, some constant, general, and irrefragable laws of right—laws, which based upon man's nature, not upon his knowledge, may possess so far the unchangeableness of the one, as that neither the increase nor imperfection of the other may be able to assault or invalidate them.

There are, perhaps, no such laws peculiar to any one art. Their range necessarily includes the entire horizon of man's action. But they have modified forms and operations belonging to each of his pursuits, and the extent of their authority cannot surely be considered as a diminution of its weight. Those peculiar aspects of them which belong to the first of the arts, I have endeavored to trace in the following pages ; and since, if truly stated, they must necessarily be, not only safeguards against every form of error, but sources of every measure of success, I do not think that I claim too much for them in calling them the Lamps of Architecture, nor that it is indolence, in endeavoring to ascertain the true nature and nobility of their fire, to refuse to enter into any curious or special questioning of the innumerable hindrances by which their light has been too often distorted or overpowered.

Had this farther examination been attempted, the work would have become certainly more invidious, and perhaps less useful, as liable to errors which are avoided by the present simplicity of its plan. Simple though it be, its extent is too great to admit of any adequate accomplishment, unless by a devotion of time which the writer did not feel justified in withdrawing from branches of inquiry in which the prosecution of works already undertaken has engaged him. Both arrangements and nomenclature are those of convenience rather than of system ; the one is arbitrary and the other illogical : nor is it pretended that all, or even the greater number of, the prin⸱ ciples necessary to the well-being of the art, are included in the inquiry.   Many, however, of considerable importance will be found to develope themselves incidentally from those more specially brought forward.

Graver apology is necessary for an apparently graver fault. It has been just said, that there is no branch of human work whose constant laws have not close analogy with those which govern every other mode of man's exertion.   But, more than this, exactly as we reduce to greater simplicity and surety any one group of these practical laws, we shall find them passing the mere condition of connection or analogy, and becoming the actual expression of some ultimate nerve or fibre of the mighty laws which govern the moral world.   However mean or inconsiderable the act, there is something in the well doing of it, which has fellowship with the noblest forms of manly virtue ; and the truth, decision, and temperance, which we reverently regard as honorable conditions of the spiritual being, have a representative or derivative influence over the works of the hand, the movements of the frame, and the action of the intellect.

And as thus every action, down even to the drawing of a line or utterance of a syllable, is capable of a peculiar dignity in the manner of it, which we sometimes express by saying it is truly done (as a line or tone is true), so also it is capable of dignity still higher in the motive of it.   For there is no action so slight, nor so mean, but it may be done to a great purpose, and ennobled therefore ; nor is any purpose so great but that slight actions may help it, and may be so done as to help it much, most especially that chief of all purposes, the pleasing of God.   Hence George Herbert—

> " A servant with this clause
>   Makes drudgery divine ;
> Who sweeps a room, as for thy laws,
>   Makes that and the action fine."

Therefore, in the pressing or recommending of any act or manner of acting, we have choice of two separate lines of ar⸱

gument : one based on representation of the expediency or inherent value of the work, which is often small, and always disputable ; the other based on proofs of its relations to the higher orders of human virtue, and of its acceptableness, so far as it goes, to Him who is the origin of virtue. The former is commonly the more persuasive method, the latter assuredly the more conclusive ; only it is liable to give offence, as if there were irreverence in adducing considerations so weighty in treating subjects of small temporal importance. I believe, however, that no error is more thoughtless than this. We treat God with irreverence by banishing Him from our thoughts, not by referring to His will on slight occasions. His is not the finite authority or intelligence which cannot be troubled with small things. There is nothing so small but that we may honor God by asking His guidance of it, or insult Him by taking it into our own hands ; and what is true of the Deity is equally true of His Revelation. We use it most reverently when most habitually : our insolence is in ever acting without reference to it, our true honoring of it is in its universal application. I have been blamed for the familiar introduction of its sacred words. I am grieved to have given pain by so doing ; but my excuse must be my wish that those words were made the ground of every argument and the test of every action. We have them not often enough on our lips, nor deeply enough in our memories, nor loyally enough in our lives. The snow, the vapor, and the stormy wind fulfil His word. Are our acts and thoughts lighter and wilder than these—that we should forget it ?

I have therefore ventured, at the risk of giving to some passages the appearance of irreverence, to take the higher line of argument wherever it appeared clearly traceable : and this, I would ask the reader especially to observe, not merely because I think it the best mode of reaching ultimate truth, still less because I think the subject of more importance than many others ; but because every subject should surely, at a period like the present, be taken up in this spirit, or not at all. The aspect of the years that approach us is as solemn as it is full of mystery ; and the weight of evil against which we have to contend, is increasing like the letting out of water. It is no time for the idleness of metaphysics, or the entertainment of the arts. The blasphemies of the earth are sounding louder, and its miseries heaped heavier every day; and if, in the midst of the exertion which every good man is called upon to put forth for their repression or relief, it is lawful to ask for a thought, for a moment, for a lifting of the finger, in any direction but that of the immediate and overwhelming need, it is at least incumbent upon us to approach the questions in which we would engage him, in the spirit which has become the habit of his mind, and in the hope that neither his zeal nor his usefulness may be checked by the withdrawal of an hour which has shown him how even those things which seemed mechanical, indifferent, or contemptible, depend for their perfection upon the acknowledgment of the sacred principles of faith, truth, and obedience, for which it has become the occupation of his life to contend.

THE

SEVEN LAMPS OF ARCHITECTURE.

CHAPTER I.

I. Architecture is the art which so disposes and adorns the edifices raised by man for whatsoever uses, that the sight or them contributes to his mental health, power and pleasure.

It is very necessary, in the outset of all inquiry, to distinguish carefully between Architecture and Building.

To build, literally to confirm, is by common understanding to put together and adjust the several pieces of any edifice or receptacle of a considerable size. Thus we have church building, house building, ship building, and coach building. That one edifice stands, another floats, and another is suspended on iron springs, makes no difference in the nature of the art, if so it may be called, of building or edification. The persons who profess that art, are severally builders, ecclesiastical, naval, or of whatever other name their work may justify ; but building does not become architecture merely by the stability of what it erects ; and it is no more architecture which raises a church, or which fits it to receive and contain with comfort a required number of persons occupied in certain religious offices, than it is architecture which makes a carriage commodious or a ship swift. I do not, of course, mean that the word is not often, or even may not be legitimately, applied in such a sense (as we speak of naval architecture) ; but in that sense architecture ceases to be one of the fine arts, and it is therefore better not to run the risk, by loose nomenclature, of the confusion which would arise, and has often arisen, from extending principles which belong altogether to building, into the sphere of architecture proper.

Let us, therefore, at once confine the name to that art which, taking up and admitting, as conditions of its working, the necessities and common uses of the building, impresses on its form certain characters venerable or beautiful, but other-wise unnecessary. Thus, I suppose, no one would call the laws architectural which determine the height of a breastwork or the position of a bastion. But if to the stone facing of that bastion be added an unnecessary feature, as a cable moulding, *that* is Architecture. It would be similarly unreasonable to call battlements or machicolations architectural features, so long as they consist only of an advanced gallery supported on projecting masses, with open intervals beneath for offence. But if these projecting masses be carved beneath into rounded courses, which are useless, and if the headings of the intervals be arched and trefoiled, which is useless, *that* is Architecture. It may not be always easy to draw the line so sharply and simply, because there are few buildings which have not some pretence or color of being architectural; neither can there be any architecture which is not based on building, nor any good architecture which is not based on good building ; but it is perfectly easy and very necessary to keep the ideas dis-tinct, and to understand fully that Architecture concerns itself only with those characters of an edifice which are above and beyond its common use. I say common ; because a building raised to the honor of God, or in memory of men, has surely a use to which its architectural adornment fits it ; but not a use which limits, by any inevitable necessities, its plan or details.

II. Architecture proper, then, naturally arranges itself un-der five heads :—

Devotional ; including all buildings raised for God's ser-vice or honor.

Memorial ; including both monuments and tombs.

Civil ; including every edifice raised by nations or societies, for purposes of common business or pleasure.

Military ; including all private and public architecture of defence.

Domestic; including every rank and kind of dwelling-place.

Now, of the principles which I would endeavor to develope, while all must be, as I have said, applicable to every stage and style of the art, some, and especially those which are exciting rather than directing, have necessarily fuller reference to one kind of building than another ; and among these I would place first that spirit which, having influence in all, has nevertheless such especial reference to devotional and memorial architecture—the spirit which offers for such work precious things simply because they are precious ; not as being necessary to the building, but as an offering, surrendering, and sacrifice of what is to ourselves desirable. It seems to me, not only that this feeling is in most cases wholly wanting in those who forward the devotional buildings of the present day ; but that it would even be regarded as an ignorant, dangerous, or perhaps criminal principle by many among us. I have not space to enter into dispute of all the various objections which may be urged against it—they are many and spacious; but I may, perhaps, ask the reader's patience while I set down those simple reasons which cause me to believe it a good and just feeling, and as well-pleasing to God and honorable in men, as it is beyond all dispute necessary to the production of any great work in the kind with which we are at present concerned,

III. Now, first, to define this Lamp, or Spirit of Sacrifice, clearly. I have said that it prompts us to the offering of precious things merely because they are precious, not because they are useful or necessary. It is a spirit, for instance, which of two marbles, equally beautiful, applicable and durable, would choose the more costly because it was so, and of two kinds of decoration, equally effective, would choose the more elaborate because it was so, in order that it might in the same compass present more cost and more thought. It is therefore most unreasoning and enthusiastic, and perhaps best negatively defined, as the opposite of the prevalent feeling of modern times, which desires to produce the largest results at the least cost.

Of this feeling, then, there are two distinct forms : the first, the wish to exercise self-denial for the sake of self-discipline merely, a wish acted upon in the abandonment of things loved or desired, there being no direct call or purpose to be answered by so doing ; and the second, the desire to honor or please some one else by the costliness of the sacrifice. The practice is, in the first case, either private or public ; but most frequently, and perhaps most properly, private ; while, in the latter case, the act is commonly, and with greatest advantage, public. Now, it cannot but at first appear futile to assert the expediency of self-denial for its own sake, when, for so many sakes, it is every day necessary to a far greater degree than any of us practise it. But I believe it is just because we do not enough acknowledge or contemplate it as a good in itself, that we are apt to fail in its duties when they become imperative, and to calculate, with some partiality, whether the good proposed to others measures or warrants the amount of grievance to ourselves, instead of accepting with gladness the opportunity of sacrifice as a personal advantage. Be this as it may, it is not necessary to insist upon the matter here ; since there are always higher and more useful channels of self-sacrifice, for those who choose to practise it, than any connected with the arts.

While in its second branch, that which is especially concerned with the arts, the justice of the feeling is still more doubtful ; it depends on our answer to the broad question, Can the Deity be indeed honored by the presentation to Him of any material objects of value, or by any direction of zeal or wisdom which is not immediately beneficial to men ?

For, observe, it is not now the question whether the fairness and majesty of a building may or may not answer any moral purpose ; it is not the *result* of labor in any sort of which we are speaking, but the bare and mere costliness—the substance and labor and time themselves : are these, we ask, independently of their result, acceptable offerings to God, and considered by Him as doing Him honor ? So long as we refer this question to the decision of feeling, or of conscience, or of reason merely, it will be contradictorily or imperfectly answered ; it admits of entire answer only when we have met another and a far different question, whether the Bible be indeed one book or two, and whether the character of God revealed in the Old Testament be other than His character revealed in the New.

IV. Now, it is a most secure truth, that, although the particular ordinances divinely appointed for special purposes at any given period of man's history, may be by the same divine authority abrogated at another, it is impossible that any character of God, appealed to or described in any ordinance past or present, can ever be changed, or understood as changed, by the abrogation of that ordinance. God is one and the same, and is pleased or displeased by the same things for ever, although one part of His pleasure may be expressed at one time rather than another, and although the mode in which His pleasure is to be consulted may be by Him graciously modified to the circumstances of men. Thus, for instance, it was necessary that, in order to the understanding by man of the scheme of Redemption, that scheme should be foreshown from the beginning by the type of bloody sacrifice. But God had no more pleasure in such sacrifice in the time of Moses than He has now ; He never accepted as a propitiation for sin any sacrifice but the single one in prospective ; and that we may not entertain any shadow of doubt on this subject, the worthlessness of all other sacrifice than this is proclaimed at the very time when typical sacrifice was most imperatively demanded. God was a spirit, and could be worshipped only in spirit and in truth, as singly and exclusively when every day brought its claim of typical and material service or offering, as now when He asks for none but that of the heart.

So, therefore, it is a most safe and sure principle that, if in the manner of performing any rite at any time, circumstances can be traced which we are either told, or may legitimately conclude, *pleased* God at that time, those same circumstances will please Him at all times, in the performance of all rites or offices to which they may be attached in like manner; unless it has been afterwards revealed that, for some special purpose, it is now His will that such circumstances should be withdrawn. And this argument will have all the more force if it can be shown that such conditions were not essential to the completeness of the rite in its human uses and bearings, and only were added to it as being in *themselves* pleasing to God.

V. Now, was it necessary to the completeness, as a type, of the Levitical sacrifice, or to its utility as an explanation of divine purposes, that it should cost anything to the person in whose behalf it was offered? On the contrary, the sacrifice which it foreshowed was to be God's free gift; and the cost of, or difficulty of obtaining, the sacrificial type, could only render that type in a measure obscure, and less expressive of the offering which God would in the end provide for all men. Yet this costliness was *generally* a condition of the acceptableness of the sacrifice. "Neither will I offer unto the Lord my God of that which doth cost me nothing." * That costliness, therefore, must be an acceptable condition in all human offerings at all times; for if it was pleasing to God once, it must please Him always, unless directly forbidden by Him afterwards, which it has never been.

Again, was it necessary to the typical perfection of the Levitical offering, that it should be the best of the flock? Doubtless the spotlessness of the sacrifice renders it more expressive to the Christian mind; but was it because so expressive that it was actually, and in so many words, demanded by God? Not at all. It was demanded by Him expressly on the same grounds on which an earthly governor would demand it, as a testimony of respect. "Offer it now unto thy governor." † And the less valuable offering was rejected, not because it did not image Christ, nor fulfil the purposes of sacrifice, but because it indicated a feeling that would grudge the best of its possessions to Him who gave them; and because it was a bold dishonoring of God in the sight of man. Whence it may be infallibly concluded, that in whatever offerings we may now see reason to present unto God (I say not what these may be), a condition of their acceptableness will be now, as it was then, that they should be the best of their kind.

VI. But farther, was it necessary to the carrying out of the Mosaical system, that there should be either art or splendor in the form or services of the tabernacle or temple? Was it

* 2 Sam. xxiv. 24.　Deut. xvi. 16, 17.　　　　† Mal. i. 8.

necessary to the perfection of any one of their typical offices, that there should be that hanging of blue, and purple, and scarlet? those taches of brass and sockets of silver? that working in cedar and overlaying with gold? One thing at least is evident: there was a deep and awful danger in it; a danger that the God whom they so worshipped, might be associated in the minds of the serfs of Egypt with the gods to whom they had seen similar gifts offered and similar honors paid. The probability, in our times, of fellowship with the feelings of the idolatrous Romanist is absolutely as nothing compared with the danger to the Israelite of a sympathy with the idolatrous Egyptian;[1] no speculative, no unproved danger; but proved fatally by their fall during a month's abandonment to their own will; a fall into the most servile idolatry; yet marked by such offerings to their idol as their leader was, in the close sequel, instructed to bid them offer to God. This danger was imminent, perpetual, and of the most awful kind: it was the one against which God made provision, not only by commandments, by threatenings, by promises, the most urgent, repeated, and impressive; but by temporary ordinances of a severity so terrible as almost to dim for a time, in the eyes of His people, His attribute of mercy. The principal object of every instituted law of that Theocracy, of every judgment sent forth in its vindication, was to mark to the people His hatred of idolatry; a hatred written under their advancing steps, in the blood of the Canaanite, and more sternly still in the darkness of their own desolation, when the children and the sucklings swooned in the streets of Jerusalem, and the lion tracked his prey in the dust of Samaria.[*] Yet against this mortal danger provision was not made in one way (to man's thoughts the simplest, the most natural, the most effective), by withdrawing from the worship of the Divine Being whatever could delight the sense, or shape the imagination, or limit the idea of Deity to place. This one way God refused, demanding for Himself such honors, and accepting for Himself such local dwelling, as had been paid and dedicated to idol gods by heathen worshippers;

* *Lam.* ii. 11. 2 Kings xvii. 25.

and for what reason? Was the glory of the tabernacle nec
essary to set forth or image His divine glory to the minds of
His people? What! purple or scarlet necessary to the people who had seen the great river of Egypt run scarlet to the
sea, under His condemnation? What! golden lamp and
cherub necessary for those who had seen the fires of heaven
falling like a mantle on Mount Sinai, and its golden courts
opened to receive their mortal lawgiver? What! silver clasp
and fillet necessary when they had seen the silver waves of the
Red Sea clasp in their arched hollows the corpses of the
horse and his rider? Nay—not so. There was but one reason, and that an eternal one; that as the covenant that He
made with men was accompanied with some external sign of
its continuance, and of His remembrance of it, so the acceptance of that covenant might be marked and signified by use,
in some external sign of their love and obedience, and surrender of themselves and theirs to His will; and that their gratitude to Him, and continual remembrance of Him, might
have at once their expression and their enduring testimony in
the presentation to Him, not only of the firstlings of the herd
and fold, not only of the fruits of the earth and the tithe of
time, but of all treasures of wisdom and beauty; of the
thought that invents, and the hand that labors; of wealth of
wood, and weight of stone; of the strength of iron, and of the
light of gold.

And let us not now lose sight of this broad and unabrogated
principle—I might say, incapable of being abrogated, so long
as men shall receive earthly gifts from God. Of all that they
have His tithe must be rendered to Him, or in so far and in
so much He is forgotten: of the skill and of the treasure, of
the strength and of the mind, of the time and of the toil, offering must be made reverently; and if there be any difference between the Levitical and the Christian offering, it is
that the latter may be just so much the wider in its range as
it is less typical in its meaning, as it is thankful instead of
sacrificial. There can be no excuse accepted because the
Deity does not now visibly dwell in His temple; if He is invisible it is only through our failing faith: nor any excuse

because other calls are more immediate or more sacred ; this ought to be done, and not the other left undone. Yet this objection, as frequent as feeble, must be more specifically answered.

VII. It has been said—it ought always to be said, for it is true—that a better and more honorable offering is made to our Master in ministry to the poor, in extending the knowledge of His name, in the practice of the virtues by which that name is hallowed, than in material presents to His temple. Assuredly it is so : woe to all who think that any other kind or manner of offering may in any wise take the place of these ! Do the people need place to pray, and calls to hear His word ? Then it is no time for smoothing pillars or carving pulpits ; let us have enough first of walls and roofs. Do the people need teaching from house to house, and bread from day to day? Then they are deacons and ministers we want, not architects. I insist on this, I plead for this ; but let us examine ourselves, and see if this be indeed the reason for our backwardness in the lesser work. The question is not between God's house and His poor : it is not between God's house and His Gospel. It is between God's house and ours. Have we no tesselated colors on our floors ? no frescoed fancies on our roofs ? no niched statuary in our corridors? no gilded furniture in our chambers? no costly stones in our cabinets ? Has even the tithe of these been offered ? They are, or they ought to be, the signs that enough has been devoted to the great purposes of human stewardship, and that there remains to us what we can spend in luxury ; but there is a greater and prouder luxury than this selfish one—that of bringing a portion of such things as these into sacred service, and presenting them for a memorial * that our pleasure as well as our toil has been hallowed by the remembrance of Him who gave both the strength and the reward. And until this has been done, I do not see how such possessions can be retained in happiness. I do not understand the feeling which would arch our own gates and pave our own thresholds, and leave the church with its narrow door and foot-worn sill ; the feeling which enriches

* Num. xxxi. 54. Psa. lxxvi. 11.

our own chambers with all manner of costliness, and endures the bare wall and mean compass of the temple. There is seldom even so severe a choice to be made, seldom so much self-denial to be exercised. There are isolated cases, in which men's happiness and mental activity depend upon a certain degree of luxury in their houses ; but then this is true luxury, felt and tasted, and profited by. In the plurality of instances nothing of the kind is attempted, nor can be enjoyed ; men's average resources cannot reach it ; and that which they *can* reach, gives them no pleasure, and might be spared. It will be seen, in the course of the following chapters, that I am no advocate for meanness of private habitation. I would fain introduce into it all magnificence, care, and beauty, where they are possible ; but I would not have that useless expense in unnoticed fineries or formalities ; cornicings of ceilings and graining of doors, and fringing of curtains, and thousands such ; things which have become foolishly and apathetically habitual —things on whose common appliance hang whole trades, to which there never yet belonged the blessing of giving one ray of real pleasure, or becoming of the remotest or most contemptible use—things which cause half the expense of life, and destroy more than half its comfort, manliness, respectability, freshness, and facility. I speak from experience : I know what it is to live in a cottage with a deal floor and roof, and a hearth of mica slate ; and I know it to be in many respects healthier and happier than living between a Turkey carpet and gilded ceiling, beside a steel grate and polished fender. I do not say that such things have not their place and propriety ; but I say this, emphatically, that the tenth part of the expense which is sacrificed in domestic vanities, if not absolutely and meaninglessly lost in domestic discomforts, and incumbrances, would, if collectively offered and wisely employed, build a marble church for every town in England ; such a church as it should be a joy and a blessing even to pass near in our daily ways and walks, and as it would bring the light into the eyes to see from afar, lifting its fair height above the purple crowd of humble roofs.

VIII. I have said for every town : I do not want a marble

church for every village ; nay, I do not want marble churches at all for their own sake, but for the sake of the spirit that would build them. The church has no need of any visible splendors ; her power is independent of them, her purity is in some degree opposed to them. The simplicity of a pastoral sanctuary is lovelier than the majesty of an urban temple ; and it may be more than questioned whether, to the people, such majesty has ever been the source of any increase of effective piety ; but to the builders it has been, and must ever be. It is not the church we want, but the sacrifice ; not the emotion of admiration, but the act of adoration : not the gift, but the giving.' And see how much more charity the full understanding of this might admit, among classes of men of naturally opposite feelings ; and how much more nobleness in the work. There is no need to offend by importunate, self-proclaiming splendor. Your gift may be given in an unpresuming way. Cut one or two shafts out of a porphyry whose preciousness those only would know who would desire it to be so used ; add another month's labor to the undercutting of a few capitals, whose delicacy will not be seen nor loved by one beholder of ten thousand ; see that the simplest masonry of the edifice be perfect and substantial ; and to those who regard such things, their witness will be clear and impressive ; to those who regard them not, all will at least be inoffensive. But do not think the feeling itself a folly, or the act itself useless. Of what use was that dearly-bought water of the well of Bethlehem with which the King of Israel slaked the dust of Adullam ?—yet was not thus better than if he had drunk it ? Of what use was that passionate act of Christian sacrifice, against which, first uttered by the false tongue, the very objection we would now conquer took a sullen tone for ever ? * So also let us not ask of what use our offering is to the church : it is at least better for *us* than if it had been retained for ourselves. It may be better for others also: there is, at any rate, a chance of this ; though we must always fearfully and widely shun the thought that the magnificence of the temple can materially add to the efficiency of the worship or to the power

* John xii. 5.

of the ministry. Whatever we do, or whatever we offer, let it not interfere with the simplicity of the one, or abate, as if replacing, the zeal of the other. That is the abuse and fallacy of Romanism, by which the true spirit of Christian offering is directly contradicted. The treatment of the Papists' temple is eminently exhibitory ; it is surface work throughout ; and the danger and evil of their church decoration lie, not in its reality —not in the true wealth and art of it, of which the lower people are never cognizant—but in its tinsel and glitter, in the gilding of the shrine and painting of the image, in embroidery of dingy robes and crowding of imitated gems ; all this being frequently thrust forward to the concealment of what is really good or great in their buildings.[3] Of an offering of gratitude which is neither to be exhibited nor rewarded, which is neither to win praise nor purchase salvation, the Romanist (as such) has no conception.

IX. While, however, I would especially deprecate the imputation of any other acceptableness or usefulness to the gift itself than that which it receives from the spirit of its presentation, it may be well to observe, that there is a lower advantage which never fails to accompany a dutiful observance of any right abstract principle. While the first fruits of his possessions were required from the Israelite as a testimony of fidelity, the payment of those first fruits was nevertheless rewarded, and that connectedly and specifically, by the increase of those possessions. Wealth, and length of days, and peace, were the promised and experienced rewards of his offering, though they were not to be the objects of it. The tithe paid into the storehouse was the expressed condition of the blessing which there should not be room enough to receive. And it will be thus always : God never forgets any work or labor of love ; and whatever it may be of which the first and best proportions or powers have been presented to Him, he will multiply and increase sevenfold. Therefore, though it may not be necessarily the interest of religion to admit the service of the arts, the arts will never flourish until they have been primarily devoted to that service—devoted, both by architect and employer ; by the one in scrupulous, earnest, affectionate design ; by the other in expenditure at least more frank, at least less calculating, than that which he would admit in the indulgence of his own private feelings. Let this principle be but once fairly acknowledged among us ; and however it may be chilled and repressed in practice, however feeble may be its real influence, however the sacredness of it may be diminished by counter-workings of vanity and self-interest, yet its mere acknowledgment would bring a reward ; and with our present accumulation of means and of intellect, there would be such an impulse and vitality given to art as it has not felt since the thirteenth century. And I do not assert this as other than a national consequence : I should, indeed, expect a larger measure of every great and spiritual faculty to be always given where those faculties had been wisely and religiously employed ; but the impulse to which I refer, would be, humanly speaking, certain ; and would naturally result from obedience to the two great conditions enforced by the Spirit of Sacrifice, first, that we should in everything do our best ; and, secondly, that we should consider increase of apparent labor as an increase of beauty in the building. A few practical deductions from these two conditions, and I have done.

X. For the first : it is alone enough to secure success, and it is for want of observing it that we continually fail. We are none of us so good architects as to be able to work habitually beneath our strength ; and yet there is not a building that I know of, lately raised, wherein it is not sufficiently evident that neither architect nor builder has done his best. It is the especial characteristic of modern work. All old work nearly has been hard work. It may be the hard work of children, of barbarians, of rustics ; but it is always their utmost. Ours has as constantly the look of money's worth, of a stopping short wherever and whenever we can, of a lazy compliance with low conditions ; never of a fair putting forth of our strength. Let us have done with this kind of work at once : cast off every temptation to it : do not let us degrade ourselves voluntarily, and then mutter and mourn over our short comings ; let us confess our poverty or our parsimony.

but not belie our human intellect. It is not even a question of how *much* we are to do, but of how it is to be done ; it is not a question of doing more, but of doing better. Do not let us boss our roofs with wretched, half-worked, blunt-edged rosettes ; do not let us flank our gates with rigid imitations of mediæval statuary. Such things are mere insults to common sense, and only unfit us for feeling the nobility of their prototypes. We have so much, suppose, to be spent in decoration ; let us go to the Flaxman of his time, whoever he may be, and bid him carve for us a single statue, frieze or capital, or as many as we can afford, compelling upon him the one condition, that they shall be the best he can do ; place them where they will be of the most value, and be content. Our other capitals may be mere blocks, and our other niches empty. No matter : better our work unfinished than all bad. It may be that we do not desire ornament of so high · an order ; choose, then, a less developed style, also, if you will, rougher material ; the law which we are enforcing requires only that what we pretend to do and to give, shall both be the best of their kind ; choose, therefore, the Norman hatchet work, instead of the Flaxman frieze and statue, but let it be the best hatchet work ; and if you cannot afford marble, use Caen stone, but from the best bed ; and if not stone, brick, but the best brick ; preferring always what is good of a lower order of work or material, to what is bad of a higher ; for this is not only the way to improve every kind of work, and to put every kind of material to better use ; but it is more honest and unpretending, and is in harmony with other just, upright, and manly principles, whose range we shall have presently to take into consideration.

XI. The other condition which we had to notice, was the value of the appearance of labor upon architecture. I have spoken of this before ; * and it is, indeed, one of the most frequent sources of pleasure which belong to the art, always, however, within certain somewhat remarkable limits. For it does not at first appear easily to be explained why labor, as represented by materials of value, should, without sense of

* Mod. Painters, Part I. Sec. 1, Chap. 3.

wrong or error, bear being wasted ; while the waste of actual workmanship is always painful, so soon as it is apparent. But so it is, that, while precious materials may, with a certain profusion and negligence, be employed for the magnificence of what is seldom seen, the work of man cannot be carelessly and idly bestowed, without an immediate sense of wrong ; as if the strength of the living creature were never intended by its Maker to be sacrificed in vain, though it is well for us sometimes to part with what we esteem precious of substance, as showing that in such a service it becomes but dross and dust. And in the nice balance between the straitening of effort or enthusiasm on the one hand, and vainly casting it away upon the other, there are more questions than can be met by any but very just and watchful feeling. In general it is less the mere loss of labor that offends us, than the lack of judgment implied by such loss ; so that if men confessedly work for work's sake, and it does not appear that they are ignorant where or how to make their labor tell, we shall not be grossly offended. On the contrary, we shall be pleased if the work be lost in carrying out a principle, or in avoiding a deception. It, indeed, is a law properly belonging to another part of our subject, but it may be allowably stated here, that, whenever, by the construction of a building, some parts of it are hidden from the eye which are the continuation of others bearing some consistent ornament, it is not well that the ornament should cease in the parts concealed ; credit is given for it, and it should not be deceptively withdrawn : as, for instance, in the sculpture of the backs of the statues of a temple pediment ; never, perhaps, to be seen, but yet not lawfully to be left unfinished. And so in the working out of ornaments in dark concealed places, in which it is best to err on the side of completion ; and in the carrying round of string courses, and other such continuous work ; not but that they may stop sometimes, on the point of going into some palpably impenetrable recess, but then let them stop boldly and markedly, on some distinct terminal ornament, and never be supposed to exist where they do not. The arches of the towers which flank the transepts of Rouen Cathedral have rosette ornaments on their spandrils, on the three visible sides ; none on the side towards the roof. The right of this is rather a nice point for question.

XII. Visibility, however, we must remember, depends, not only on situation, but on distance ; and there is no way in which work is more painfully and unwisely lost than in its over delicacy on parts distant from the eye. Here, again, the principle of honesty must govern our treatment : we must not work any kind of ornament which is, perhaps, to cover the whole building (or at least to occur on all parts of it) delicately where it is near the eye, and rudely where it is removed from it. That is trickery and dishonesty. Consider, first, what kinds of ornaments will tell in the distance and what near, and so distribute them, keeping such as by their nature are delicate, down near the eye, and throwing the bold and rough kinds of work to the top ; and if there be any kind which is to be both near and far off, take care that it be as boldly and rudely wrought where it is well seen as where it is distant, so that the spectator may know exactly what it is, and what it is worth. Thus chequered patterns, and in general such ornaments as common workmen can execute, may extend over the whole building ; but bas-reliefs, and fine niches and capitals, should be kept down, and the common sense of this will always give a building dignity, even though there be some abruptness or awkwardness, in the resulting arrangements. Thus at San Zeno at Verona, the bas-reliefs, full of incident and interest are confined to a parallelogram of the front, reaching to the height of the capitals of the columns of the porch. Above these, we find a simple though most lovely, little arcade ; and above that, only blank wall, with square face shafts. The whole effect is tenfold grander and better than if the entire façade had been covered with bad work, and may serve for an example of the way to place little where we cannot afford much. So, again, the transept gates of Rouen * are covered with delicate bas-reliefs (of which I

---

* Henceforward, for the sake of convenience, when I name any cathedral town in this manner, let me be understood to speak of its cathedral church.

shall speak at greater length presently) up to about once and a half a man's height; and above that come the usual and more visible statues and niches. So in the campanile at Florence, the circuit of bas-reliefs is on its lowest story; above that come its statues; and above them all its pattern mosaic, and twisted columns, exquisitely finished, like all Italian work of the time, but still, in the eye of the Florentine, rough and commonplace by comparison with the bas-reliefs. So generally the most delicate niche work and best mouldings of the French Gothic are in gates and low windows well within sight; although, it being the very spirit of that style to trust to its exuberance for effect, there is occasionally a burst upwards and blossoming unrestrainably to the sky, as in the pediment of the west front of Rouen, and in the recess of the rose window behind it, where there are some most elaborate flower-mouldings, all but invisible from below, and only adding a general enrichment to the deep shadows that relieve the shafts of the advanced pediment. It is observable, however, that this very work is bad flamboyant, and has corrupt renaissance characters in its detail as well as use; while in the earlier and grander north and south gates, there is a very noble proportioning of the work to the distance, the niches and statues which crown the northern one, at a height of about one hundred feet from the ground, being alike colossal and simple; visibly so from below, so as to induce no deception, and yet honestly and well-finished above, and all that they are expected to be; the features very beautiful, full of expression, and as delicately wrought as any work of the period.

XIII. It is to be remembered, however, that while the ornaments in every fine ancient building, without exception so far as I am aware, are most delicate at the base, they are often in greater effective *quantity* on the upper parts. In high towers this is perfectly natural and right, the solidity of the foundation being as necessary as the division and penetration of the superstructure; hence the lighter work and richly pierced crowns of late Gothic towers. The campanile of Giotto at Florence, already alluded to, is an exquisite instance

of the union of the two principles, delicate bas-reliefs adorn-
ing its massy foundation, while the open tracery of the upper
windows attracts the eye by its slender intricacy, and a rich
cornice crowns the whole. In such truly fine cases of this
disposition the upper work is effective by its quantity and intricacy only, as the lower portions by delicacy ; so also in the
Tour de Beurre at Rouen, where, however, the detail is massy
throughout, subdividing into rich meshes as it ascends. In
the bodies of buildings the principle is less safe, but its discussion is not connected with our present subject.

XIV. Finally, work may be wasted by being too good for
its material, or too fine to bear exposure ; and this, generally a
characteristic of late, especially of renaissance, work, is perhaps the worst fault of all. I do not know anything more
painful or pitiful than the kind of ivory carving with which
the Certosa of Pavia, and part of the Colleone sepulchral
chapel at Bergamo, and other such buildings, are incrusted,
of which it is not possible so much as to think without ex-
haustion ; and a heavy sense of the misery it would be, to be
forced to look at it at all. And this is not from the quantity
of it, nor because it is bad work—much of it is inventive and
able ; but because it looks as if it were only fit to be put in
inlaid cabinets and velveted caskets, and as if it could not
bear one drifting shower or gnawing frost. We are afraid for
it, anxious about it, and tormented by it ; and we feel that a
massy shaft and a bold shadow would be worth it all. Nevertheless, even in cases like these, much depends on the accomplishment of the great ends of decoration. If the ornament
does its duty—if it *is* ornament, and its points of shade and
light tell in the general effect, we shall not be offended by
finding that the sculptor in his fulness of fancy has chosen to
give much more than these mere points of light, and has
composed them of groups of figures. But if the ornament
does not answer its purpose, if it have no distant, no truly
decorative power ; if generally seen it be a mere incrustation
and meaningless roughness, we shall only be chagrined by
finding when we look close, that the incrustation has cost
years of labor, and has millions of figures and histories in it

and would be the better of being seen through a Stanhope lens. Hence the greatness of the northern Gothic as con-trasted with the latest Italian. It reaches nearly the same extreme of detail ; but it never loses sight of its architectural purpose, never fails in its decorative power ; not a leaflet in it but speaks, and speaks far off, too ; and so long as this be the case, there is no limit to the luxuriance in which such work may legitimately and nobly be bestowed.

XV. No limit : it is one of the affectations of architects to speak of overcharged ornament. Ornament cannot be over-charged if it be good, and is always overcharged when it is bad. I have given, on the opposite page (fig. 1), one of the smallest niches of the central gate of Rouen. That gate I suppose to be the most exquisite piece of pure flamboyant work existing ; for though I have spoken of the upper por-tions, especially the receding window, as degenerate, the gate itself is of a purer period, and has hardly any renaissance taint. There are four strings of these niches (each with two figures beneath it) round the porch, from the ground to the top of the arch, with three intermediate rows of larger niches, far more elaborate ; besides the six principal canopies of each outer pier. The total number of the subordinate niches alone, each worked like that in the plate, and each with a different pattern of traceries in each compartment, is one hundred and seventy-six.⁴ Yet in all this ornament there is not one cusp, one finial that is useless—not a stroke of the chisel is in vain ; the grace and luxuriance of it all are visible—sensible rather —even to the uninquiring eye ; and all its minuteness does not diminish the majesty, while it increases the mystery, of the noble and unbroken vault. It is not less the boast of some styles that they can bear ornament, than of others that they can do without it ; but we do not often enough reflect that those very styles, of so haughty simplicity, owe part of their pleasurableness to contrast, and would be wearisome if universal. They are but the rests and monotones of the art , it is to its far happier, far higher, exaltation that we owe those fair fronts of variegated mosaic, charged with wild fan-cies and dark hosts of imagery, thicker and quainter than

ever filled the depth of midsummer dream ; those vaulted
gates, trellised with close leaves ; those window-labyrinths of
twisted tracery and starry light ; those misty masses of multitudinous pinnacle and diademed tower ; the only witnesses,
perhaps that remain to us of the faith and fear of nations.
All else for which the builders sacrificed, has passed away—
all their living interests, and aims, and achievements.   We
know not for what they labored, and we see no evidence of
their reward.   Victory, wealth, authority, happiness—all have
departed, though bought by many a bitter sacrifice.   But of
them, and their life, and their toil upon the earth, one reward, one evidence, is left to us in those gray heaps of deep-
wrought stone.   They have taken with them to the grave
their powers, their honors, and their errors ; but they have
left us their adoration.

CHAPTER II.

THE LAMP OF TRUTH.

I. There is a marked likeness between the virtues of man
and the enlightenment of the globe he inhabits—the same
diminishing gradation in vigor up to the limits of their do-
mains, the same essential separation from their contraries—
the same twilight at the meeting of the two : a something
wider belt than the line where the world rolls into night, that
strange twilight of the virtues ; that dusky debateable land,
wherein zeal becomes impatience, and temperance becomes
severity, and justice becomes cruelty, and faith superstition,
and each and all vanish into gloom.

Nevertheless, with the greater number of them, though
their dimness increases gradually, we may mark the moment
of their sunset ; and, happily, may turn the shadow back by
the way by which it had gone down : but for one, the line of
the horizon is irregular and undefined ; and this, too, the very
equator and girdle of them all—Truth ; that only one of
which there are no degrees, but breaks and rents continually ,
that pillar of the earth, yet a cloudy pillar ; that golden and
narrow line, which the very powers and virtues that lean upon

it bend, which policy and prudence conceal, which kindness and courtesy modify, which courage overshadows with his shield, imagination covers with her wings, and charity dims with her tears. How difficult must the maintenance of that authority be, which, while it has to restrain the hostility of all the worst principles of man, has also to restrain the disorders of his best—which is continually assaulted by the one and betrayed by the other, and which regards with the same severity the lightest and the boldest violations of its law! There are some faults slight in the sight of love, some errors slight in the estimate of wisdom ; but truth forgives no insult, and endures no stain.

We do not enough consider this ; nor enough dread the slight and continual occasions of offence against her. We are too much in the habit of looking at falsehood in its darkest associations, and through the color of its worst purposes. That indignation which we profess to feel at deceit absolute, is indeed only at deceit malicious. We resent calumny, hypocrisy and treachery, because they harm us, not because they are untrue. Take the detraction and the mischief from the untruth, and we are little offended by it ; turn it into praise, and we may be pleased with it. And yet it is not calumny nor treachery that does the largest sum of mischief in the world ; they are continually crushed, and are felt only in being conquered. But it is the glistening and softly spoken lie ; the amiable fallacy ; the patriotic lie of the historian, the provident lie of the politician, the zealous lie of the partizan, the merciful lie of the friend, and the careless lie of each man to himself, that cast that black mystery over humanity, through which any man who pierces, we thank as we would thank one who dug a well in a desert ; happy in that the thirst for truth still remains with us, even when we have wilfully left the fountains of it.

It would be well if moralists less frequently confused the greatness of a sin with its unpardonableness. The two characters are altogether distinct. The greatness of a fault depends partly on the nature of the person against whom it is committed, partly upon the extent of its consequences. Its par-

donableness depends, humanly speaking, on the degree of
temptation to it.   One class of circumstances determines the
weight of the attaching punishment ; the other, the claim to
remission of punishment : and since it is not easy for men to
estimate the relative weight, nor possible for them to know
the relative consequences, of crime, it is usually wise in them
to quit the care of such nice measurements, and to look to
the other and clearer condition of culpability ; esteeming
those faults worst which are committed under least temptation.   I do not mean to diminish the blame of the injurious
and malicious sin, of the selfish and deliberate falsity ; yet it
seems to me, that the shortest way to check the darker forms
of deceit is to set watch more scrupulous against those which
have mingled, unregarded and unchastised, with the current
of our life.   Do not let us lie at all.   Do not think of one
falsity as harmless, and another as slight, and another as un-
intended.   Cast them all aside : they may be light and accidental ; but they are an ugly soot from the smoke of the pit,
for all that ; and it is better that our hearts should be swept
clean of them, without over care as to which is largest or
blackest.   Speaking truth is like writing fair, and comes only
by practice ; it is less a matter of will than of habit, and I
doubt if any occasion can be trivial which permits the practice
and formation of such a habit.   To speak and act truth with
constancy and precision is nearly as difficult, and perhaps as
meritorious, as to speak it under intimidation or penalty ;
and it is a strange thought how many men there are, as I
trust, who would hold to it at the cost of fortune or life, for
one who would hold to it at the cost of a little daily trouble.
And seeing that of all sin there is, perhaps, no one more flatly
opposite to the Almighty, no one more "wanting the good of
virtue and of being," than this of lying, it is surely a strange
insolence to fall into the foulness of it on light or on no temptation, and surely becoming an honorable man to resolve that,
whatever semblances or fallacies the necessary course of his
life may compel him to bear or to believe, none shall disturb
the serenity of his voluntary actions, nor diminish the reality
of his chosen delights.

II. If this be just and wise for truth's sake, much more is it necessary for the sake of the delights over which she has influence. For, as I advocated the expression of the Spirit of Sacrifice in the acts and pleasures of men, not as if thereby those acts could further the cause of religion, but because most assuredly they might therein be infinitely ennobled themselves, so I would have the Spirit or Lamp of Truth clear in the hearts of our artists and handicraftsmen, not as if the truthful practice of handicrafts could far advance the cause of truth, but because I would fain see the handicrafts themselves urged by the spurs of chivalry : and it is, indeed, marvellous to see what power and universality there is in this single principle, and how in the consulting or forgetting of it lies half the dignity or decline of every art and act of man. I have before endeavored to show its range and power in painting ; and I believe a volume, instead of a chapter, might be written on its authority over all that is great in architecture. But I must be content with the force of instances few and familiar, believing that the occasions of its manifestation may be more easily discovered by a desire to be true, than embraced by an analysis of truth.

Only it is very necessary in the outset to mark clearly wherein consists the essence of fallacy as distinguished from supposition.

III. For it might be at first thought that the whole kingdom of imagination was one of deception also. Not so : the action of the imagination is a voluntary summoning of the conceptions of things absent or impossible ; and the pleasure and nobility of the imagination partly consist in its knowledge and contemplation of them as such, *i.e.* in the knowledge of their actual absence or impossibility at the moment of their apparent presence or reality. When the imagination deceives it becomes madness. It is a noble faculty so long as it confesses its own ideality ; when it ceases to confess this, it is insanity. All the difference lies in the fact of the confession, in there being *no* deception. It is necessary to our rank as spiritual creatures, that we should be able to invent and to behold what is not ; and to our rank as moral creatures that we should know and confess at the same time that it is not.

IV. Again, it might be thought, and has been thought, that the whole art of painting is nothing else than an endeavor to deceive. Not so : it is, on the contrary, a statement of certain facts, in the clearest possible way. For instance : I desire to give an account of a mountain or of a rock ; I begin by telling its shape. But words will not do this distinctly, and I draw its shape, and say, " This was its shape." Next : I would fain represent its color ; but words will not do this either, and I dye the paper, and say, " This was its color." Such a process may be carried on until the scene appears to exist, and a high pleasure may be taken in its apparent existence. This is a communicated act of imagination, but no lie. The lie can consist only in an *assertion* of its existence (which is never for one instant made, implied, or believed), or else in false statements of forms and colors (which are, indeed, made and believed to our great loss, continually). And observe, also, that so degrading a thing is deception in even the approach and appearance of it, that all painting which even reaches the mark of apparent realization, is degraded in so doing. I have enough insisted on this point in another place.

V. The violations of truth, which dishonor poetry and painting, are thus for the most part confined to the treatment of their subjects. But in architecture another and a less subtle, more contemptible, violation of truth is possible ; a direct falsity of assertion respecting the nature of material, or the quantity of labor. And this is, in the full sense of the word, wrong ; it is as truly deserving of reprobation as any other moral delinquency ; it is unworthy alike of architects and of nations ; and it has been a sign, wherever it has widely and with toleration existed, of a singular debasement of the arts ; that it is not a sign of worse than this, of a general want of severe probity, can be accounted for only by our knowledge of the strange separation which has for some centuries existed between the arts and all other subjects of human intellect, as matters of conscience. This withdrawal of conscientiousness from among the faculties concerned with art, while it has destroyed the arts themselves, has also rendered in a measure nugatory the evidence which otherwise they might have presented respecting the character of the respective nations among whom they have been cultivated ; otherwise, it might appear more than strange that a nation so distinguished for its general uprightness and faith as the English, should admit in their architecture more of pretence, concealment, and deceit, than any other of this or of past time.

They are admitted in thoughtlessness, but with fatal effect upon the art in which they are practised. If there were no other causes for the failures which of late have marked every great occasion for architectural exertion, these petty dishonesties would be enough to account for all. It is the first step and not the least, towards greatness to do away with these ; the first, because so evidently and easily in our power. We may not be able to command good, or beautiful, or inventive architecture ; but we *can* command an honest architecture : the meagreness of poverty may be pardoned, the sternness of utility respected ; but what is there but scorn for the meanness of deception ?

VI. Architectural Deceits are broadly to be considered under three heads :—

1st. The suggestion of a mode of structure or support, other than the true one ; as in pendants of late Gothic roofs.

2d. The painting of surfaces to represent some other material than that of which they actually consist (as in the marbling of wood), or the deceptive representation of sculptured ornament upon them.

3d. The use of cast or machine-made ornaments of any kind.

Now, it may be broadly stated, that architecture will be noble exactly in the degree in which all these false expedients are avoided. Nevertheless, there are certain degrees of them, which, owing to their frequent usage, or to other causes, have so far lost the nature of deceit as to be admissible ; as, for instance, gilding, which is in architecture no deceit, because it is therein not understood for gold ; while in jewellery it is a deceit, because it is so understood, and therefore altogether to be reprehended. So that there arise, in the application of the strict rules of right, many exceptions and niceties of con science ; which let us as briefly as possible examine.

VII. 1st. Structural Deceits.   I have limited these to the determined and purposed suggestion of a mode of support other than the true one.   The architect is not *bound* to exhibit structure ; nor are we to complain of him for concealing it, any more than we should regret that the outer surfaces of the human frame conceal much of its anatomy ; nevertheless, that building will generally be the noblest, which to an intelligent eye discovers the great secrets of its structure, as an animal form does, although from a careless observer they may be concealed.   In the vaulting of a Gothic roof it is no deceit to throw the strength into the ribs of it, and make the intermediate vault a mere shell.   Such a structure would be presumed by an intelligent observer, the first time he saw such a roof ; and the beauty of its traceries would be enhanced to him if they confessed and followed the lines of its main strength.   If, however, the intermediate shell were made of wood instead of stone, and whitewashed to look like the rest, —this would, of course, be direct deceit, and altogether unpardonable.

There is, however, a certain deception necessarily occurring in Gothic architecture, which relates, not to the points, but to the manner, of support.   The resemblance in its shafts and ribs to the external relations of stems and branches, which has been the ground of so much foolish speculation, necessarily induces in the mind of the spectator a sense or belief of a correspondent internal structure ; that is to say, of a fibrous and continuous strength from the root into the limbs, and an elasticity communicated *upwards,* sufficient for the support of the ramified portions.   The idea of the real conditions, of a great weight of ceiling thrown upon certain narrow, jointed lines, which have a tendency partly to be crushed, and partly to separate and be pushed outwards, is with difficulty received ; and the more so when the pillars would be, if unassisted, too slight for the weight, and are supported by external flying buttresses, as in the apse of Beauvais, and other such achievements of the bolder Gothic.   Now, there is a nice question of conscience in this, which we shall hardly settle but by considering that, when the mind is informed beyond the possibility of mistake as to the true nature of things, the affecting it with a contrary impression, however distinct, is no dishonesty, but on the contrary, a legitimate appeal to the imagination. For instance, the greater part of the happiness which we have in contemplating clouds, results from the impression of their having massive, luminous, warm, and mountain-like surfaces; and our delight in the sky frequently depends upon our considering it as a blue vault. But we know the contrary, in both instances; we know the cloud to be a damp fog, or a drift of snow flakes; and the sky to be a lightless abyss. There is, therefore, no dishonesty, while there is much delight, in the irresistibly contrary impression. In the same way, so long as we see the stones and joints, and are not deceived as to the points of support in any piece of architecture, we may rather praise than regret the dextrous artifices which compel us to feel as if there were fibre in its shafts and life in its branches. Nor is even the concealment of the support of the external buttress reprehensible, so long as the pillars are not sensibly inadequate to their duty. For the weight of a roof is a circumstance of which the spectator generally has no idea, and the provisions for it, consequently, circumstances whose necessity or adaptation he could not understand. It is no deceit, therefore, when the weight to be borne is necessarily unknown, to conceal also the means of bearing it, leaving only to be perceived so much of the support as is indeed adequate to the weight supposed. For the shafts do, indeed, bear as much as they are ever imagined to bear, and the system of added support is no more, as a matter of conscience, to be exhibited, than, in the human or any other form, mechanical provisions for those functions which are themselves unperceived.

But the moment that the conditions of weight are comprehended, both truth and feeling require that the conditions of support should be also comprehended. Nothing can be worse, either as judged by the taste or the conscience, than affectedly inadequate supports—suspensions in air, and other such tricks and vanities. Mr. Hope wisely reprehends, for this reason, the arrangement of the main piers of St. Sophia at Constantinople. King's College Chapel, Cambridge, is a piece of architectural juggling, if possible still more to be condemned, because less sublime.

VIII. With deceptive concealments of structure are to be classed, though still more blameable, deceptive assumptions of it—the introduction of members which should have, or profess to have, a duty, and have none. One of the most general instances of this will be found in the form of the flying buttress in late Gothic. The use of that member is, of course, to convey support from one pier to another when the plan of the building renders it necessary or desirable that the supporting masses should be divided into groups, the most frequent necessity of this kind arising from the intermediate range of chapels or aisles between the nave or choir walls and their supporting piers. The natural, healthy, and beautiful arrangement is that of a steeply sloping bar of stone, sustained by an arch with its spandril carried farthest down on the lowest side, and dying into the vertical of the outer pier; that pier being, of course, not square, but rather a piece of wall set at right angles to the supported walls, and, if need be, crowned by a pinnacle to give it greater weight. The whole arrangement is exquisitely carried out in the choir of Beauvais. In later Gothic the pinnacle became gradually a decorative member, and was used in all places merely for the sake of its beauty. There is no objection to this; it is just as lawful to build a pinnacle for its beauty as a tower; but also the buttress became a decorative member; and was used, first, where it was not wanted, and, secondly, in forms in which it could be of no use, becoming a mere tie, not between the pier and wall, but between the wall and the top of the decorative pinnacle, thus attaching itself to the very point where its thrust, if it made any, could not be resisted. The most flagrant instance of this barbarism that I remember (though it prevails partially in all the spires of the Netherlands), is the lantern of St. Ouen at Rouen, where the pierced buttress, having an ogee curve, looks about as much calculated to bear a thrust as a switch of willow; and the pinnacles, huge and richly decorated, have evidently no work to do whatsoever, but stand round the central tower, like four idle servants, as they are—heraldic supporters, that central tower being merely a hollow crown, which needs no more buttressing than a basket does. In fact, I do not know anything more strange or unwise than the praise lavished upon this lantern; it is one of the basest pieces of Gothic in Europe; its flamboyant traceries of the last and most degraded forms;[5] and its entire plan and decoration resembling, and deserving little more credit than, the burnt sugar ornaments of elaborate confectionery. There are hardly any of the magnificent and serene constructions of the early Gothic which have not, in the course of time, been gradually thinned and pared away into these skeletons, which sometimes indeed, when their lines truly follow the structure of the original masses, have an interest like that of the fibrous framework of leaves from which the substance has been dissolved, but which are usually distorted as well as emaciated, and remain but the sickly phantoms and mockeries of things that were; they are to true architecture what the Greek ghost was to the armed and living frame; and the very winds that whistle through the threads of them, are to the diapasoned echoes of the ancient walls, as to the voice of the man was the pining of the spectre.[6]

IX. Perhaps the most fruitful source of these kinds of corruption which we have to guard against in recent times, is one which, nevertheless, comes in a "questionable shape," and of which it is not easy to determine the proper laws and limits; I mean the use of iron. The definition of the art of architecture, given in the first chapter, is independent of its materials: nevertheless, that art having been, up to the beginning of the present century, practised for the most part in clay, stone, or wood, it has resulted that the sense of proportion and the laws of structure have been based, the one altogether, the other in great part, on the necessities consequent on the employment of those materials; and that the entire or principal employment of metallic framework would, therefore, be generally felt as a departure from the first principles of the art. Abstract edly there appears no reason why iron should not be used as well as wood ; and the time is probably near when a new system of architectural laws will be developed, adapted entirely to metallic construction. But I believe that the tendency of all present sympathy and association is to limit the idea of architecture to non-metallic work ; and that not without reason. For architecture being in its perfection the earliest, as in its elements it is necessarily the first, of arts, will always precede, in any barbarous nation, the possession of the science necessary either for the obtaining or the management of iron. Its first existence and its earliest laws must, therefore, depend upon the use of materials accessible in quantity, and on the surface of the earth ; that is to say, clay, wood, or stone : and as I think it cannot but be generally felt that one of the chief dignities of architecture is its historical use; and since the latter is partly dependent on consistency of style, it will be felt right to retain as far as may be, even in periods of more advanced science, the materials and principles of earlier ages.

X. But whether this be granted me or not, the fact is, that every idea respecting size, proportion, decoration, or construction, on which we are at present in the habit of acting or judging, depends on presupposition of such materials : and as I both feel myself unable to escape the influence of these prejudices, and believe that my readers will be equally so, it may be perhaps permitted to me to assume that true architecture does not admit iron as a constructive material,[7] and that such works as the cast-iron central spire of Rouen Cathedral, or the iron roofs and pillars of our railway stations, and of some of our churches, are not architecture at all. Yet it is evident that metals may, and sometimes must, enter into the construction to a certain extent, as nails in wooden architecture, and therefore as legitimately rivets and solderings in stone ; neither can we well deny to the Gothic architect the power of supporting statues, pinnacles, or traceries by iron bars ; and if we grant this I do not see how we can help allowing Brunelleschi his iron chain around the dome of Florence, or the builders of Salisbury their elaborate iron binding of the central tower.[8] If, however, we would not fall into the old sophistry of the grains of corn and the heap, we must find a rule which may enable us to stop somewhere. This rule is, I think, that metals may be used as a *cement* but not as a *support.* For as cements of other kinds are often so strong that the stones may easier be broken than separated, and the wall becomes a solid mass without for that reason losing the character of architecture, there is no reason why, when a nation has obtained the knowledge and practice of iron work, metal rods or rivets should not be used in the place of cement, and establish the same or a greater strength and adherence, without in any wise inducing departure from the types and system of architecture before established; nor does it make any difference except as to sightliness, whether the metal bands or rods so employed, be in the body of the wall or on its exterior, or set as stays and cross-bands; so only that the use of them be always and distinctly one which might be superseded by mere strength of cement; as for instance if a pinnacle or mullion be propped or tied by an iron band, it is evident that the iron only prevents the separation of the stones by lateral force, which the cement would have done, had it been strong enough. But the moment that the iron in the least degree takes the place of the stone, and acts by its resistance to crushing, and bears superincumbent weight, or if it acts by its own weight as a counterpoise, and so supersedes the use of pinnacles or buttresses in resisting a lateral thrust, or if, in the form of a rod or girder, it is used to do what wooden beams would have done as well, that instant the building ceases, so far as such applications of metal extend, to be true architecture.

XI. The limit, however, thus determined, is an ultimate one, and it is well in all things to be cautious how we approach the utmost limit of lawfulness; so that, although the employment of metal within this limit cannot be considered as destroying the very being and nature of architecture, it will, if, extravagant and frequent, derogate from the dignity of the work, as well as (which is especially to our present point) from its honesty. For although the spectator is not informed as to the quantity or strength of the cement employed, he will generally conceive the stones of the building to be separable.

and his estimate of the skill of the architect will be based in a great measure on his supposition of this condition, and of the difficulties attendant upon it : so that it is always more honorable, and it has a tendency to render the style of architecture both more masculine and more scientific, to employ stone and mortar simply as such, and to do as much as possible with the weight of the one and the strength of the other, and rather sometimes to forego a grace, or to confess a weakness, than attain the one, or conceal the other, by means verging upon dishonesty.

Nevertheless, where the design is of such delicacy and slightness as, in some parts of very fair and finished edifices, it is desirable that it should be ; and where both its completion and security are in a measure dependent on the use of metal, let not such use be reprehended ; so only that as much is done as may be, by good mortar and good masonry ; and no slovenly workmanship admitted through confidence in the iron helps ; for it is in this license as in that of wine, a man may use it for his infirmities, but not for his nourishment.

XII. And, in order to avoid an over use of this liberty, it would be well to consider what application may be conveniently made of the dovetailing and various adjusting of stones ; for when any artifice is necessary to help the mortar, certainly this ought to come before the use of metal, for it is both safer and more honest. I cannot see that any objection can be made to the fitting of the stones in any shapes the architect pleases : for although it would not be desirable to see buildings put together like Chinese puzzles, there must always be a check upon such an abuse of the practice in its difficulty ; nor is it necessary that it should be always exhibited, so that it be understood by the spectator as an admitted help, and that no principal stones are introduced in positions apparently impossible for them to retain, although a riddle here and there, in unimportant features, may sometimes serve to draw the eye to the masonry, and make it interesting, as well as to give a delightful sense of a kind of necromantic power in the architect. There is a pretty one **in the** lintel of the lateral door of the cathedral of Prato

(Plate IV. fig. 4.) ; where the maintenance of the visibly separate stones, alternate marble and serpentine, cannot be understood until their cross-cutting is seen below. Each block is, of course, of the form given in fig. 5.

XIII. Lastly, before leaving the subject of structural deceits, I would remind the architect who thinks that I am unnecessarily and narrowly limiting his resources or his art, that the highest greatness and the highest wisdom are shown, the first by a noble submission to, the second by a thoughtful providence for, certain voluntarily admitted restraints. Nothing is more evident than this, in that supreme government which is the example, as it is the centre, of all others. The Divine Wisdom is, and can be, shown to us only in its meeting and contending with the difficulties which are voluntarily, and *for the sake of that contest,* admitted by the Divine Omnipotence : and these difficulties, observe, occur in the form of natural laws or ordinances, which might, at many times and in countless ways, be infringed with apparent advantage, but which are never infringed, whatever costly arrangements or adaptations their observance may necessitate for the accomplishment of given purposes. The example most apposite to our present subject is the structure of the bones of animals. No reason can be given, I believe, why the system of the higher animals should not have been made capable, as that of the *Infusoria* is, of secreting flint, instead of phosphate of lime, or more naturally still, carbon ; so framing the bones of adamant at once. The elephant or rhinoceros, had the earthy part of their bones been made of diamond, might have been as agile and light as grasshoppers, and other animals might have been framed far more magnificently colossal than any that walk the earth. In other worlds we may, perhaps, see such creations ; a creation for every element, and elements infinite. But the architecture of animals *here*, is appointed by God to be a marble architecture, not a flint nor adamant architecture ; and all manner of expedients are adopted to attain the utmost degree of strength and size possible under that great limitation. The jaw of the ichthyosaurus is pieced and riveted, the leg of the megatherium is a foot thick, and

the head of the myodon has a double skull; we, in our wis
dom, should, doubtless, have given the lizard a steel jaw, and
the myodon a cast-iron headpiece, and forgotten the great
principle to which all creation bears witness, that order and
system are nobler things than power. But God shows us in
Himself, strange as it may seem, not only authoritative perfection, but even the perfection of Obedience—an obedience
to His own laws: and in the cumbrous movement of those
unwieldiest of His creatures we are reminded, even in His
divine essence, of that attribute of uprightness in the human creature "that sweareth to his own hurt and changeth
not."

XIV. 2d. Surface Deceits. These may be generally defined
as the inducing the supposition of some form or material
which does not actually exist; as commonly in the painting
of wood to represent marble, or in the painting of ornaments
in deceptive relief, &c. But we must be careful to observe,
that the evil of them consists always in definitely attempted
deception, and that it is a matter of some nicety to mark the
point where deception begins or ends.

Thus, for instance, the roof of Milan Cathedral is seemingly
covered with elaborate fan tracery, forcibly enough painted to
enable it, in its dark and removed position, to deceive a careless observer. This is, of course, gross degradation; it destroys much of the dignity even of the rest of the building,
and is in the very strongest terms to be reprehended.

The roof of the Sistine Chapel has much architectural design in grissaille mingled with the figures of its frescoes; and
the effect is increase of dignity.

In what lies the distinctive character?

In two points, principally:—First. That the architecture
is so closely associated with the figures, and has so grand fellowship with them in its forms and cast shadows, that both
are at once felt to be of a piece; and as the figures must necessarily be painted, the architecture is known to be so too
There is thus no deception.

Second. That so great a painter as Michael Angelo would
always stop short in such minor parts of his design, of the de-

gree of vulgar force which would be necessary to induce the
supposition of their reality ; and, strangely as it may sound,
would never paint badly enough to deceive.

But though right and wrong are thus found broadly opposed
in works severally so mean and so mighty as the roof of Milan
and that of the Sistine, there are works neither so great nor so
mean, in which the limits of right are vaguely defined, and
will need some care to determine ; care only, however, to apply accurately the broad principle with which we set out, that
no form nor material is to be *deceptively* represented.

XV. Evidently, then, painting, confessedly such, is no deception : it does not assert any material whatever. Whether
it be on wood or on stone, or, as will naturally be supposed,
on plaster, does not matter. Whatever the material, good
painting makes it more precious ; nor can it ever be said to
deceive respecting the ground of which it gives us no informa-
tion. To cover brick with plaster, and this plaster with fresco,
is, therefore, perfectly legitimate ; and as desirable a mode of
decoration as it is constant in the great periods. Verona and
Venice are now seen deprived of more than half their former
splendor ; it depended far more on their frescoes than their
marbles. The plaster, in this case, is to be considered as the
gesso ground on panel or canvas. But to cover brick with
cement, and to divide this cement with joints that it may look
like stone, is to tell a falsehood ; and is just as contemptible a
procedure as the other is noble.

It being lawful to paint then, is it lawful to paint everything ? So long as the painting is confessed—yes ; but if,
even in the slightest degree, the sense of it be lost, and the
thing painted be supposed real—no. Let us take a few instances. In the Campo Santo at Pisa, each fresco is surrounded with a border composed of flat colored patterns of
great elegance—no part of it in attempted relief. The certainty of flat surface being thus secured, the figures, though
the size of life, do not deceive, and the artist thenceforward is
at liberty to put forth his whole power, and to lead us through
fields and groves, and depths of pleasant landscape, and to
soothe us with the sweet clearness of far off sky, and yet

never lose the severity of his primal purpose of architectural decoration.

In the Camera di Correggio of San Lodovico at Parma, the trellises of vine shadow the walls, as if with an actual arbor ; and the troops of children, peeping through the oval openings, luscious in color and faint in light, may well be expected every instant to break through, or hide behind the covert. The grace of their attitudes, and the evident greatness of the whole work, mark that it is painting, and barely redeem it from the charge of falsehood ; but even so saved, it is utterly unworthy to take a place among noble or legitimate architectural decoration.

In the cupola of the duomo of Parma the same painter has represented the Assumption with so much deceptive power, that he has made a dome of some thirty feet diameter look like a cloud-wrapt opening in the seventh heaven, crowded with a rushing sea of angels. Is this wrong? Not so : for the subject at once precludes the possibility of deception. We might have taken the vines for a veritable pergoda, and the children for its haunting ragazzi ; but we know the stayed clouds and moveless angels must be man's work ; let him put his utmost strength to it and welcome, he can enchant us, but cannot betray.

We may thus apply the rule to the highest, as well as the art of daily occurrence, always remembering that more is to be forgiven to the great painter than to the mere decorative workman ; and this especially, because the former, even in deceptive portions, will not trick us so grossly ; as we have just seen in Correggio, where a worse painter would have made the thing look like life at once. There is, however, in room, villa, or garden decoration, some fitting admission of trickeries of this kind, as of pictured landscapes at the extremities of alleys and arcades, and ceilings like skies, or painted with prolongations upwards of the architecture of the walls, which things have sometimes a certain luxury and pleasureableness in places meant for idleness, and are innocent enough as long as they are regarded as mere toys.

XVI. Touching the false representation of material, the

question is infinitely more simple, and the law more sweeping ; all such imitations are utterly base and inadmissible. It is melancholy to think of the time and expense lost in marbling the shop fronts of London alone, and of the waste of our resources in absolute vanities, in things about which no mortal cares, by which no eye is ever arrested, unless painfully, and which do not add one whit to comfort or cleanliness, or even to that great object of commercial art—conspicuousness. But in architecture of a higher rank, how much more is it to be condemned? I have made it a rule in the present work not to blame specifically ; but I may, perhaps, be permitted, while I express my sincere admiration of the very noble entrance and general architecture of the British Museum, to express also my regret that the noble granite foundation of the staircase should be mocked at its landing by an imitation, the more blameable because tolerably successful. The only effect of it is to cast a suspicion upon the true stones below, and upon every bit of granite afterwards encountered. One feels a doubt, after it, of the honesty of Memnon himself. But even this, however derogatory to the noble architecture around it, is less painful than the want of feeling with which, in our cheap modern churches, we suffer the wall decorator to erect about the altar frameworks and pediments daubed with mottled color, and to dye in the same fashions such skeletons or caricatures of columns as may emerge above the pews ; this is not merely bad taste ; it is no unimportant or excusable error which brings even these shadows of vanity and falsehood into the house of prayer. The first condition which just feeling requires in church furniture is, that it should be simple and unaffected, not fictitious nor tawdry. It may be in our power to make it beautiful, but let it at least be pure ; and if we cannot permit much to the architect, do not let us permit anything to the upholsterer ; if we keep to solid stone and solid wood, whitewashed, if we like, for cleanliness' sake (for whitewash has so often been used as the dress of noble things that it has thence received a kind of nobility itself), it must be a bad design indeed which is grossly offensive. I recollect no instance of a

want of sacred character, or of any marked and painful ugliness
in the simplest or the most awkwardly built village church,
where stone and wood were roughly and nakedly used, and the
windows latticed with white glass. But the smoothly stuc-
coed walls, the flat roofs with ventilator ornaments, the
barred windows with jaundiced borders and dead ground
square panes, the gilded or bronzed wood, the painted iron,
the wretched upholstery of curtains and cushions, and pew
heads and altar railings, and Birmingham metal candlesticks,
and, above all, the green and yellow sickness of the false
marble—disguises all, observe ; falsehoods all—who are they
who like these things ? who defend them ? who do them ? I
have never spoken to any one who *did* like them, though to
many who thought them matters of no consequence.   Perhaps not to religion (though I cannot but believe that there
are many to whom, as to myself, such things are serious obstacles to the repose of mind and temper which should precede devotional exercises) ; but to the general tone of our
judgment and feeling—yes ; for assuredly we shall regard,
with tolerance, if not with affection, whatever forms of material things we have been in the habit of associating with our
worship, and be little prepared to detect or blame hypocrisy,
meanness, and disguise in other kinds of decoration when we
suffer objects belonging to the most solemn of all services to
be tricked out in a fashion so fictitious and unseemly.

XVII. Painting, however, is not the only mode in which
material may be concealed, or rather simulated ; for merely
to conceal is, as we have seen, no wrong.   Whitewash, for instance, though often (by no means always) to be regretted as
a concealment, is not to be blamed as a falsity.   It shows itself for what it is, and asserts nothing of what is beneath it.
Gilding has become, from its frequent use, equally innocent.
It is understood for what it is, a film merely, and is, therefore,
allowable to any extent.   I do not say expedient : it is one of
the most abused means of magnificence we possess, and I
much doubt whether any use we ever make of it, balances
that loss of pleasure, which, from the frequent sight and perpetual suspicion of it, we suffer in the contemplation of any

thing that is verily of gold. I think gold was meant to be seldom seen and to be admired as a precious thing; and I sometimes wish that truth should so far literally prevail as that all
should be gold that glittered, or rather that nothing should
glitter that was not gold. Nevertheless, nature herself does
not dispense with such semblance, but uses light for it; and
I have too great a love for old and saintly art to part with its
burnished field, or radiant nimbus; only it should be used
with respect, and to express magnificence, or sacredness, and
not in lavish vanity, or in sign painting. Of its expedience,
however, any more than of that of color, it is not here the place
to speak; we are endeavoring to determine what is lawful, not
what is desirable. Of other and less common modes of dis-
guising surface, as of powder of lapis lazuli, or mosaic imitations of colored stones, I need hardly speak. The rule will
apply to all alike, that whatever is pretended, is wrong; commonly enforced also by the exceeding ugliness and insufficient
appearance of such methods, as lately in the style of renova-
tion by which half the houses in Venice have been defaced,
the brick covered first with stucco, and this painted with
zigzag veins in imitation of alabaster. But there is one more
form of architectural fiction, which is so constant in the great
periods that it needs respectful judgment. I mean the facing
of brick with precious stone.

XVIII. It is well known, that what is meant by a church's
being built of marble is, in nearly all cases, only that a veneering of marble has been fastened on the rough brick wall, built
with certain projections to receive it; and that what appear
to be massy stones, are nothing more than external slabs.

Now, it is evident, that, in this case, the question of right
is on the same ground as in that of gilding. If it be clearly
understood that a marble facing does not pretend or imply a
marble wall, there is no harm in it; and as it is also evident
that, when very precious stones are used, as jaspers and ser-
pentines, it must become, not only an extravagant and vain
increase of expense, but sometimes an actual impossibility, to
obtain mass of them enough to build with, there is no resource
but this of veneering; nor is there anything to be alleged

against it on the head of durability, such work having been by experience found to last as long, and in as perfect condition, as any kind of masonry. It is, therefore, to be considered as simply an art of mosaic on a large scale, the ground being of brick, or any other material; and when lovely stones are to be obtained, it is a manner which should be thoroughly understood, and often practised. Nevertheless, as we esteem the shaft of a column more highly for its being of a single block, and as we do not regret the loss of substance and value which there is in things of solid gold, silver, agate, or ivory; so I think the walls themselves may be regarded with a more just complacency if they are known to be all of noble substance; and that rightly weighing the demands of the two principles of which we have hitherto spoken—Sacrifice and Truth, we should sometimes rather spare external ornament than diminish the unseen value and consistency of what we do; and I believe that a better manner of design, and a more careful and studious, if less abundant decoration would follow, upon the consciousness of thoroughness in the substance. And, indeed, this is to be remembered, with respect to all the points we have examined; that while we have traced the limits of license, we have not fixed those of that high rectitude which refuses license. It is thus true that there is no falsity, and much beauty in the use of external color, and that it is lawful to paint either pictures or patterns on whatever surfaces may seem to need enrichment. But it is not less true, that such practices are essentially unarchitectural; and while we cannot say that there is actual danger in an over use of them, seeing that they have been *always* used most lavishly in the times of most noble art, yet they divide the work into two parts and kinds, one of less durability than the other, which dies away from it in process of ages, and leaves it, unless it have noble qualities of its own, naked and bare. That enduring noblesse I should, therefore, call truly architectural; and it is not until this has been secured that the accessory power of painting may be called in, for the delight of the immediate time; nor this, as I think, until every resource of a more stable kind has been exhausted. The true colors of architecture are those of natural stone, and

I would fain see these taken advantage of to the full. Every variety of hue, from pale yellow to purple, passing through orange, red, and brown, is entirely at our command ; nearly every kind of green and gray is also attainable : and with these, and pure white, what harmonies might we not achieve ? Of stained and variegated stone, the quantity is unlimited, the kinds innumerable ; where brighter colors are required, let glass, and gold protected by glass, be used in mosaic—a kind of work as durable as the solid stone, and incapable of losing its lustre by time—and let the painter's work be reserved for the shadowed *loggia* and inner chamber. This is the true and faithful way of building ; where this cannot be, the device of external coloring may, indeed, be employed without dishonor ; but it must be with the warning reflection, that a time will come when such aids must pass away, and when the building will be judged in its lifelessness, dying the death of the dolphin. Better the less bright, more enduring fabric. The transparent alabasters of San Miniato, and the mosaics of St. Mark's, are more warmly filled, and more brightly touched, by every return of morning and evening rays ; while the hues of our cathedrals have died like the iris out of the cloud ; and the temples whose azure and purple once flamed above the Grecian promontories, stand in their faded whiteness, like snows which the sunset has left cold.

XIX. The last form of fallacy which it will be remembered we had to deprecate, was the substitution of cast or machine work for that of the hand, generally expressible as Operative Deceit.

There are two reasons, both weighty, against this practice ; one, that all cast and machine work is bad, as work ; the other, that it is dishonest. Of its badness, I shall speak in another place, that being evidently no efficient reason against its use when other cannot be had. Its dishonesty, however, which, to my mind, is of the grossest kind, is, I think, a sufficient reason to determine absolute and unconditional rejection of it.

Ornament, as I have often before observed, has two entirely distinct sources of agreeableness : one, that of the ab-

stract beauty of its forms, which, for the present, we will suppose to be the same whether they come from the hand or the machine ; the other, the sense of human labor and care spent upon it. How great this latter influence we may perhaps judge, by considering that there is not a cluster of weeds growing in any cranny of ruin which has not a beauty in all respects *nearly* equal, and, in some, immeasurably superior, to that of the most elaborate sculpture of its stones : and that all our interest in the carved work, our sense of its richness, though it is tenfold less rich than the knots of grass beside it ; of its delicacy, though it is a thousand fold less delicate ; of its admirableness, though a millionfold less admirable ; results from our consciousness of its being the work of poor, clumsy, toilsome man. Its true delightfulness depends on our discovering in it the record of thoughts, and intents, and trials, and heart-breakings—of recoveries and joyfulnesses of success : all this *can* be traced by a practised eye ; but, granting it even obscure, it is presumed or understood ; and in that is the worth of the thing, just as much as the worth of anything else we call precious. The worth of a diamond is simply the understanding of the time it must take to look for it before it can be cut. It has an intrinsic value besides, which the diamond has not (for a diamond has no more real beauty than a piece of glass) ; but I do not speak of that at present ; I place the two on the same ground ; and I suppose that hand-wrought ornament can no more be generally known from machine work, than a diamond can be known from paste ; nay, that the latter may deceive, for a moment, the mason's, as the other the jeweller's eye ; and that it can be detected only by the closest examination. Yet exactly as a woman of feeling would not wear false jewels, so would a builder of honor disdain false ornaments. The using of them is just as downright and inexcusable a lie. You use that which pretends to a worth which it has not ; which pretends to have cost, and to be, what it did not, and is not ; it is an imposition, a vulgarity, an impertinence, and a sin. Down with it to the ground, grind it to powder, leave its ragged place upon the wall, rather ; you have not paid for it, you have no business with it, you do not want it. Nobody wants ornaments in this world, but everybody wants integrity. All the fair devices that ever were fancied, are not worth a lie. Leave your walls as bare as a planed board, or build them or baked mud and chopped straw, if need be ; but do not rough-cast them with falsehood.

This, then, being our general law, and I hold it for a more imperative one than any other I have asserted ; and this kind of dishonesty the meanest, as the least necessary ; for ornament is an extravagant and inessential thing ; and, therefore, if fallacious, utterly base—this, I say, being our general law, there are, nevertheless, certain exceptions respecting particular substances and their uses.

XX. Thus in the use of brick ; since that is known to be originally moulded, there is no reason why it should not be moulded into diverse forms. It will never be supposed to have been cut, and therefore, will cause no deception ; it will have only the credit it deserves. In flat countries, far from any quarry of stone, cast brick may be legitimately, and most successfully, used in decoration, and that elaborate, and even refined. The brick mouldings of the Palazzo Pepoli at Bologna, and those which run round the market-place of Vercelli, are among the richest in Italy. So also, tile and porcelain work, of which the former is grotesquely, but successfully, employed in the domestic architecture of France, colored tiles being inserted in the diamond spaces between the crossing timbers ; and the latter admirably in Tuscany, in external bas-reliefs, by the Robbia family, in which works, while we cannot but sometimes regret the useless and ill-arranged colors, we would by no means blame the employment of a material which, whatever its defects, excels every other in permanence, and, perhaps, requires even greater skill in its management than marble. For it is not the material, but the absence of the human labor, which makes the thing worthless; and a piece of terra cotta, or of plaster of Paris, which has been wrought by human hand, is worth all the stone in Carrara, cut by machinery. It is, indeed, possible, and even usual, for men to sink into machines themselves, so that even hand-work has all the characters of mechanism ; of the difference between living and dead hand-work I shall speak presently ; all that I ask at present is, what it is always in our power to secure—the confession of what we have done, and what we have given ; so that when we use stone at all, since all stone is naturally supposed to be carved by hand, we must not carve it by machinery ; neither must we use any artificial stone cast into shape, nor any stucco ornaments of the color of stone, or which might in anywise be mistaken for it, as the stucco mouldings in the cortile of the Palazzo Vecchio at Florence, which cast a shame and suspicion over every part of the building. But for ductile and fusible materials, as clay, iron, and bronze, since these will usually be supposed to have been cast or stamped, it is at our pleasure to employ them as we will ; remembering that they become precious, or otherwise, just in proportion to the hand-work upon them, or to the clearness of their reception of the hand-work of their mould.

But I believe no cause to have been more active in the degradation of our natural feeling for beauty, than the constant use of cast iron ornaments. The common iron work of the middle ages was as simple as it was effective, composed of leafage cut flat out of sheet iron, and twisted at the workman's will. No ornaments, on the contrary, are so cold, clumsy, and vulgar, so essentially incapable of a fine line, or shadow, as those of cast iron ; and while, on the score of truth, we can hardly allege anything against them, since they are always distinguishable, at a glance, from wrought and hammered work, and stand only for what they are, yet I feel very strongly that there is no hope of the progress of the arts of any nation which indulges in these vulgar and cheap substitutes for real decoration. Their inefficiency and paltriness I shall endeavor to show more conclusively in another place, enforcing only, at present, the general conclusion that, if even honest or allowable, they are things in which we can never take just pride or pleasure, and must never be employed in any place wherein they might either themselves obtain the credit of being other and better than they are, or be associated with the downright work to which it would be a disgrace to be found in their company.

Such are, I believe, the three principal kinds of fallacy by which architecture is liable to be corrupted ; there are, however, other and more subtle forms of it, against which it is less easy to guard by definite law, than by the watchfulness of a manly and unaffected spirit. For, as it has been above noticed, there are certain kinds of deception which extend to impressions and ideas only ; of which some are, indeed, of a noble use, as that above referred to, the arborescent look of lofty Gothic aisles ; but of which the most part have so much of legerdemain and trickery about them, that they will lower any style in which they considerably prevail ; and they are likely to prevail when once they are admitted, being apt to catch the fancy alike of uninventive architects and feelingless spectators ; just as mean and shallow minds are, in other matters, delighted with the sense of over-reaching, or tickled with the conceit of detecting the intention to over-reach ; and when subtleties of this kind are accompanied by the display of such dextrous stone-cutting, or architectural sleight of hand, as may become, even by itself, a subject of admiration, it is a great chance if the pursuit of them do not gradually draw us away from all regard and care for the nobler character of the art, and end in its total paralysis or extinction. And against this there is no guarding, but by stern disdain of all display of dexterity and ingenious device, and by putting the whole force of our fancy into the arrangement of masses and forms, caring no more how these masses and forms are wrought out, than a great painter cares which way his pencil strikes. It would be easy to give many instances of the danger of these tricks and vanities ; but I shall confine myself to the examination of one which has, as I think, been the cause of the fall of Gothic architecture throughout Europe. I mean the system of intersectional mouldings, which, on account of its great importance, and for the sake of the general reader, I may, perhaps, be pardoned for explaining elementarily.

XXI. I must, in the first place, however, refer to Professor

Willis's account of the origin of tracery, given in the sixth
chapter of his Architecture of the Middle Ages; since the
publication of which I have been not a little amazed to hear
of any attempts made to resuscitate the inexcusably absurd
theory of its derivation from imitated vegetable form—inexcusably, I say, because the smallest acquaintance with early
Gothic architecture would have informed the supporters of
that theory of the simple fact, that, exactly in proportion to
the antiquity of the work, the imitation of such organic forms
is less, and in the earliest examples does not exist at all.
There cannot be the shadow of a question, in the mind of a
person familiarised with any single series of consecutive examples, that tracery arose from the gradual enlargement of
the penetrations of the shield of stone which, usually supported by a central pillar, occupied the head of early windows.
Professor Willis, perhaps, confines his observations somewhat
too absolutely to the double sub-arch. I have given, in Plat
VII. fig. 2, an interesting case of rude penetration of a high
and simply trefoiled shield, from the church of the Eremitani
at Padua. But the more frequent and typical form is that of
the double sub-arch, decorated with various piercings of the
space between it and the superior arch ; with a simple trefoil
under a round arch, in the Abbaye aux Hommes, Caen °
(Plate III. fig. 1) ; with a very beautifully proportioned quatrefoil, in the triforium of Eu, and that of the choir of Lisieux ;
with quatrefoils, sixfoils, and septfoils, in the transept towers
of Rouen (Plate III. fig. 2) ; with a trefoil awkwardly, and very
small quatrefoil above, at Coutances, (Plate III. fig. 3) ; then,
with multiplications of the same figures, pointed or round, giving very clumsy shapes of the intermediate stone (fig. 4, from
one of the nave chapels of Rouen, fig. 5, from one of the nave
chapels of Bayeaux), and finally, by thinning out the stony
ribs, reaching conditions like that of the glorious typical form
of the clerestory of the apse of Beauvais (fig. 6).

XXII. Now, it will be noticed that, during the whole of
this process, the attention is kept fixed on the forms of the
penetrations, that is to say, of the lights as seen from the interior, not of the intermediate stone. All the grace of the

window is in the outline of its light; and I have drawn all
these traceries as seen from within, in order to show the effect
of the light thus treated, at first in far off and separate stars,
and then gradually enlarging, approaching, until they come
and stand over us, as it were, filling the whole space with their
effulgence. And it is in this pause of the star, that we have
the great, pure, and perfect form of French Gothic; it was
at the instant when the rudeness of the intermediate space
had been finally conquered, when the light had expanded to
its fullest, and yet had not lost its radiant unity, principality,
and visible first causing of the whole, that we have the most
exquisite feeling and most faultless judgments in the management alike of the tracery and decorations. I have given, in
Plate X., an exquisite example of it, from a panel decoration
of the buttresses of the north door of Rouen; and in order
that the reader may understand what truly fine Gothic work
is, and how nobly it unites fantasy and law, as well as for our
immediate purpose, it will be well that he should examine its
sections and mouldings in detail (they are described in the
fourth Chapter, § xxvii.), and that the more carefully, because
this design belongs to a period in which the most important
change took place in the spirit of Gothic architecture, which,
perhaps, ever resulted from the natural progress of any art.
That tracery marks a pause between the laying aside of one
great ruling principle, and the taking up of another; a pause
as marked, as clear, as conspicuous to the distant view of
after times, as to the distant glance of the traveller is the
culminating ridge of the mountain chain over which he has
passed. It was the great watershed of Gothic art. Before it,
all had been ascent; after it, all was decline; both, indeed,
by winding paths and varied slopes; both interrupted, like
the gradual rise and fall of the passes of the Alps, by great
mountain outliers, isolated or branching from the central
chain, and by retrograde or parallel directions of the valleys
of access. But the track of the human mind is traceable up
to that glorious ridge, in a continuous line, and thence down-
wards. Like a silver zone—

> "Flung about carelessly, it shines afar,
> Catching the eye in many a broken link,
> In many a turn and traverse, as it glides.
> And oft above, and oft below, appears—
> *   *   *   *   to him who journeys up
> As though it were another."

And at that point, and that instant, reaching the place that was nearest heaven, the builders looked back, for the last time, to the way by which they had come, and the scenes through which their early course had passed. They turned away from them and their morning light, and descended to-wards a new horizon, for a time in the warmth of western sun, but plunging with every forward step into more cold and melancholy shade.

XXIII. The change of which I speak, is inexpressible in few words, but one more important, more radically influential, could not be. It was the substitution of the *line* for the *mass,* as the element of decoration.

We have seen the mode in which the openings or penetra-tion of the window expanded, until what were, at first, awk-ward forms of intermediate stone, became delicate lines of tracery : and I have been careful in pointing out the peculiar attention bestowed on the proportion and decoration of the mouldings of the window at Rouen, in Plate X., as compared with earlier mouldings, because that beauty and care are sin-gularly significant. They mark that the traceries had *caught the eye* of the architect. Up to that time, up to the very last instant in which the reduction and thinning of the intervening stone was consummated, his eye had been on the openings only, on the stars of light. He did not care about the stone, a rude border of moulding was all he needed, it was the penetrating shape which he was watching. But when that shape had re-ceived its last possible expansion, and when the stone-work became an arrangement of graceful and parallel lines, that arrangement, like some form in a picture, unseen and acciden-tally developed, struck suddenly, inevitably, on the sight. It nad literally not been seen before. It flashed out in an in-stant as an independent form. It became a feature of the work. The architect took it under his care, thought over it, and distributed its members as we see.

Now, the great pause was at the moment when the space and the dividing stone-work were both equally considered. It did not last fifty years. The forms of the tracery were seized with a childish delight in the novel source of beauty ; and the intervening space was cast aside, as an element of decoration, for ever. I have confined myself, in following this change, to the window, as the feature in which it is clearest. But the transition is the same in every member of architecture ; and its importance can hardly be understood, unless we take the pains to trace it in the universality, of which illustrations, irrelevant to our present purpose, will be found in the third Chapter. I pursue here the question of truth, relating to the treatment of the mouldings.

XXIV. The reader will observe that, up to the last expansion of the penetrations, the stone-work was necessarily considered, as it actually is, *stiff*, and unyielding. It was so, also, during the pause of which I have spoken, when the forms of the tracery were still severe and pure ; delicate indeed, but perfectly firm.

At the close of the period of pause, the first sign of serious change was like a low breeze, passing through the emaciated tracery, and making it tremble. It began to undulate like the threads of a cobweb lifted by the wind. It lost its essence as a structure of stone. Reduced to the slenderness of threads, it began to be considered as possessing also their flexibility. The architect was pleased with this his new fancy, and set himself to carry it out ; and in a little time, the bars of tracery were caused to appear to the eye as if they had been woven together like a net. This was a change which sacrificed a great principle of truth ; it sacrificed the expression of the qualities of the material ; and, however delightful its results in their first developments, it was ultimately ruinous.

For, observe the difference between the supposition of ductility, and that of elastic structure noticed above in the resemblance to tree form. That resemblance was not sought, but **necessary** ; it resulted from the natural conditions of strength in the pier or trunk, and slenderness in the ribs or branches, while many of the other suggested conditions of resemblance were perfectly true. A tree branch, though in a certain sense flexible, is not ductile; it is as firm in its own form as the rib of stone; both of them will yield up to certain limits, both of them breaking when those limits are exceeded; while the tree trunk will bend no more than the stone pillar. But when the tracery is assumed to be as yielding as a silken cord; when the whole fragility, elasticity, and weight of the material are to the eye, if not in terms, denied; when all the art of the architect is applied to disprove the first conditions of his working, and the first attributes of his materials; *this* is a deliberate treachery, only redeemed from the charge of direct falsehood by the visibility of the stone surface, and degrading all the traceries it affects exactly in the degree of its presence.

XXV. But the declining and morbid taste of the later architects, was not satisfied with thus much deception. They were delighted with the subtle charm they had created, and thought only of increasing its power. The next step was to consider and represent the tracery, as not only ductile, but penetrable; and when two mouldings met each other, to manage their intersection, so that one should appear to pass through the other, retaining its independence; or when two ran parallel to each other, to represent the one as partly contained within the other, and partly apparent above it. This form of falsity was that which crushed the art. The flexible traceries were often beautiful, though they were ignoble; but the penetrated traceries, rendered, as they finally were, merely the means of exhibiting the dexterity of the stone-cutter, annihilated both the beauty and dignity of the Gothic types. A system so momentous in its consequences deserves some detailed examination.

XXVI. In the drawing of the shafts of the door at Lisieux, under the spandril, in Plate VII., the reader will see the mode of managing the intersection of similar mouldings, which was universal in the great periods. They melted into each other, and became *one* at the point of crossing, or of contact; and even the suggestion of so sharp intersection as this of Lisieux is usually avoided (this design being, of course, only a pointed form of the earlier Norman arcade, in which the arches are interlaced, and lie each over the preceding, and under the following, one, as in Anselm's tower at Canterbury), since, in the plurality of designs, when mouldings meet each other, they coincide through some considerable portion of their curves, meeting by contact, rather than by intersection; and at the point of coincidence the section of each separate moulding becomes common to the two thus melted into each other. Thus, in the junction of the circles of the window of the Palazzo Foscari, Plate VIII., given accurately in fig. 8, Plate IV., the section across the line s, is exactly the same as that across any break of the separated moulding above, as $\bar{s}$. It sometimes, however, happens, that two different mouldings meet each other. This was seldom permitted in the great periods, and, when it took place, was most awkwardly managed. Fig. 1, Plate IV. gives the junction of the mouldings of the gable and vertical, in the window of the *spire* of Salisbury. That of the gable is composed of a single, and that of the vertical of a double cavetto, decorated with ball-flowers; and the larger single moulding swallows up one of the double ones, and pushes forward among the smaller balls with the most blundering and clumsy simplicity. In comparing the sections it is to be observed that, in the upper one, the line $a\,b$ represents an actual vertical in the plane of the window; while, in the lower one, the line $e\,d$ represents the horizontal, in the plane of the window, indicated by the perspective line $d\,e$.

XXVII. The very awkwardness with which such occurrences of difficulty are met by the earlier builder, marks his dislike of the system, and unwillingness to attract the eye to such arrangements. There is another very clumsy one, in the junction of the upper and sub-arches of the triforium of Salisbury; but it is kept in the shade, and all the prominent junctions are of mouldings like each other, and managed with perfect simplicity. But so soon as the attention of the builders became, as we have just seen, fixed upon the lines of mouldings instead of the enclosed spaces, those lines began to preserve an independent existence wherever they met; and different mouldings were studiously associated, in order to obtain variety of intersectional line.   We must, however, do the late builders the justice to note that, in one case, the habit grew out of a feeling of proportion, more refined than that of earlier workmen.   It shows itself first in the bases of divided pillars, or arch mouldings, whose smaller shafts had originally bases formed by the continued base of the central, or other larger, columns with which they were grouped; but it being felt, when the eye of the architect became fastidious, that the dimension of moulding which was right for the base of a large shaft, was wrong for that of a small one, each shaft had an independent base ; at first, those of the smaller died simply down on that of the larger ; but when the vertical sections of both became complicated, the bases of the smaller shafts were considered to exist within those of the larger, and the places of their emergence, on this supposition, were calculated with the utmost nicety, and cut with singular precision ; so that an elaborate late base of a divided column, as, for instance, of those in the nave of Abbeville, looks exactly as if its smaller shafts had all been finished to the ground first, each with its complete and intricate base, and then the comprehending base of the central pier had been moulded over them in clay, leaving their points and angles sticking out here and there, like the edges of sharp crystals out of a nodule of earth.   The exhibition of technical dexterity in work of this kind is often marvellous, the strangest possible shapes of sections being calculated to a hair's-breadth, and the occurrence of the under and emergent forms being rendered, even in places where they are so slight that they can hardly be detected but by the touch.   It is impossible to render a very elaborate example of this kind intelligible, without some fifty measured sections; but fig. 6, Plate IV. is a very interesting and simple one, from the west gate of Rouen.   It is part of the base of one of the narrow piers between its principal niches.   The square column k, having a base with the profile $p\ r$, is supposed to contain within itself another similar one, set diagonally, and lifted so far above the inclosing one, as that the recessed part of its profile $\bar{p}\ r$ shall fall behind the projecting part of the outer one.   The angle of its upper por-

tion exactly meets the plane of the side of the upper inclosing
shaft 4, and would, therefore, not be seen, unless two vertical
cuts were made to exhibit it, which form two dark lines the
whole way up the shaft. Two small pilasters are run, like
fastening stitches, through the junction on the front of the
shafts. The sections $\bar{k}$ n taken respectively at the levels k, n,
will explain the hypothetical construction of the whole. Fig.
7 is a base, or joint rather (for passages of this form occur
again and again, on the shafts of flamboyant work), of one of
the smallest piers of the pedestals which support the lost statues of the porch ; its section below would be the same as $\bar{n}$,
and its construction, after what has been said of the other
base, will be at once perceived.

XXVIII. There was, however, in this kind of involution,
much to be admired as well as reprehended, the proportions
of quantities were always as beautiful as they were intricate ;
and, though the lines of intersection were harsh, they were
exquisitely opposed to the flower-work of the interposing
mouldings. But the fancy did not stop here ; it rose from
the bases into the arches ; and there, not finding room enough
for its exhibition, it withdrew the capitals from the heads
even of cylindrical shafts, (we cannot but admire, while we
regret, the boldness of the men who could defy the authority
and custom of all the nations of the earth for a space of some
three thousand years,) in order that the arch mouldings might
appear to emerge from the pillar, as at its base they had been
lost in it, and not to terminate on the abacus of the capital ;
then they ran the mouldings across and through each other,
at the point of the arch ; and finally, not finding their natural
directions enough to furnish as many occasions of intersection
as they wished, bent them hither and thither, and cut off their
ends short, when they had passed the point of intersection.
Fig. 2, Plate IV. is part of a flying buttress from the apse of
St. Gervais at Falaise, in which the moulding whose section
is rudely given above at $\bar{f}$, (taken vertically through the point
f,) is carried thrice through itself, in the cross-bar and two
arches ; and the flat fillet is cut off sharp at the end of the
cross-bar, for the mere pleasure of the truncation. Fig. 3 is

half of the head of a door in the Stadthaus of Sursee, in which
the shaded part of the section of the joint g g, is that of the
arch-moulding, which is three times reduplicated, and six
times intersected by itself, the ends being cut off when they
become unmanageable, This style is, indeed, earlier exag-
gerated in Switzerland and Germany, owing to the imitation
in stone of the dovetailing of wood, particularly of the inter-
secting of beams at the angles of châlets ; but it only furnishes
the more plain instance of the danger of the fallacious system
which, from the beginning, repressed the German, and, in
the end, ruined the French Gothic. It would be too painful
a task to follow further the caricatures of form, and eccen-
tricities of treatment, which grow out of this singular abuse
—the flattened arch, the shrunken pillar, the lifeless ornament, the liny moulding, the distorted and extravagant foliation, until the time came when, over these wrecks and remnants, deprived of all unity and principle, rose the foul torrent
of the renaissance, and swept them all away.   So fell the great
dynasty of mediæval architecture. It was because it had lost
its own strength, and disobeyed its own laws—because its order,
and consistency, and organization, had been broken through
—that it could oppose no resistance to the rush of overwhelming innovation. And this, observe, all because it had sacrificed a single truth.   From that one surrender of its integrity,
from that one endeavor to assume the semblance of what it
was not, arose the multitudinous forms of disease and decrep-
itude, which rotted away the pillars of its supremacy.   It was
not because its time was come ; it was not because it was
scorned by the classical Romanist, or dreaded by the faithful
Protestant.   That scorn and that fear it might have survived,
and lived ; it would have stood forth in stern comparison with
the enervated sensuality of the renaissance ; it would have
risen in renewed and purified honor, and with a new soul,
from the ashes into which it sank, giving up its glory, as it
had received it, for the honor of God—but its own truth was
gone, and it sank forever.   There was no wisdom nor strength
left in it, to raise it from the dust ; and the error of zeal, and
the softness of luxury smote it down and dissolved it away

It is good for us to remember this, as we tread upon the bare ground of its foundations, and stumble over its scattered stones. Those rent skeletons of pierced wall, through which our sea-winds moan and murmur, strewing them joint by joint, and bone by bone, along the bleak promontories on which the Pharos lights came once from houses of prayer— those grey arches and quiet isles under which the sheep of our valleys feed and rest on the turf that has buried their altars—those shapeless heaps, that are not of the Earth, which lift our fields into strange and sudden banks of flowers, and stay our mountain streams with stones that are not their own, have other thoughts to ask from us than those of mourning for the rage that despoiled, or the fear that forsook them. It was not the robber, not the fanatic, not the blasphemer, who sealed the destruction that they had wrought ; the war, the wrath, the terror, might have worked their worst, and the strong walls would have risen, and the slight pillars would have started again, from under the hand of the destroyer. But they could not rise out of the ruins of their own violated truth.

CHAPTER III.

THE LAMP OF POWER.

I. In recalling the impressions we have received from the works of man, after a lapse of time long enough to involve in obscurity all but the most vivid, it often happens that we find a strange pre-eminence and durability in many upon whose strength we had little calculated, and that points of character which had escaped the detection of the judgment, become developed under the waste of memory ; as veins of harder rock, whose places could not at first have been discovered by the eye, are left salient under the action of frosts and streams. The traveller who desires to correct the errors of his judgment, necessitated by inequalities of temper, infelicities of circumstance, and accidents of association, has no other resource than to wait for the calm verdict of interposing years ; and to watch for the new arrangements of eminence and shape

in the images which remain latest in his memory; as in the
ebbing of a mountain lake, he would watch the varying outlines of its successive shore, and trace, in the form of its de-
parting waters, the true direction of the forces which had
cleft, or the currents which had excavated, the deepest recesses of its primal bed.

In thus reverting to the memories of those works of architecture by which we have been most pleasurably impressed, it
will generally happen that they fall into two broad classes:
the one characterized by an exceeding preciousness and delicacy, to which we recur with a sense of affectionate admiration ; and the other by a severe, and, in many cases, mysterious, majesty, which we remember with an undiminished
awe, like that felt at the presence and operation of some great
Spiritual Power.   From about these two groups, more or less
harmonised by intermediate examples, but always distinctively marked by features of beauty or of power, there will be
swept away, in multitudes, the memories of buildings, perhaps, in their first address to our minds, of no inferior pretension, but owing their impressiveness to characters of less
enduring nobility—to value of material, accumulation of ornament, or ingenuity of mechanical construction.   Especial
interest may, indeed, have been awakened by such circumstances, and the memory may have been, consequently, rendered tenacious of particular parts or effects of the structure;
but it will recall even these only by an active effort, and then
without emotion ; while in passive moments, and with thrill-
ing influence, the image of purer beauty, and of more spiritual power, will return in a fair and solemn company ; and
while the pride of many a stately palace, and the wealth of
many a jewelled shrine, perish from our thoughts in a dust of
gold, there will rise, through their dimness, the white image
of some secluded marble chapel, by river or forest side, with
the fretted flower-work shrinking under its arches, as if under
vaults of late-fallen snow ; or the vast weariness of some shadowy wall whose separate stones are like mountain foundations,
and yet numberless.

II. Now, the difference between these two orders of building is not merely that which there is in nature between things beautiful and sublime. It is, also, the difference between what is derivative and original in man's work ; for whatever is in architecture fair or beautiful, is imitated from natural forms ; and what is not so derived, but depends for its dignity upon arrangement and government received from human mind, becomes the expression of the power of that mind, and receives a sublimity high in proportion to the power expressed. All building, therefore, shows man either as gathering or governing : and the secrets of his success are his knowing what to gather, and how to rule. These are the two great intellectual Lamps of Architecture ; the one consisting in a just and humble veneration for the works of God upon the earth, and the other in an understanding of the dominion over those works which has been vested in man.

III. Besides this expression of living authority and power, there is, however, a sympathy in the forms of noble building, with what is most sublime in natural things ; and it is the governing Power directed by this sympathy, whose operation I shall at present endeavor to trace, abandoning all inquiry into the more abstract fields of invention : for this latter faculty, and the questions of proportion and arrangement connected with its discussion, can only be rightly examined in a general view of all arts ; but its sympathy, in architecture, with the vast controlling powers of Nature herself, is special, and may shortly be considered ; and that with the more advantage, that it has, of late, been little felt or regarded by architects. I have seen, in recent efforts, much contest between two schools, one affecting originality, and the other legality— many attempts at beauty of design—many ingenious adaptations of construction ; but I have never seen any aim at the expression of abstract power ; never any appearance of a consciousness that, in this primal art of man, there is room for the marking of his relations with the mightiest, as well as the fairest, works of God ; and that those works themselves have been permitted, by their Master and his, to receive an added glory from their association with earnest efforts of human thought. In the edifices of Man there should be found rever-

ent worship and following, not only of the spirit which rounds
the pillars of the forest, and arches the vault of the avenue—
which gives veining to the leaf, and polish to the shell, and
grace to every pulse that agitates animal organization,—but
of that also which reproves the pillars of the earth, and builds
up her barren precipices into the coldness of the clouds, and
lifts her shadowy cones of mountain purple into the pale arch
of the sky ; for these, and other glories more than these, refuse not to connect themselves, in his thoughts, with the work
of his own hand ; the grey cliff loses not its nobleness when it
reminds us of some Cyclopean waste of mural stone ; the pinnacles of the rocky promontory arrange themselves, unde-
graded, into fantastic semblances of fortress towers ; and even
the awful cone of the far-off mountain has a melancholy mixed
with that of its own solitude, which is cast from the images of
nameless tumuli on white sea-shores, and of the heaps of reedy
clay, into which chambered cities melt in their mortality.

IV. Let us, then, see what is this power and majesty, which
Nature herself does not disdain to accept from the works of
man ; and what that sublimity in the masses built up by his
coralline-like energy, which is honorable, even when trans-
ferred by association to the dateless hills, which it needed
earthquakes to lift, and deluges to mould.

And, first of mere size : It might not be thought possible
to emulate the sublimity of natural objects in this respect ; nor
would it be, if the architect contended with them in pitched
battle.   It would not be well to build pyramids in the valley
of Chamouni ; and St. Peter's, among its many other errors,
counts for not the least injurious its position on the slope of
an inconsiderable hill.   But imagine it placed on the plain of
Marengo, or, like the Superga of Turin, or like La Salute at
Venice !   The fact is, that the apprehension of the size of natural objects, as well as of architecture, depends more on fortunate excitement of the imagination than on measurements
by the eye ; and the architect has a peculiar advantage in being
able to press close upon the sight, such magnitude as he can
command.   There are few rocks, even among the Alps, that
have a clear vertical fall as high as the choir of Beauvais ; and

if we secure a good precipice of wall, or a sheer and unbroken
flank of tower, and place them where there are no enormous
natural features to oppose them, we shall feel in them no want
of sublimity of size. And it may be matter of encouragement
in this respect, though one also of regret, to observe how much
oftener man destroys natural sublimity, than nature crushes
human power. It does not need much to humiliate a mountain. A hut will sometimes do it; I never look up to the Col
de Balme from Chamouni, without a violent feeling of provo-
cation against its hospitable little cabin, whose bright white
walls form a visibly four-square spot on the green ridge, and
entirely destroy all idea of its elevation. A single villa will
often mar a whole landscape, and dethrone a dynasty of hills,
and the Acropolis of Athens, Parthenon and all, has, I believe,
been dwarfed into a model by the palace lately built beneath
it. The fact is, that hills are not so high as we fancy them,
and, when to the actual impression of no mean comparative
size, is added the sense of the toil of manly hand and thought,
a sublimity is reached, which nothing but gross error in arrangement of its parts can destroy.

V. While, therefore, it is not to be supposed that mere size
will ennoble a mean design, yet every increase of magnitude
will bestow upon it a certain degree of nobleness : so that it
is well to determine at first, whether the building is to be
markedly beautiful or markedly sublime ; and if the latter,
not to be withheld by respect to smaller parts from reaching
largeness of scale ; provided only, that it be evidently in the
architect's power to reach at least that degree of magnitude
which is the lowest at which sublimity begins, rudely definable
as that which will make a living figure look less than life beside it. It is the misfortune of most of our modern buildings
that we would fain have an universal excellence in them ; and
so part of the funds must go in painting, part in gilding, part
in fitting up, part in painted windows, part in small steeples,
part in ornaments here and there ; and neither the windows,
nor the steeple, nor the ornaments, are worth their materials.
For there is a crust about the impressible part of men's minds,
which must be pierced through before they can be touched

to the quick ; and though we may prick at it and scratch it
in a thousand separate places, we might as well have let it
alone if we do not come through somewhere with a deep
thrust : and if we can give such a thrust anywhere, there is
no need of another ; it need not be even so " wide as a church
door," so that it be *enough.* And mere weight will do this ;
it is a clumsy way of doing it, but an effectual one, too ; and
the apathy which cannot be pierced through by a small steeple,
nor shone through by a small window, can be broken through
in a moment by the mere weight of a great wall. Let, therefore, the architect who has not large resources, choose his
point of attack first, and, if he choose size, let him abandon
decoration ; for, unless they are concentrated, and numerous
enough to make their concentration conspicuous, all his ornaments together would not be worth one huge stone. And the
choice must be a decided one, without compromise. It must
be no question whether his capitals would not look better with
a little carving—let him leave them huge as blocks ; or whether
his arches should not have richer architraves—let him throw
them a foot higher, if he can ; a yard more across the nave
will be worth more to him than a tesselated pavement ; and
another fathom of outer wall, than an army of pinnacles. The
limitation of size must be only in the uses of the building, or
in the ground at his disposal.

VI. That limitation, however, being by such circumstances
determined, by what means, it is to be next asked, may the
actual magnitude be best displayed ; since it is seldom, perhaps never, that a building of any pretension to size looks so
large as it is. The appearance of a figure in any distant, more
especially in any upper, parts of it will almost always prove
that we have under-estimated the magnitude of those parts.

It has often been observed that a building, in order to show
its magnitude, must be seen all at once. It would, perhaps,
be better to say, must be bounded as much as possible by
continuous lines, and that its extreme points should be seen
all at once ; or we may state, in simpler terms still, that it
must have one visible bounding line from top to bottom, and
from end to end. This bounding line from top to bottom may

either be inclined inwards, and the mass, therefore, pyramidical; or vertical, and the mass form one grand cliff; or inclined outwards, as in the advancing fronts of old houses, and, in a sort, in the Greek temple, and in all buildings with heavy cornices or heads. Now, in all these cases, if the bounding line be violently broken; if the cornice project, or the upper portion of the pyramid recede, too violently, majesty will be lost; not because the building cannot be seen all at once,—for in the case of a heavy cornice no part of it is necessarily concealed—but because the continuity of its terminal line is broken, and the *length of that line*, therefore, cannot be estimated. But the error is, of course, more fatal when much of the building is also concealed; as in the well-known case of the recession of the dome of St. Peter's, and, from the greater number of points of view, in churches whose highest portions, whether dome or tower, are over their cross. Thus there is only one point from which the size of the Cathedral of Florence is felt; and that is from the corner of the Via de' Balestrieri, opposite the south-east angle, where it happens that the dome is seen rising instantly above the apse and transepts. In all cases in which the tower is over the cross, the grandeur and height of the tower itself are lost, because there is but one line down which the eye can trace the whole height, and that is in the inner angle of the cross, not easily discerned. Hence, while, in symmetry and feeling, such designs may often have pre-eminence, yet, where the height of the tower itself is to be made apparent, it must be at the west end, or better still, detached as a campanile. Imagine the loss to the Lombard churches if their campaniles were carried only to their present height over their crosses; or to the Cathedral of Rouen, if the Tour de Beurre were made central, in the place of its present debased spire !

VII. Whether, therefore, we have to do with tower or wall, there must be one bounding line from base to coping; and I am much inclined, myself, to love the true vertical, or the vertical, with a solemn frown of projection (not a scowl), as in the Palazzo Vecchio of Florence. This character is always given to rocks by the poets; with slight foundation indeed,

real rocks being little given to overhanging—but with excel
ient judgment; for the sense of threatening conveyed by this
form is a nobler character than that of mere size. And, in
buildings, this threatening should be somewhat carried down
into their mass. A mere projecting shelf is not enough, the
whole wall must, Jupiter like, nod as well as frown. Hence,
I think the propped machicolations of the Palazzo Vecchio
and Duomo of Florence far grander headings than any form
of Greek cornice. Sometimes the projection may be thrown
lower, as in the Doge's palace of Venice, where the chief appearance of it is above the second arcade; or it may become
a grand swell from the ground, as the head of a ship of the
line rises from the sea. This is very nobly attained by the
projection of the niches in the third story of the Tour de
Beurre at Rouen.

VIII. What is needful in the setting forth of magnitude in
height, is right also in the marking it in area—let it be gathered well together. It is especially to be noted with respect
to the Palazzo Vecchio and other mighty buildings of its
order, how mistakenly it has been stated that dimension, in
order to become impressive, should be expanded either in
height or length, but not equally: whereas, rather it will be
found that those buildings seem on the whole the vastest
which have been gathered up into a mighty square, and which
look as if they had been measured by the angel's rod, " the
length, and the breadth, and the height of it are equal," and
herein something is to be taken notice of, which I believe
not to be sufficiently, if at all, considered among our architects.

Of the many broad divisions under which architecture may
be considered, none appear to me more significant than that
into buildings whose interest is in their walls, and those
whose interest is in the lines dividing their walls. In the
Greek temple the wall is as nothing; the entire interest is in
the detached columns and the frieze they bear; in French
Flamboyant, and in our detestable Perpendicular, the object
is to get rid of the wall surface, and keep the eye altogether
on tracery of line; in Romanesque work and Egyptian, the

wall is a confessed and honored member, and the light is often allowed to fall on large areas of it, variously decorated. Now, both these principles are admitted by Nature, the one in her woods and thickets, the other in her plains, and cliffs, and waters; but the latter is pre-eminently the principle of power, and, in some sense, of beauty also. For, whatever infinity of fair form there may be in the maze of the forest, there is a fairer, as I think, in the surface of the quiet lake; and I hardly know that association of shaft or tracery, for which I would exchange the warm sleep of sunshine on some smooth, broad, human-like front of marble. Nevertheless, if breadth is to be beautiful, its substance must in some sort be beautiful; and we must not hastily condemn the exclusive resting of the northern architects in divided lines, until at least we have remembered the difference between a blank surface of Caen stone, and one mixed from Genoa and Carrara, of serpentine with snow: but as regards abstract power and awfulness, there is no question; without breadth of surface it is in vain to seek them, and it matters little, so that the surface be wide, bold and unbroken, whether it be of brick or of jasper; the light of heaven upon it, and the weight of earth in it, are all we need: for it is singular how forgetful the mind may become both of material and workmanship, if only it have space enough over which to range, and to remind it, however feebly, of the joy that it has in contemplating the flatness and sweep of great plains and broad seas. And it is a noble thing for men to do this with their cut stone or moulded clay, and to make the face of a wall look infinite, and its edge against the sky like an horizon: or even if less than this be reached, it is still delightful to mark the play of passing light on its broad surface, and to see by how many artifices and gradations of tinting and shadow, time and storm will set their wild signatures upon it; and how in the rising or declining of the day the unbroken twilight rests long and luridly on its high lineless forehead, and fades away untraceably down its tiers of confused and countless stone.

IX. This, then, being, as I think, one of the peculiar elements of sublime architecture, it may be easily seen how neces-

sarily consequent upon the love of it will be the choice of a
form approaching to the square for the main outline.

For, in whatever direction the building is contracted, in
that direction the eye will be drawn to its terminal lines ; and
the sense of surface will only be at its fullest when those lines
are removed, in every direction, as far as possible.   Thus the
square and circle are pre-eminently the areas of power among
those bounded by purely straight or curved lines ; and these,
with their relative solids, the cube and sphere, and relative
solids of progression (as in the investigation of the laws of
proportion I shall call those masses which are generated by
the progression of an area of given form along a line in a
given direction), the square and cylindrical column, are the
elements of utmost power in all architectural arrangements.
On the other hand, grace and perfect proportion require an
elongation in some one direction : and a sense of power may
be communicated to this form of magnitude by a continuous
series of any marked features, such as the eye may be unable
to number ; while yet we feel, from their boldness, decision,
and simplicity, that it is indeed their multitude which has
embarrassed us, not any confusion or indistinctness of form.
This expedient of continued series forms the sublimity of
arcades and aisles, of all ranges of columns, and, on a smaller
scale, of those Greek mouldings, of which, repeated as they
now are in all the meanest and most familiar forms of our furniture, it is impossible altogether to weary.   Now, it is evident that the architect has choice of two types of form, each
properly associated with its own kind of interest or decoration : the square, or greatest area, to be chosen especially
when the *surface* is to be the subject of thought ; and the
elongated area, when the *divisions* of the surface are to be the
subjects of thought.   Both these orders of form, as I think
nearly every other source of power and beauty, are marvellously united in that building which I fear to weary the reader
by bringing forward too frequently, as a model of all perfection—the Doge's palace at Venice : its general arrangement,
a hollow square ; its principal façade, an oblong, elongated to
the eye by a range of thirty-four small arches, and thirty-five

columns, while it is separated by a richly-canopied window in the centre, into two massive divisions, whose height and length are nearly as four to five; the arcades which give it length being confined to the lower stories, and the upper, between its broad windows, left a mighty surface of smooth marble, chequered with blocks of alternate rose-color and white. It would be impossible, I believe, to invent a more magnificent arrangement of all that is in building most dignified and most fair.

X. In the Lombard Romanesque, the two principles are more fused into each other, as most characteristically in the Cathedral of Pisa: length of proportion, exhibited by an arcade of twenty-one arches above, and fifteen below, at the side of the nave; bold square proportion in the front; that front divided into arcades, placed one above the other, the lowest with its pillars engaged, of seven arches, the four uppermost thrown out boldly from the receding wall, and casting deep shadows; the first, above the basement, of nineteen arches; the second of twenty-one; the third and fourth of eight each; sixty-three arches in all; all *circular* headed, all with cylindrical shafts, and the lowest with *square* panellings, set diagonally under their semicircles, an universal ornament in this style (Plate XII., fig. 7); the apse, a semicircle, with a semidome for its roof, and three ranges of circular arches for its exterior ornament; in the interior of the nave, a range of circular arches below a circular-arched triforium, and a vast flat *surface*, observe, of wall decorated with striped marble above; the whole arrangement (not a peculiar one, but characteristic of every church of the period; and, to my feeling, the most majestic; not perhaps the fairest, but the mightiest type of form which the mind of man has ever conceived) based exclusively on associations of the circle and the square.

I am now, however, trenching upon ground which I desire to reserve for more careful examination, in connection with other æsthetic questions: but I believe the examples I have given will justify my vindication of the square form from the reprobation which has been lightly thrown upon it; nor might this be done for it only as a ruling outline, but as occurring

constantly in the best mosaics, and in a thousand forms of
minor decoration, which I cannot now examine ; my chief
assertion of its majesty being always as it is an exponent of
space and surface, and therefore to be chosen, either to rule in
their outlines, or to adorn by masses of light and shade those
portions of buildings in which surface is to be rendered precious or honorable.

XI. Thus far, then, of general forms, and of the modes in
which the scale of architecture is best to be exhibited. Let
us next consider the manifestations of power which belong to
its details and lesser divisions.

The first division we have to regard, is the inevitable one
of masonry. It is true that this division may, by great art, be
concealed ; but I think it unwise (as well as dishonest) to do
so ; for this reason, that there is a very noble character always
to be obtained by the opposition of large stones to divided
masonry, as by shafts and columns of one piece, or massy
lintels and architraves, to wall work of bricks or smaller stones ;
and there is a certain organization in the management of such
parts, like that of the continuous bones of the skeleton, opposed to the vertebræ, which it is not well to surrender. I
hold, therefore, that, for this and other reasons, the masonry
of a building is to be shown : and also that, with certain rare
exceptions (as in the cases of chapels and shrines of most finished workmanship), the smaller the building, the more necessary it is that its masonry should be bold, and *vice versâ*.
For if a building be under the mark of average magnitude, it
is not in our power to increase its apparent size (too easily
measurable) by any proportionate diminution in the scale of
its masonry. But it may be often in our power to give it a
certain nobility by building it of massy stones, or, at all events,
introducing such into its make. Thus it is impossible that
there should ever be majesty in a cottage built of brick ; but
there is a marked element of sublimity in the rude and irregular piling of the rocky walls of the mountain cottages of
Wales, Cumberland, and Scotland. Their size is not one whit
diminished, though four or five stones reach at their angles
from the ground to the eaves, or though a native rock happen

to project conveniently, and to be built into the framework of the wall. On the other hand, after a building has once reached the mark of majestic size, it matters, indeed, comparatively little whether its masonry be large or small, but if it be altogether large, it will sometimes diminish the magnitude for want of a measure ; if altogether small, it will suggest ideas of poverty in material, or deficiency in mechanical resource, besides interfering in many cases with the lines of the design, and delicacy of the workmanship. A very unhappy instance of such interference exists in the façade of the church of St. Madeleine at Paris, where the columns, being built of very small stones of nearly equal size, with visible joints, look as if they were covered with a close trellis. So, then, that masonry will be generally the most magnificent which, without the use of materials systematically small or large, accommodates itself, naturally and frankly, to the conditions and structure of its work, and displays alike its power of dealing with the vastest masses, and of accomplishing its purpose with the smallest, sometimes heaping rock upon rock with Titanic commandment, and anon binding the dusty remnants and edgy splinters into springing vaults and swelling domes. And if the nobility of this confessed and natural masonry were more commonly felt, we should not lose the dignity of it by smoothing surfaces and fitting joints. The sums which we waste in chiselling and polishing stones which would have been better left as they came from the quarry would often raise a building a story higher. Only in this there is to be a certain respect for material also : for if we build in marble, or in any limestone, the known ease of the workmanship will make its absence seem slovenly ; it will be well to take advantage of the stone's softness, and to make the design delicate and dependent upon smoothness of chiselled surfaces : but if we build in granite or lava, it is a folly, in most cases, to cast away the labor necessary to smooth it ; it is wiser to make the design granitic itself, and to leave the blocks rudely squared. I do not deny a certain splendor and sense of power in the smoothing of granite, and in the entire subduing of its iron resistance to the human supremacy. But in most cases, I believe, the labor

and time necessary to do this would be better spent in another
way ; and that to raise a building to a height of a hundred
feet with rough blocks, is better than to raise it to seventy
with smooth ones.   There is also a magnificence in the natural
cleavage of the stone to which the art must indeed be great
that pretends to be equivalent ; and a stern expression of
brotherhood with the mountain heart from which it has been
rent, ill-exchanged for a glistering obedience to the rule and
measure of men.   His eye must be delicate indeed, who would
desire to see the Pitti palace polished.

XII. Next to those of the masonry, we have to consider
the divisions of the design itself.   Those divisions are, necessarily, either into masses of light and shade, or else by traced
lines ; which latter must be, indeed, themselves produced by
incisions or projections which, in some lights, cast a certain
breadth of shade, but which may, nevertheless, if finely enough
cut, be always true lines, in distant effect.   I call, for instance,
such panelling as that of Henry the Seventh's chapel, pure
linear division.

Now, it does not seem to me sufficiently recollected, that a
wall surface is to an architect simply what a white canvas is to
a painter, with this only difference, that the wall has already a
sublimity in its height, substance, and other characters already
considered, on which it is more dangerous to break than to
touch with shade the canvas surface.   And, for my own part,
I think a smooth, broad, freshly laid surface of gesso a fairer
thing than most pictures I see painted on it ; much more, a
noble surface of stone than most architectural features which
it is caused to assume.   But however this may be, the canvas
and wall are supposed to be given, and it is our craft to divide
them.

And the principles on which this division is to be made, are
as regards relation of quantities, the same in architecture as
in painting, or indeed, in any other art whatsoever, only the
painter is by his varied subject partly permitted, partly compelled, to dispense with the symmetry of architectural light
and shade, and to adopt arrangements apparently free and
accidental. So that in modes of grouping there is much dif-

ference (though no opposition) between the two arts ; but in rules of quantity, both are alike, so far forth as their commands of means are alike. For the architect, not being able to secure always the same depth or decision of shadow, nor to add to its sadness by color (because even when color is employed, it cannot follow the moving shade), is compelled to make many allowances, and avail himself of many contrivances, which the painter needs neither consider nor employ.

XIII. Of these limitations the first consequence is, that positive shade is a more necessary and more sublime thing in an architect's hands than in a painter's. For the latter being able to temper his light with an under-tone throughout, and to make it delightful with sweet color, or awful with lurid color, and to represent distance, and air, and sun, by the depth of it, and fill its whole space with expression, can deal with an enormous, nay, almost with an universal extent of it, and the best painters most delight in such extent ; but as light, with the architect, is nearly always liable to become full and untempered sunshine seen upon solid surface, his only rests, and his chief means of sublimity, are definite shades. So that, after size and weight, the Power of architecture may be said to depend on the quantity (whether measured in space or intenseness) of its shadow ; and it seems to me, that the reality of its works, and the use and influence they have in the daily life of men (as opposed to those works of art with which we have nothing to do but in times of rest or of pleasure) require of it that it should express a kind of human sympathy, by a measure of darkness as great as there is in human life : and that as the great poem and great fiction generally affect us most by the majesty of their masses of shade, and cannot take hold upon us if they affect a continuance of lyric sprightliness, but must be serious often, and sometimes melancholy, else they do not express the truth of this wild world of ours ; so there must be, in this magnificently human art of architecture, some equivalent expression for the trouble and wrath of life, for its sorrow and its mystery : and this it can only give by depth or diffusion of gloom, by the frown upon its front, and the shadow of its recess. So that Rembrandtism is a noble manner in architecture, though a false one in painting ; and I do not believe that ever any building was truly great, unless it had mighty masses, vigorous and deep, of shadow mingled with its surface. And among the first habits that a young architect should learn, is that of thinking in shadow, not looking at a design in its miserable liny skeleton ; but conceiving it as it will be when the dawn lights it, and the dusk leaves it ; when its stones will be hot and its crannies cool ; when the lizards will bask on the one, and the birds build in the other. Let him design with the sense of cold and heat upon him ; let him cut out the shadows, as men dig wells in unwatered plains ; and lead along the lights, as a founder does his hot metal ; let him keep the full command of both, and see that he knows how they fall, and where they fade. His paper lines and proportions are of no value : all that he has to do must be done by spaces of light and darkness ; and his business is to see that the one is broad and bold enough not to be swallowed up by twilight, and the other deep enough not to be dried like a shallow pool by a noon-day sun.

And that this may be, the first necessity is that the quantities of shade or light, whatever they may be, shall be thrown into masses, either of something like equal weight, or else large masses of the one relieved with small of the other ; but masses of one or other kind there must be. No design that is divided at all, and is not divided into masses, can ever be of the smallest value : this great law respecting breadth, precisely the same in architecture and painting, is so important, that the examination of its two principal applications will include most of the conditions of majestic design on which I would at present insist.

XIV. Painters are in the habit of speaking loosely of masses of light and shade, meaning thereby any large spaces of either. Nevertheless, it is convenient sometimes to restrict the term " mass" to the portions to which proper form belongs, and to call the field on which such forms are traced, interval. Thus, in foliage with projecting boughs or stems, we have masses of light, with intervals of shade ; and, in light skies with dark clouds upon them, masses of shade with intervals of light.

This distinction is, in architecture, still more necessary; for there are two marked styles dependent upon it : one in which the forms are drawn with light upon darkness, as in Greek sculpture and pillars ; the other in which they are drawn with darkness upon light, as in early Gothic foliation. Now, it is not in the designer's power determinately to vary degrees and places of darkness, but it is altogether in his power to vary in determined directions his degrees of light. Hence, the use of the dark mass characterises, generally, a trenchant style of design, in which the darks and lights are both flat, and terminated by sharp edges ; while the use of the light mass is in the same way associated with a softened and full manner of design, in which the darks are much warmed by reflected lights, and the lights are rounded and melt into them. The term applied by Milton to Doric bas-relief—" bossy," is, as is generally the case with Milton's epithets, the most comprehensive and expressive of this manner, which the English language contains ; while the term which specifically describes the chief member of early Gothic decoration, feuille, foil or leaf, is equally significative of a flat space of shade.

XV. We shall shortly consider the actual modes in which these two kinds of mass have been treated. And, first, of the light, or rounded, mass. The modes in which relief was secured for the more projecting forms of bas-relief, by the Greeks, have been too well described by Mr. Eastlake * to need recapitulation ; the conclusion which forces itself upon us from the facts he has remarked, being one on which I shall have occasion farther to insist presently, that the Greek workman cared for shadow only as a dark field wherefrom his light figure or design might be intelligibly detached : his attention was concentrated on the one aim at readableness, and clearness of accent ; and all composition, all harmony, nay, the very vitality and energy of separate groups were, when necessary, sacrificed to plain speaking. Nor was there any predilection for one kind

* Literature of the Fine Arts.—Essay on Bas-relief.

of form rather than another. Rounded forms were, in the columns and principal decorative members, adopted, not for their own sake, but as characteristic of the things represented. They were beautifully rounded, because the Greek habitually did well what he had to do, not because he loved roundness more than squareness; severely rectilinear forms were associated with the curved ones in the cornice and triglyph, and the mass of the pillar was divided by a fluting, which, in distant effect, destroyed much of its breadth. What power of light these primal arrangements left, was diminished in successive refinements and additions of ornament; and continued to diminish through Roman work, until the confirmation of the circular arch as a decorative feature. Its lovely and simple line taught the eye to ask for a similar boundary of solid form; the dome followed, and necessarily the decorative masses were thenceforward managed with reference to, and in sympathy with, the chief feature of the building. Hence arose, among the Byzantine architects, a system of ornament, entirely restrained within the superfices of curvilinear masses, on which the light fell with as unbroken gradation as on a dome or column, while the illumined surface was nevertheless cut into details of singular and most ingenious intricacy. Something is, of course, to be allowed for the less dexterity of the workmen; it being easier to cut down into a solid block, than to arrange the projecting portions of leaf on the Greek capital: such leafy capitals are nevertheless executed by the Byzantines with skill enough to show that their preference of the massive form was by no means compulsory, nor can I think it unwise. On the contrary, while the arrangements of *line* are far more artful in the Greek capital, the Byzantine light and shade are as incontestably more grand and masculine, based on that quality of pure gradation, which nearly all natural objects possess, and the attainment of which is, in fact, the first and most palpable purpose in natural arrangements of grand form. The rolling heap of the thunder-cloud, divided by rents, and multiplied by wreaths, yet gathering them all into its broad, torrid, and towering zone, and its midnight darkness opposite; the scarcely less majestic heave of the mountain side, all torn and traversed by depth of defile and ridge of rock, yet never losing.the unity of its illumined swell and shadowy decline ; and the head of every mighty tree, rich with tracery of leaf and bough, yet terminated against the sky by a true line, and rounded by a green horizon, which, multiplied in the distant forest, makes it look bossy from above ; all these mark, for a great and honored law, that diffusion of light for which the Byzantine ornaments were designed ; and show us that those builders had truer sympathy with what God made majestic, than the self-contemplating and self-contented Greek. I know that they are barbaric in comparison ; but there is a power in their barbarism of sterner tone, a power not sophistic nor penetrative, but embracing and mysterious ; a power faithful more than thoughtful, which conceived and felt more than it created ; a power that neither comprehended nor ruled itself, but worked and wandered as it listed, like mountain streams and winds ; and which could not rest in the expression or seizure of finite form. It could not bury itself in acanthus leaves. Its imagery was taken from the shadows of the storms and hills, and had fellowship with the night and day of the earth itself.

XVI. I have endeavored to give some idea of one of the hollow balls of stone which, surrounded by flowing leafage, occur in varied succession on the architrave of the central gate of St. Mark's at Venice, in Plate I. fig. 2. It seems to me singularly beautiful in its unity of lightness, and delicacy of detail, with breadth of light. It looks as if its leaves had been sensitive, and had risen and shut themselves into a bud at some sudden touch, and would presently fall back again into their wild flow. The cornices of San Michele of Lucca, seen above and below the arch, in Plate VI., show the effect of heavy leafage and thick stems arranged on a surface whose curve is a simple quadrant, the light dying from off them as it turns. It would be difficult, as I think, to invent anything more noble ; and I insist on the broad character of their arrangement the more earnestly, because, afterwards modified by greater skill in its management, it became characteristic of the richest pieces of Gothic design. The capital, given in

Plate V., is of the noblest period of the Venetian Gothic ; and it is interesting to see the play of leafage so luxuriant, absolutely subordinated to the breadth of two masses of light and shade. What is done by the Venetian architect, with a power as irresistible as that of the waves of his surrounding sea, is done by the masters of the Cis-Alpine Gothic, more timidly, and with a manner somewhat cramped and cold, but not less expressing their assent to the same great law. The ice spiculæ of the North, and its broken sunshine, seem to have image in, and influence on the work ; and the leaves which, under the Italian's hand, roll, and flow, and bow down over their black shadows, as in the weariness of noon-day heat, are, in the North, crisped and frost-bitten, wrinkled on the edges, and sparkling as if with dew. But the rounding of the ruling form is not less sought and felt. In the lower part of Plate I. is the finial of the pediment given in Plate II., from the cathedral of St. Lo. It is exactly similar in feeling to the Byzantine capital, being rounded under the abacus by four branches of thistle leaves, whose stems, springing from the angles, bend outwards and fall back to the head, throwing their jaggy spines down upon the full light, forming two sharp quatrefoils. I could not get near enough to this finial to see with what degree of delicacy the spines were cut ; but I have sketched a natural group of thistle-leaves beside it, that the reader may compare the types, and see with what mastery they are subjected to the broad form of the whole. The small capital from Coutances, Plate XIII. fig. 4, which is of earlier date, is of simpler elements, and exhibits the principle still more clearly ; but the St. Lo finial is only one of a thousand instances which might be gathered even from the fully developed flamboyant, the feeling of breadth being retained in minor ornaments long after it had been lost in the main design, and sometimes capriciously renewing itself throughout, as in the cylindrical niches and pedestals which enrich the porches of Caudebec and Rouen. Fig. 1, Plate I. is the simplest of those of Rouen ; in the more elaborate there are four projecting sides, divided by buttresses into eight rounded compartments of tracery ; even the whole bulk of the outer pier is treated with the same feeling ; and though composed partly of concave recesses, party of square shafts, partly of statues and tabernacle work, arranges itself as a whole into one richly rounded tower.

XVII. I cannot here enter into the curious questions connected with the management of larger curved surfaces ; into the causes of the difference in proportion necessary to be observed between round and square towers ; nor into the reasons why a column or ball may be richly ornamented, while surface decorations would be inexpedient on masses like the Castle of St. Angelo, the tomb of Cecilia Metella, or the dome of St. Peter's. But what has been above said of the desireableness of serenity in plane surfaces, applies still more forcibly to those which are curved ; and it is to be remembered that we are, at present, considering how this serenity and power may be carried into minor divisions, not how the ornamental character of the lower form may, upon occasion, be permitted to fret the calmness of the higher. Nor, though the instances we have examined are of globular or cylindrical masses chiefly, is it to be thought that breadth can only be secured by such alone : many of the noblest forms are of subdued curvature, sometimes hardly visible ; but curvature of some degree there must be, in order to secure any measure of grandeur in a small mass of light. One of the most marked distinctions between one artist and another, in the point of skill, will be found in their relative delicacy of perception of rounded surface ; the full power of expressing the perspective, foreshortening and various undulation of such surface is, perhaps, the last and most difficult attainment of the hand and eye. For instance : there is, perhaps, no tree which has baffled the landscape painter more than the common black spruce fir. It is rare that we see any representation of it other than caricature. It is conceived as if it grew in one plane, or as a section of a tree, with a set of boughs symmetrically dependent on opposite sides. It is thought formal, unmanageable, and ugly. It would be so, if it grew as it is drawn. But the power of the tree is not in that chandelier-like section. It is in the dark, flat, solid tables of leafage, which it holds out on its strong arms, curved slightly over them like shields, and spreading towards the extremity like a hand. It is vain to endeavor to paint the sharp, grassy, intricate leafage, until this ruling form has been secured : and in the boughs that approach the spectator, the foreshortening of it is like that of a wide hill country, ridge just rising over ridge in successive distances ; and the finger-like extremities, foreshortened to absolute bluntness, require a delicacy in the rendering of them like that of the drawing of the hand of the Magdalene upon the vase in Mr. Rogers's Titian. Get but the back of that foliage, and you have the tree ; but I cannot name the artist who has thoroughly felt it. So, in all drawing and sculpture, it is the power of rounding, softly and perfectly, every inferior mass which preserves the serenity, as it follows the truth, of Nature, and which demands the highest knowledge and skill from the workman. A noble design may always be told by the back of a single leaf, and it was the sacrifice of this breadth and refinement of surface for sharp edges and extravagant undercutting, which destroyed the Gothic mouldings, as the substitution of the line for the light destroyed the Gothic tracery. This change, however, we shall better comprehend after we have glanced at the chief conditions of arrangement of the second kind of mass ; that which is flat, and of shadow only.

XVIII. We have noted above how the wall surface, composed of rich materials, and covered with costly work, in modes which we shall examine in the next Chapter, became a subject of peculiar interest to the Christian architects. Its broad flat lights could only be made valuable by points or masses of energetic shadow, which were obtained by the Romanesque architect by means of ranges of recessed arcade, in the management of which, however, though all the effect depends upon the shadow so obtained, the eye is still, as in classical architecture, caused to dwell upon the projecting columns, capitals, and wall, as in Plate VI. But with the enlargement of the window, which, in the Lombard and Romanesque churches, is usually little more than an arched slit, came the conception of the simpler mode of decoration, by penetrations which, seen from within, are forms of light, and, from without, are forms of shade. In Italian traceries the eye is exclusively fixed upon the dark forms of the penetrations, and the whole proportion and power of the design are caused to depend upon them. The intermediate spaces are, indeed, in the most perfect early examples, filled with elaborate ornament; but this ornament was so subdued as never to disturb the simplicity and force of the dark masses; and in many instances is entirely wanting. The composition of the whole depends on the proportioning and shaping of the darks; and it is impossible that anything can be more exquisite than their placing in the head window of the Giotto campanile, Plate IX., or the church of Or San Michele. So entirely does the effect depend upon them, that it is quite useless to draw Italian tracery in outline; if with any intention of rendering its effect, it is better to mark the black spots, and let the rest alone. Of course, when it is desired to obtain an accurate rendering of the design, its lines and mouldings are enough; but it often happens that works on architecture are of little use, because they afford the reader no means of judging of the effective intention of the arrangements which they state. No person, looking at an architectural drawing of the richly foliaged cusps and intervals of Or San Michele, would understand that all this sculpture was extraneous, was a mere added grace, and had nothing to do with the real anatomy of the work, and that by a few bold cuttings through a slab of stone he might reach the main effect of it all at once. I have, therefore, in the plate of the design of Giotto, endeavored especially to mark these points of *purpose;* there, as in every other instance, black shadows of a graceful form lying on the white surface of the stone, like dark leaves laid upon snow. Hence, as before observed, the universal name of foil applied to such ornaments.

XIX. In order to the obtaining their full effect, it is evident that much caution is necessary in the management of the glass. In the finest instances, the traceries are open lights, either in towers, as in this design of Giotto's or in external arcades like that of the Campo Santo at Pisa or the Doge's palace at Venice ; and it is thus only that their full beauty is shown. In domestic buildings, or in windows of churches necessarily glazed, the glass was usually withdrawn entirely behind the traceries. Those of the Cathedral of Florence stand quite clear of it, casting their shadows in well detached lines, so as in most lights to give the appearance of a double tracery. In those few instances in which the glass was set in the tracery itself, as in Or San Michele, the effect of the latter is half destroyed : perhaps the especial attention paid by Orgagna to his surface ornament, was connected with the intention of so glazing them. It is singular to see, in late architecture, the glass, which tormented the older architects, considered as a valuable means of making the lines of tracery more slender ; as in the smallest intervals of the windows of Merton College, Oxford, where the glass is advanced about two inches from the centre of the tracery bar (that in the larger spaces being in the middle, as usual), in order to prevent the depth of shadow from farther diminishing the apparent interval. Much of the lightness of the effect of the traceries is owing to this seemingly unimportant arrangement. But, generally speaking, glass spoils all traceries ; and it is much to be wished that it should be kept well within them, when it cannot be dispensed with, and that the most careful and beautiful designs should be reserved for situations where no glass would be needed.

XX. The method of decoration by shadow was, as far as we have hitherto traced it, common to the northern and southern Gothic. But in the carrying out of the system they instantly diverged. Having marble at his command, and classical decoration in his sight, the southern architect was able to carve the intermediate spaces with exquisite leafage, or to vary his wall surface with inlaid stones. The northern architect neither knew the ancient work, nor possessed the delicate material ; and he had no resource but to cover his walls with holes, cut into foiled shapes like those of the windows. This he did, often with great clumsiness, but always with a vigorous sense of composition, and always, observe, depending on the *shadows* for effect. Where the wall was thick and could not be cut through, and the foilings were large, those shadows did not fill the entire space ; but the form was, nevertheless, drawn on the eye by means of them, and when it was possible, they were cut clear through, as in raised screens of pediment, like those on the west front of Bayeux ; cut so deep in every case, as to secure, in all but a direct low front light, great breadth of shadow.

The spandril, given at the top of Plate VII., is from the southwestern entrance of the Cathedral of Lisieux ; one of the most quaint and interesting doors in Normandy, probably soon to be lost forever, by the continuance of the masonic operations which have already destroyed the northern tower. Its work is altogether rude, but full of spirit ; the opposite spandrils have different, though balanced, ornaments very inaccurately adjusted, each rosette or star (as the five-rayed figure, now quite defaced, in the upper portion appears to have been) cut on its own block of stone and fitted in with small nicety, especially illustrating the point I have above insisted upon—the architect's utter neglect of the forms of intermediate stone, at this early period.

The arcade, of which a single arch and shaft are given on the left, forms the flank of the door ; three outer shafts bearing three orders within the spandril which I have drawn, and each of these shafts carried over an inner arcade, decorated above with quatre-foils, cut concave and filled with leaves, the whole disposition exquisitely picturesque and full of strange play of light and shade.

For some time the penetrative ornaments, if so they may be for convenience called, maintained their bold and independent character. Then they multiplied and enlarged, becoming shallower as they did so ; then they began to run together, one swallowing up, or hanging on to, another, like bubbles in expiring foam—fig. 4, from a spandril at Bayeux, looks as if it had been blown from a pipe ; finally, they lost their individual character altogether, and the eye was made to rest on the separating lines of tracery, as we saw before in the window ; and then came the great change and the fall of the Gothic power.

XXI. Figs. 2 and 3, the one a quadrant of the star window of the little chapel close to St. Anastasia at Verona, and the other a very singular example from the church of the Eremitani at Padua, compared with fig. 5, one of the ornaments of the transept towers of Rouen, show the closely correspondent conditions of the early Northern and Southern Gothic.[10] But, as we have said, the Italian architects, not being embarrassed for decoration of wall surface, and not being obliged, like the Northmen, to multiply their penetrations, held to the system for some time longer ; and while they increased the refinement of the ornament, kept the purity of the plan. That refinement of ornament was their weak point, however, and opened the way for the renaissance attack. They fell, like the old Romans, by their luxury, except in the separate instance of the magnificent school of Venice. That architecture began with the luxuriance in which all others expired : it founded itself on the Byzantine mosaic and fretwork ; and laying aside its ornaments, one by one, while it fixed its forms by laws more and more severe, stood forth, at last, a model of domestic Gothic, so grand, so complete, so nobly systematised, that, to my mind, there never existed an architecture with so stern a claim to our reverence. I do not except even the Greek Doric ; the Doric had cast nothing away ; the fourteenth century Venetian had cast away, one by one, for a succession of centuries, every splendor that art and wealth could give it. It had laid down its crown and its jewels, its gold and its color, like a king disrobing ; it had resigned its exertion, like an athlete reposing ; once capricious and fantastic, it had bound itself by laws inviolable and serene as those of nature herself. It retained nothing but its beauty and its power ; both the highest, but both restrained. The Doric flutings were of irregular number—the Venetian mouldings were unchangeable. The Doric manner of ornament admitted no temptation, it was the fasting of an anchorite—the Venetian ornament embraced, while it governed, all vegetable and animal forms ; it was the temperance of a man, the command of Adam over creation. I do not know so magnificent a marking of human authority as the iron grasp of the Vene

tian over his own exuberance of imagination ; the calm and
solemn restraint with which, his mind filled with thoughts of
flowing leafage and fiery life, he gives those thoughts expression for an instant, and then withdraws within those massy
bars and level cusps of stone.[11]

And his power to do this depended altogether on his retaining the forms of the shadows in his sight. Far from carrying the eye to the ornaments, upon the stone, he abandoned
these latter one by one ; and while his mouldings received
the most shapely order and symmetry, closely correspondent
with that of the Rouen tracery, compare Plates III. and VIII.,
he kept the cusps within them perfectly flat, decorated, if at
all, with a trefoil (Palazzo Foscari), or fillet (Doge's Palace)
just traceable and no more, so that the quatrefoil, cut as
sharply through them as if it had been struck out by a stamp,
told upon the eye, with all its four black leaves, miles away.
No knots of flowerwork, no ornaments of any kind, were suffered to interfere with the purity of its form : the cusp is
usually quite sharp ; but slightly truncated in the Palazzo
Foscari, and charged with a simple ball in that of the Doge ;
and the glass of the window, where there was any, was, as
we have seen, thrown back behind the stone-work, that no
flashes of light might interfere with its depth. Corrupted
forms, like those of the Casa d'Oro and Palazzo Pisani, and
several others, only serve to show the majesty of the common
design.

XXII. Such are the principal circumstances traceable in the
treatment of the two kinds of masses of light and darkness,
in the hands of the earlier architects ; gradation in the one,
flatness in the other, and breadth in both, being the qualities
sought and exhibited by every possible expedient, up to the
period when, as we have before stated, the line was substituted
for the mass, as the means of division of surface. Enough
has been said to illustrate this, as regards tracery ; but a word
or two is still necessary respecting the mouldings.

Those of the earlier times were, in the plurality of instances,
composed of alternate square and cylindrical shafts, variously
associated and proportioned. Where concave cuttings occur,

as in the beautiful west doors of Bayeux, they are between cylindrical shafts, which they throw out into broad light. The eye in all cases dwells on broad surfaces, and commonly upon few. In course of time, a low ridgy process is seen emerging along the outer edge of the cylindrical shaft, forming a line of light upon it and destroying its gradation. Hardly traceable at first (as on the alternate rolls of the north door of Rouen), it grows and pushes out as gradually as a stag's horns : sharp at first on the edge ; but, becoming prominent, it receives a truncation, and becomes a definite fillet on the face of the roll. Not yet to be checked, it pushes forward until the roll itself becomes subordinate to it, and is finally lost in a slight swell upon its sides, while the concavities have all the time been deepening and enlarging behind it, until, from a succession of square or cylindrical masses, the whole moulding has become a series of *concavities* edged by delicate fillets, upon which (sharp *lines* of light, observe) the eye exclusively rests. While this has been taking place, a similar, though less total, change has affected the flowerwork itself. In Plate I. fig. 2 (*a*), I have given two from the transepts of Rouen. It will be observed how absolutely the eye rests on the forms of the leaves, and on the three berries in the angle, being in light exactly what the trefoil is in darkness. These mouldings nearly adhere to the stone ; and are very slightly, though sharply, undercut. In process of time, the attention of the architect, instead of resting on the leaves, went to the *stalks*. These latter were elongated (*b*, from the south door of St. Lo) ; and to exhibit them better, the deep concavity was cut behind, so as to throw them out in lines of light. The system was carried out into continually increasing intricacy, until, in the transepts of Beauvais, we have brackets and flamboyant traceries, composed of twigs without any leaves at all. This, however, is a partial, though a sufficiently characteristic, caprice, the leaf being never generally banished, and in the mouldings round those same doors, beautifully managed, but itself rendered liny by bold marking of its ribs and veins, and by turning up, and crisping its edges, large intermediate spaces being always left to be occupied by intertwining stems (*c*, from Caudebec).

The trefoil of light formed by berries or acorns, though diminished in value, was never lost up to the last period of living Gothic.

XXIII. It is interesting to follow into its many ramifications, the influence of the corrupting principle ; but we have seen enough of it to enable us to draw our practical conclusion —a conclusion a thousand times felt and reiterated in the experience and advice of every practised artist, but never often enough repeated, never profoundly enough felt. Of composition and invention much has been written, it seems to me vainly, for men cannot be taught to compose or to invent ; of these, the highest elements of Power in architecture, I do not, therefore, speak ; nor, here, of that peculiar restraint in the imitation of natural forms, which constitutes the dignity of even the most luxuriant work of the great periods. Of this restraint I shall say a word or two in the next Chapter ; pressing now only the conclusion, as practically useful as it is certain, that the relative majesty of buildings depends more on the weight and vigor of their masses than on any other attribute of their design : mass of everything, of bulk, of light, of darkness, of color, not mere sum of any of these, but breadth of them ; not broken light, nor scattered darkness, nor divided weight, but solid stone, broad sunshine, starless shade. Time would fail me altogether, if I attempted to follow out the range of the principle ; there is not a feature, however apparently trifling, to which it cannot give power. The wooden fillings of belfry lights, necessary to protect their interiors from rain, are in England usually divided into a number of neatly executed cross-bars, like those of Venetian blinds, which, of course, become as conspicuous in their sharpness as they are uninteresting in their precise carpentry, multiplying, moreover, the horizontal lines which directly contradict those of the architecture. Abroad, such necessities are met by three or four downright penthouse roofs, reaching each from within the window to the outside shafts of its mouldings ; instead of the horrible row of ruled lines, the space is thus divided into four or five grand masses of shadow, with grey slopes of roof above, bent or yielding into all kinds of delicious swells and curves, and covered with warm tones of moss and lichen. Very often the thing is more delightful than the stone-work itself, and all because it is broad, dark, and simple. It matters not how clumsy, how common, the means are, that get weight and shadow—sloping roof, jutting porch, projecting balcony, hollow niche, massy gargoyle, frowning parapet; get but gloom and simplicity, and all good things will follow in their place and time ; do but design with the owl's eyes first, and you will gain the falcon's afterwards.

XXIV. I am grieved to have to insist upon what seems so simple ; it looks trite and commonplace when it is written, but pardon me this : for it is anything but an accepted or understood principle in practice, and the less excusably forgotten, because it is, of all the great and true laws of art, the easiest to obey. The executive facility of complying with its demands cannot be too earnestly, too frankly asserted. There are not five men in the kingdom who could compose, not twenty who could cut, the foliage with which the windows of Or San Michele are adorned ; but there is many a village clergyman who could invent and dispose its black openings, and not a village mason who could not cut them. Lay a few clover or wood-roof leaves on white paper, and a little alteration in their positions will suggest figures which, cut boldly through a slab of marble, would be worth more window traceries than an architect could draw in a summer's day. There are few men in the world who could design a Greek capital ; there are few who could not produce some vigor of effect with leaf designs on Byzantine block : few who could design a Palladian front, or a flamboyant pediment ; many who could build a square mass like the Strozzi palace. But I know not how it is, unless that our English hearts have more oak than stone in them, and have more filial sympathy with acorns than Alps ; but all that we do is small and mean, if not worse—thin, and wasted, and unsubstantial. It is not modern work only ; we have built like frogs and mice since the thirteenth century (except only in our castles). What a contrast between the pitiful little pigeon-holes which stand for doors in the east front of Salisbury, looking like the entrances to a bee-

hive or a wasp's nest, and the soaring arches and kingly
crowning of the gates of Abbeville, Rouen, and Rheims, or the
rock-hewn piers of Chartres, or the dark and vaulted porches
and writhed pillars of Verona! Of domestic architecture
what need is there to speak? How small, how cramped, how
poor, how miserable in its petty neatness is our best! how
beneath the mark of attack, and the level of contempt, that
which is common with us! What a strange sense of formalised deformity, of shrivelled precision, of starved accuracy, of minute misanthropy have we, as we leave even the
rude streets of Picardy for the market towns of Kent! Until
that street architecture of ours is bettered, until we give it
some size and boldness, until we give our windows recess,
and our walls thickness, I know not how we can blame our
architects for their feebleness in more important work; their
eyes are inured to narrowness and slightness: can we expect
them at a word to conceive and deal with breadth and solidity?
They ought not to live in our cities; there is that in their
miserable walls which bricks up to death men's imaginations,
as surely as ever perished forsworn nun. An architect should
live as little in cities as a painter. Send him to our hills, and
let him study there what nature understands by a buttress,
and what by a dome. There was something in the old power
of architecture, which it had from the recluse more than from
the citizen. The buildings of which I have spoken with chief
praise, rose, indeed, out of the war of the piazza, and above
the fury of the populace: and Heaven forbid that for such
cause we should ever have to lay a larger stone, or rivet a
firmer bar, in our England! But we have other sources of
power, in the imagery of our iron coasts and azure hills; of
power more pure, nor less serene, than that of the hermit
spirit which once lighted with white lines of cloisters the
glades of the Alpine pine, and raised into ordered spires the
wild rocks of the Norman sea; which gave to the temple gate
the depth and darkness of Elijah's Horeb cave; and lifted,
out of the populous city, grey cliffs of lonely stone, into the
midst of sailing birds and silent air.

CHAPTER IV.

THE LAMP OF BEAUTY.

I. It was stated, in the outset of the preceding chapter that the value of architecture depended on two distinct characters : the one, the impression it receives from human power ; the other, the image it bears of the natural creation. I have endeavored to show in what manner its majesty was attributable to a sympathy with the effort and trouble of human life (a sympathy as distinctly perceived in the gloom and mystery of form, as it is in the melancholy tones of sounds). I desire now to trace that happier element of its excellence, consisting in a noble rendering of images of Beauty, derived chiefly from the external appearances of organic nature.

It is irrelevant to our present purpose to enter into any inquiry respecting the essential causes of impressions of beauty. I have partly expressed my thoughts on this matter in a previous work, and I hope to develope them hereafter.   But since all such inquiries can only be founded on the ordinary understanding of what is meant by the term Beauty, and since they presume that the feeling of mankind on this subject is universal and instinctive, I shall base my present investigation on this assumption ; and only asserting that to be beautiful which I believe will be granted me to be so without dispute, I would endeavor shortly to trace the manner in which this element of delight is to be best engrafted upon architectural design, what are the purest sources from which it is to be derived, and what the errors to be avoided in its pursuit.

II. It will be thought that I have somewhat rashly limited the elements of architectural beauty to imitative forms.   I do not mean to assert that every arrangement of line is directly suggested by a natural object ; but that all beautiful lines are adaptations of those which are commonest in the external creation ; that in proportion to the richness of their association, the resemblance to natural work, as a type and help, must be more closely attempted, and more clearly seen ; and that be

yond a certain point, and that a very low one, man cannot advance in the invention of beauty, without directly imitating
natural form. Thus, in the Doric temple, the triglyph and
cornice are unimitative ; or imitative only of artificial cuttings
of wood. No one would call these members beautiful. Their
influence over us is in their severity and simplicity. The
fluting of the column, which I doubt not was the Greek symbol of the bark of the tree, was imitative in its origin, and
feebly resembled many caniculated organic structures. Beauty
is instantly felt in it, but of a low order. The decoration
proper was sought in the true forms of organic life, and those
chiefly human. Again : the Doric capital was unimitative ;
but all the beauty it had was dependent on the precision of
its ovolo, a natural curve of the most frequent occurrence.
The Ionic capital (to my mind, as an architectural invention,
exceedingly base) nevertheless depended for all the beauty
that it had on its adoption of a spiral line, perhaps the commonest of all that characterise the inferior orders of animal
organism and habitation. Farther progress could not be
made without a direct imitation of the acanthus leaf.

Again : the Romanesque arch is beautiful as an abstract
line. Its type is always before us in that of the apparent
vault of heaven, and horizon of the earth. The cylindrical
pillar is always beautiful, for God has so moulded the stem of
every tree that it is pleasant to the eyes. The pointed arch
is beautiful ; it is the termination of every leaf that shakes in
summer wind, and its most fortunate associations are directly
borrowed from the trefoiled grass of the field, or from the
stars of its flowers. Further than this, man's invention could
not reach without frank imitation. His next step was to
gather the flowers themselves, and wreathe them in his capitals.

III. Now, I would insist especially on the fact, of which I
doubt not that further illustrations will occur to the mind of
every reader, that all most lovely forms and thoughts are directly taken from natural objects ; because I would fain be
allowed to assume also the converse of this, namely, that
forms which are *not* taken from natural objects *must* be ugly

I know this is a bold assumption ; but as I have not space to reason out the points wherein essential beauty of form consists, that being far too serious a work to be undertaken in a bye way, I have no other resource than to use this accidental mark or test of beauty, of whose truth the considerations which I hope hereafter to lay before the reader may assure him. I say an accidental mark, since forms are not beautiful *because* they are copied from nature ; only it is out of the power of man to conceive beauty without her aid. I believe the reader will grant me this, even from the examples above advanced ; the degree of confidence with which it is granted must attach also to his acceptance of the conclusions which will follow from it ; but if it be granted frankly, it will enable me to determine a matter of very essential importance, namely, what *is* or is *not* ornament. For there are many forms of so-called decoration in architecture, habitual, and received, therefore, with approval, or at all events without any venture at expression or dislike, which I have no hesitation in asserting to be not ornament at all, but to be ugly things, the expense of which ought in truth to be set down in the architect's contract, as "For Monstrification." I believe that we regard these customary deformities with a savage complacency, as an Indian does his flesh patterns and paint (all nations being in certain degrees and senses savage). I believe that I can prove them to be monstrous, and I hope hereafter to do so conclusively ; but, meantime, I can allege in defence of my persuasion nothing but this fact of their being unnatural, to which the reader must attach such weight as he thinks it deserves. There is, however, a peculiar difficulty in using this proof ; it requires the writer to assume, very impertinently, that nothing is natural but what he has seen or supposes to exist. I would not do this ; for I suppose there is no conceivable form or grouping of forms but in some part of the universe an example of it may be found. But I think I am justified in considering those forms to be *most* natural which are most frequent ; or, rather, that on the shapes which in the every-day world are familiar to the eyes of men, God has stamped those characters of beauty which He has made

It man's nature to love ; while in certain exceptional forms He has shown that the adoption of the others was not a matter of necessity, but part of the adjusted harmony of creation. I believe that thus we may reason from Frequency to Beauty, and *vice versâ ;* that knowing a thing to be frequent, we may assume it to be beautiful ; and assume that which is most frequent to be most beautiful : I mean, of course, *visibly* frequent ; for the forms of things which are hidden in caverns of the earth, or in the anatomy of animal frames, are evidently not intended by their Maker to bear the habitual gaze of man. And, again, by frequency I mean that limited and isolated frequency which is characteristic of all perfection ; not mere multitude : as a rose is a common flower, but yet there are not so many roses on the tree as there are leaves. In this respect Nature is sparing of her highest, and lavish of her less, beauty ; but I call the flower as frequent as the leaf, because, each in its allotted quantity, where the one is, there will ordinarily be the other.

IV. The first so-called ornament, then, which I would attack is that Greek fret, now, I believe, usually known by the Italian name Guilloche, which is exactly a case in point. It so happens that in crystals of bismuth formed by the unagitated cooling of the melted metal, there occurs a natural resemblance of it almost perfect. But crystals of bismuth not only are of unusual occurrence in every-day life, but their form is, as far as I know, unique among minerals ; and not only unique, but only attainable by an artificial process, the metal itself never being found pure. I do not remember any other substance or arrangement which presents a resemblance to this Greek ornament ; and I think that I may trust my remembrance as including most of the arrangements which occur in the outward forms of common and familiar things. On this ground, then, I allege that ornament to be ugly ; or, in the literal sense of the word, monstrous ; different from anything which it is the nature of man to admire : and I think an uncarved fillet or plinth infinitely preferable to one covered with this vile concatenation of straight lines : unless indeed it be employed as a foil to a true ornament, which it may, perhaps, sometimes with advantage ; or excessively small, as it occurs on coins, the harshness of its arrangement being less perceived.

V. Often in association with this horrible design we find, in Greek works, one which is as beautiful as this is painful— that egg and dart moulding, whose perfection in its place and way, has never been surpassed. And why is this? Simply because the form of which it is chiefly composed is one not only familiar to us in the soft housing of the bird's nest, but happens to be that of nearly every pebble that rolls and mur- murs under the surf of the sea, on all its endless shore. And with that a peculiar accuracy ; for the mass which bears the light in this moulding is *not* in good Greek work, as in the frieze of the Erechtheum, merely of the shape of an egg. It is *flattened* on the upper surface, with a delicacy and keen sense of variety in the curve which it is impossible too highly to praise, attaining exactly that flattened, imperfect oval, which, in nine cases out of ten, will be the form of the pebble lifted at random from the rolled beach. Leave out this flat- ness, and the moulding is vulgar instantly. It is singular also that the insertion of this rounded form in the hollow recess has a *painted* type in the plumage of the Argus pheas- ant, the eyes of whose feathers are so shaded as exactly to represent an oval form placed in a hollow.

VI. It will evidently follow, upon our application of this test of natural resemblance, that we shall at once conclude that all perfectly beautiful forms must be composed of curves; since there is hardly any common natural form in which it is possible to discover a straight line. Nevertheless, Architect- ure, having necessarily to deal with straight lines essential to its purposes in many instances and to the expression of its power in others, must frequently be content with that meas- ure of beauty which is consistent with such primal forms ; and we may presume that utmost measure of beauty to have been attained when the arrangements of such lines are con- sistent with the most frequent natural groupings of them we can discover, although, to find right lines in nature at all, we may be compelled to do violence to her finished work, break through the sculptured and colored surfaces of her crags, and examine the processes of their crystallisation.

VII. I have just convicted the Greek fret of ugliness, be-cause it has no precedent to allege for its arrangement except an artificial form of a rare metal. Let us bring into court an ornament of Lombard architects, Plate XII., fig. 7, as exclu-sively composed of right lines as the other, only, observe, with the noble element of shadow added. This ornament, taken from the front of the Cathedral of Pisa, is universal through-out the Lombard churches of Pisa, Lucca, Pistoja, and Flo-rence; and it will be a grave stain upon them if it cannot be defended. Its first apology for itself, made in a hurry, sounds marvellously like the Greek one, and highly dubious. It says that its terminal contour is the very image of a care-fully prepared artificial crystal of common salt. Salt being, however, a substance considerably more familiar to us than bismuth, the chances are somewhat in favor of the accused Lombard ornament already. But it has more to say for itself, and more to the purpose; namely, that its main outline is one not only of natural crystallisation, but among the very first and commonest of crystalline forms, being the primal condition of the occurrence of the oxides of iron, copper, and tin, of the sulphurets of iron and lead, of fluor spar, &c.; and that those projecting forms in its surface represent the conditions of structure which effect the change into another relative and equally common crystalline form, the cube. This is quite enough. We may rest assured it is as good a combination of such simple right lines as can be put together, and gracefully fitted for every place in which such lines are necessary.

VIII. The next ornament whose cause I would try is that of our Tudor work, the portcullis. Reticulation is common enough in natural form, and very beautiful; but it is either of the most delicate and gauzy texture, or of variously sized meshes and undulating lines. There is no family relation be-tween portcullis and cobwebs or beetles' wings; something like it, perhaps, may be found in some kinds of crocodile ar-mor and on the backs of the Northern divers, but always beautifully varied in size of mesh. There is a dignity in the thing itself, if its size were exhibited, and the shade given through its bars; but even these merits are taken away in the Tudor diminution of it, set on a solid surface. It has not a single syllable, I believe, to say in its defence. It is another monster, absolutely and unmitigatedly frightful. All that carving on Henry the Seventh's Chapel simply deforms the stones of it.

In the same clause with the portcullis, we may condemn all heraldic decoration, so far as beauty is its object. Its pride and significance have their proper place, fitly occurring in prominent parts of the building, as over its gates; and allowably in places where its legendary may be plainly read, as in painted windows, bosses of ceilings, &c. And sometimes, of course, the forms which it presents may be beautiful, as of animals, or simple symbols like the fleur-de-lis; but, for the most part, heraldic similitudes and arrangements are so professedly and pointedly unnatural, that it would be difficult to invent anything uglier; and the use of them as a repeated decoration will utterly destroy both the power and beauty of any building. Common sense and courtesy also forbid their repetition. It is right to tell those who enter your doors that you are such a one, and of such a rank; but to tell it to them again and again, wherever they turn, becomes soon impertinence, and at last folly. Let, therefore, the entire bearings occur in few places, and these not considered as an ornament, but as an inscription; and for frequent appliance, let any single and fair symbol be chosen out of them. Thus we may multiply as much as we choose the French fleur-de-lis, or the Florentine giglio bianco, or the English rose; but we must not multiply a King's arms.

IX. It will also follow, from these considerations, that if any one part of heraldic decoration be worse than another, it is the motto; since, of all things unlike nature, the forms of letters are, perhaps, the most so. Even graphic tellurium and felspar look, at their clearest, anything but legible. All letters are, therefore, to be considered as frightful things, and to be endured only upon occasion; that is to say, in places where the sense of the inscription is of more importance than external ornament. Inscriptions in churches, in rooms, and on pictures, are often desirable, but they are not to be considered as architectural or pictorial ornaments : they are, on the contrary, obstinate offences to the eye, not to be suffered except when their intellectual office introduces them. Place them, therefore, where they will be read, and there only; and let them be plainly written, and not turned upside down, nor wrong end first. It is an ill sacrifice to beauty to make that illegible whose only merit is in its sense. Write it as you would speak it, simply ; and do not draw the eye to it when it would fain rest elsewhere, nor recommend your sentence by anything but a little openness of place and architectural silence about it. Write the Commandments on the Church walls where they may be plainly seen, but do not put a dash and a tail to every letter ; and remember that you are an architect, not a writing master.

X. Inscriptions appear sometimes to be introduced for the sake of the scroll on which they are written ; and in late and modern painted glass, as well as in architecture, these scrolls are flourished and turned hither and thither as if they were ornamental. Ribands occur frequently in arabesques,—in some of a high order, too,—tying up flowers, or flitting in and out among the fixed forms. Is there anything like ribands in nature ? It might be thought that grass and sea-weed afforded apologetic types. They do not. There is a wide difference between their structure and that of a riband. They have a skeleton, an anatomy, a central rib, or fibre, or framework of some kind or another, which has a beginning and an end, a root and head, and whose make and strength effects every direction of their motion, and every line of their form. The loosest weed that drifts and waves under the heaving of the sea, or hangs heavily on the brown and slippery shore, has a marked strength, structure, elasticity, gradation of substance; its extremities are more finely fibred than its centre, its centre than its root ; every fork of its ramification is measured and proportioned ; every wave of its languid lines is love. It has its allotted size, and place, and function ; it is a specific creature. What is there like this in a riband ? It has no structure : it is a succession of cut threads all alike; it has no skeleton, no make, no form, no size, no will of its own. You cut it and crush it into what you will. It has no strength, no languor. It cannot fall into a single graceful form. It cannot wave, in the true sense, but only flutter : it cannot bend, in the true sense, but only turn and be wrinkled. It is a vile thing; it spoils all that is near its wretched film of an existence. Never use it. Let the flowers come loose if they cannot keep together without being tied; leave the sentence unwritten if you cannot write it on a tablet or book, or plain roll of paper. I know what authority there is against me. I remember the scrolls of Perugino's angels, and the ribands of Raphael's arabesques, and of Ghiberti's glorious bronze flowers : no matter; they are every one of them vices and uglinesses. Raphael usually felt this, and used an honest and rational tablet, as in the Madonna di Fuligno. I do not say there is any type of such tablets in nature, but all the difference lies in the fact that the tablet is not considered as an ornament, and the riband, or flying scroll, is. The tablet, as in Albert Durer's Adam and Eve, is introduced for the sake of the writing, understood and allowed as an ugly but necessary interruption. The scroll is extended as an ornamental form, which it is not, nor ever can be.

XI. But it will be said that all this want of organisation and form might be affirmed of drapery also, and that this latter is a noble subject of sculpture. By no means. When was drapery a subject of sculpture by itself, except in the form of a handkerchief on urns in the seventeenth century and in some of the baser scenic Italian decorations ? Drapery, as such, is always ignoble; it becomes a subject of interest only by the colors it bears, and the impressions which it receives from some foreign form or force. All noble draperies, either in painting or sculpture (color and texture being at present out of our consideration), have, so far as they are anything more than necessities, one of two great functions; they are the exponents of motion and of gravitation. They are the most valuable means of expressing past as well as present motion in the figure, and they are almost the only means of indicating to the eye the force of gravity which resists such motion. The Greeks used drapery in sculpture for the most part as an ugly necessity, but availed themselves of it gladly in all representation of action, exaggerating the arrangements of it which express lightness in the material, and follow gesture in the person. The Christian sculptors, caring little for the body, or disliking it, and depending exclusively on the countenance, received drapery at first contentedly as a veil, but soon perceived a capacity of expression in it which the Greek had not seen or had despised. The principal element of this expression was the entire removal of agitation from what was so pre-eminently capable of being agitated. It fell from their human forms plumb down, sweeping the ground heavily, and concealing the feet ; while the Greek drapery was often blown away from the thigh. The thick and coarse stuffs of the monkish dresses, so absolutely opposed to the thin and gauzy web of antique material, suggested simplicity of division as well as weight of fall. There was no crushing nor subdividing them. And thus the drapery gradually came to represent the spirit of repose as it before had of motion, repose saintly and severe. The wind had no power upon the garment, as the passion none upon the soul ; and the motion of the figure only bent into a softer line the stillness of the falling veil, followed by it like a slow cloud by drooping rain : only in links of lighter undulation it followed the dances of the angels.

Thus treated, drapery is indeed noble ; but it is as an exponent of other and higher things. As that of gravitation, it has especial majesty, being literally the only means we have of fully representing this mysterious natural force of earth (for falling water is less passive and less defined in its lines). So, again, in sails it is beautiful because it receives the forms of solid curved surface, and expresses the force of another invisible element. But drapery trusted to its own merits, and given for its own sake,—drapery like that of Carlo Dolci and the Caraccis,—is always base.

XII. Closely connected with the abuse of scrolls and bands, is that of garlands and festoons of flowers as an architectural

decoration, for unnatural arrangements are just as ugly as un‑
natural forms ; and architecture, in borrowing the objects of
nature, is bound to place them, as far as may be in her power,
in such associations as may befit and express their origin. She
is not to imitate directly the natural arrangement ; she is not
to carve irregular stems of ivy up her columns to account for
the leaves at the top, but she is nevertheless to place her most
exuberant vegetable ornament just where Nature would have
placed it, and to give some indication of that radical and con‑
nected structure which Nature would have given it.   Thus
the Corinthian capital is beautiful, because it expands under
the abacus just as Nature would have expanded it ; and be‑
cause it looks as if the leaves had one root, though that root
is unseen.   And the flamboyant leaf mouldings are beautiful,
because they nestle and run up the hollows, and fill the angles,
and clasp the shafts which natural leaves would have delighted
to fill and to clasp.   They are no mere cast of natural leaves ;
they are counted, orderly, and architectural : but they are
naturally, and therefore beautifully, placed.

XIII. Now I do not mean to say that Nature never uses
festoons : she loves them, and uses them lavishly ; and though
she does so only in those places of excessive luxuriance wherein
it seems to me that architectural types should seldom be sought,
yet a falling tendril or pendent bough might, if managed with
freedom and grace, be well introduced into luxuriant dec‑
oration (or if not, it is not their want of beauty, but of archi‑
tectural fitness, which incapacitates them for such uses).   But
what resemblance to such example can we trace in a mass of
all manner of fruit and flowers, tied heavily into a long bunch,
thickest in the middle, and pinned up by both ends against a
dead wall ?   For it is strange that the wildest and most fanci‑
ful of the builders of truly luxuriant architecture never ven‑
tured, so far as I know, even a pendent tendril ; while the
severest masters of the revived Greek permitted this extraor‑
dinary piece of luscious ugliness to be fastened in the middle
of their blank surfaces.   So surely as this arrangement is
adopted, the whole value of the flower work is lost.   Who
among the crowds that gaze upon the building ever pause to

admire the flower work of St. Paul's? It is as careful and as rich as it can be, yet it adds no delightfulness to the edifice. It is no part of it. It is an ugly excrescence. We always conceive the building without it, and should be happier if our conception were not disturbed by its presence. It makes the rest of the architecture look poverty-stricken, instead of sublime; and yet it is never enjoyed itself. Had it been put, where it ought, into the capitals, it would have been beheld with never-ceasing delight. I do not mean that it could have been so in the present building, for such kind of architecture has no business with rich ornament in any place; but that if those groups of flowers had been put into natural places in an edifice of another style, their value would have been felt as vividly as now their uselessness. What applies to festoons is still more sternly true of garlands. A garland is meant to be seen upon a head. There it is beautiful, because we suppose it newly gathered and joyfully worn. But it is not meant to be hung upon a wall. If you want a circular ornament, put a flat circle of colored marble, as in the Casa Doria and other such palaces at Venice; or put a star, or a medallion, or if you want a ring, put a solid one, but do not carve the images of garlands, looking as if they had been used in the last procession, and been hung up to dry, and serve next time withered. Why not also carve pegs, and hats upon them?

XIV. One of the worst enemies of modern Gothic architecture, though seemingly an unimportant feature, is an excrescence, as offensive by its poverty as the garland by its profusion, the dripstone in the shape of the handle of a chest of drawers, which is used over the square-headed windows of what we call Elizabethan buildings. In the last Chapter, it will be remembered that the square form was shown to be that of pre-eminent Power, and to be properly adapted and limited to the exhibition of space or surface. Hence, when the window is to be an exponent of power, as for instance in those by M. Angelo in the lower story of the Palazzo Ricardi at Florence, the square head is the most noble form they can assume; but then either their space must be unbroken, and their associated mouldings the most severe, or else the square must be used as a finial outline, and is chiefly to be associated with forms of tracery, in which the relative form of power, the circle, is predominant, as in Venetian, and Florentine, and Pisan Gothic. But if you break upon your terminal square, or if you cut its lines off at the top and turn them outwards, you have lost its unity and space. It is an including form no longer, but an added, isolated line, and the ugliest possible. Look abroad into the landscape and see if you can discover any one so bent and fragmentary as that of this strange windlass-looking dripstone. You cannot. It is a monster. It unites every element of ugliness, its line is harshly broken in itself, and unconnected with every other ; it has no harmony either with structure or decoration, it has no architectural support, it looks glued to the wall, and the only pleasant property it has, is the appearance of some likelihood of its dropping off.

I might proceed, but the task is a weary one, and I think I have named those false forms of decoration which are most dangerous in our modern architecture as being legal and accepted. The barbarisms of individual fancy are as countless as they are contemptible ; they neither admit attack nor are worth it ; but these above named are countenanced, some by the practice of antiquity, all by high authority : they have depressed the proudest, and contaminated the purest schools, and are so established in recent practice that I write rather for the barren satisfaction of bearing witness against them, than with hope of inducing any serious convictions to their prejudice.

XV. Thus far of what is *not* ornament. What ornament is, will without difficulty be determined by the application of the same test. It must consist of such studious arrangements of form as are imitative or suggestive of those which are commonest among natural existences, that being of course the noblest ornament which represents the highest orders of existence. Imitated flowers are nobler than imitated stones, imitated animals, than flowers ; imitated human form of all animal forms the noblest. But all are combined in the richest ornamental work ; and the rock, the fountain, the flowing river with its pebbled bed, the sea, the clouds of

Heaven, the herb of the field, the fruit-tree bearing fruit, the creeping thing, the bird, the beast, the man, and the angel, mingle their fair forms on the bronze of Ghiberti.

Every thing being then ornamental that is imitative, I would ask the reader's attention to a few general considerations, all that can here be offered relating to so vast a subject; which, for convenience sake, may be classed under the three heads of inquiry :—What is the right place for architectural ornament? What is the peculiar treatment of ornament which renders it architectural? and what is the right use of color as associated with architectural imitative form?

XVI. What is the place of ornament? Consider first that the characters of natural objects which the architect can represent are few and abstract. The greater part of those delights by which Nature recommends herself to man at all times, cannot be conveyed by him into his imitative work. He cannot make his grass green and cool and good to rest upon, which in nature is its chief use to man ; nor can he make his flowers tender and full of color and of scent, which in nature are their chief powers of giving joy. Those qualities which alone he can secure are certain severe characters of form, such as men only see in nature on deliberate examination, and by the full and set appliance of sight and thought : a man must lie down on the bank of grass on his breast and set himself to watch and penetrate the intertwining of it, before he finds that which is good to be gathered by the architect. So then while Nature is at all times pleasant to us, and while the sight and sense of her work may mingle happily with all our thoughts, and labors, and times of existence, that image of her which the architect carries away represents what we can only perceive in her by direct intellectual exertion, and demands from us, wherever it appears, an intellectual exertion of a similar kind in order to understand it and feel it. It is the written or sealed impression of a thing sought out, it is the shaped result of inquiry and bodily expression of thought.

XVII. Now let us consider for an instant what would be the effect of continually repeating an expression of a beautiful thought to any other of the senses at times when the mind could not address that sense to the understanding of it. Suppose that in time of serious occupation, of stern business, a companion should repeat in our ears continually some favorite passage of poetry, over and over again all day long. We should not only soon be utterly sick and weary of the sound of it, but that sound would at the end of the day have so sunk into the habit of the ear that the entire meaning of the passage would be dead to us, and it would ever thenceforward require some effort to fix and recover it. The music of it would not meanwhile have aided the business in hand, while its own delightfulness would thenceforward be in a measure destroyed. It is the same with every other form of definite thought. If you violently present its expression to the senses, at times when the mind is otherwise engaged, that expression will be ineffective at the time, and will have its sharpness and clearness destroyed forever. Much more if you present it to the mind at times when it is painfully affected or disturbed, or if you associate the expression of pleasant thought with incongruous circumstances, you will affect that expression thenceforward with a painful color for ever.

XVIII. Apply this to expressions of thought received by the eye. Remember that the eye is at your mercy more than the ear. "The eye it cannot choose but see." Its nerve is not so easily numbed as that of the ear, and it is often busied in tracing and watching forms when the ear is at rest. Now if you present lovely forms to it when it cannot call the mind to help it in its work, and among objects of vulgar use and unhappy position, you will neither please the eye nor elevate the vulgar object. But you will fill and weary the eye with the beautiful form, and you will infect that form itself with the vulgarity of the thing to which you have violently attached it. It will never be of much use to you any more; you have killed or defiled it; its freshness and purity are gone. You will have to pass it through the fire of much thought before you will cleanse it, and warm it with much love before it will revive.

XIX. Hence then a general law, of singular importance in
the present day, a law of simple common sense,—not to decorate things belonging to purposes of active and occupied
life. Wherever you can rest, there decorate ; where rest is
forbidden, so is beauty. You must not mix ornament with
business, any more than you may mix play. Work first, and
then rest. Work first and then gaze, but do not use golden
ploughshares, nor bind ledgers in enamel. Do not thrash
with sculptured flails : nor put bas-reliefs on millstones.
What! it will be asked, are we in the habit of doing so?
Even so ; always and everywhere. The most familiar position of Greek mouldings is in these days on shop fronts.
There is not a tradesman's sign nor shelf nor counter in all
the streets of all our cities, which has not upon it ornaments
which were invented to adorn temples and beautify kings'
palaces. There is not the smallest advantage in them where
they are. Absolutely valueless—utterly without the power
of giving pleasure, they only satiate the eye, and vulgarise
their own forms. Many of these are in themselves thoroughly good copies of fine things, which things themselves
we shall never, in consequence, enjoy any more. Many a
pretty beading and graceful bracket there is in wood or
stucco above our grocers' and cheese-mongers' and hosiers'
shops : how it is that the tradesmen cannot understand that
custom is to be had only by selling good tea and cheese and
cloth, and that people come to them for their honesty, and
their readiness, and their right wares, and not because they
have Greek cornices over their windows, or their names in
large gilt letters on their house fronts? how pleasurable it
would be to have the power of going through the streets of
London, pulling down those brackets and friezes and large
names, restoring to the tradesmen the capital they had spent
in architecture, and putting them on honest and equal terms,
each with his name in black letters over his door, not shouted
down the street from the upper stories, and each with a plain
wooden shop casement, with small panes in it that people would not think of breaking in order to be sent to
prison ! How much better for them would it be—how much

happier, how much wiser, to put their trust upon their own truth and industry, and not on the idiocy of their customers. It is curious, and it says little for our national probity on the one hand, or prudence on the other, to see the whole system of our street decoration based on the idea that people must be baited to a shop as moths are to a candle.

XX. But it will be said that much of the best wooden deco· ration of the middle ages was in shop fronts. No ; it was in *house* fronts, of which the shop was a part, and received its natural and consistent portion of the ornament. In those days men lived, and intended to live *by* their shops, and over them, all their days. They were contented with them and happy in them: they were their palaces and castles. They gave them therefore such decoration as made themselves happy in their own habitation, and they gave it for their own sake. The upper stories were always the richest, and the shop was decorated chiefly about the door, which belonged to the house more than to it. And when our tradesmen settle to their shops in the same way, and form no plans respecting future villa architecture, let their whole houses be decorated, and their shops too, but with a national and domestic decoration (I shall speak more of this point in the sixth chapter). However, our cities are for the most part too large to admit of contented dwelling in them throughout life ; and I do not say there is harm in our present system of separating the shop from the dwelling-house ; only where they are so separated, let us remember that the only reason for shop decoration is removed, and see that the decoration be removed also.

XXI. Another of the strange and evil tendencies of the present day is to the decoration of the railroad station. Now, if there be any place in the world in which people are deprived of that portion of temper and discretion which are necessary to the contemplation of beauty, it is there. It is the very temple of discomfort, and the only charity that the builder can extend to us is to show us, plainly as may be, how soonest to escape from it. The whole system of railroad travelling is addressed to people who, being in a hurry, are there-

fore, for the time being, miserable. No one would travel in
that manner who could help it—who had time to go leisurely
over hills and between hedges, instead of through tunnels and
between banks : at least those who would, have no sense of
beauty so acute as that we need consult it at the station. The
railroad is in all its relations a matter of earnest business, to
be got through as soon as possible. It transmutes a man
from a traveller into a living parcel. For the time he has
parted with the nobler characteristics of his humanity for the
sake of a planetary power of locomotion. Do not ask him to
admire anything. You might as well ask the wind. Carry
him safely, dismiss him soon : he will thank you for nothing
else. All attempts to please him in any other way are mere
mockery, and insults to the things by which you endeavor to
do so. There never was more flagrant nor impertinent folly
than the smallest portion of ornament in anything concerned
with railroads or near them. Keep them out of the way, take
them through the ugliest country you can find, confess them
the miserable things they are, and spend nothing upon them
but for safety and speed. Give large salaries to efficient servants, large prices to good manufacturers, large wages to able
workmen ; let the iron be tough, and the brickwork solid,
and the carriages strong. The time is perhaps not distant
when these first necessities may not be easily met : and to increase expense in any other direction is madness. Better
bury gold in the embankments, than put it in ornaments on
the stations. Will a single traveller be willing to pay an increased fare on the South Western, because the columns of
the terminus are covered with patterns from Nineveh ? He
will only care less for the Ninevite ivories in the British Museum : or on the North Western, because there are old Eng-
lish-looking spandrils to the roof of the station at Crewe ? He
will only have less pleasure in their prototypes at Crewe
House. Railroad architecture has or would have a dignity
of its own if it were only left to its work. You would not
put rings on the fingers of a smith at his anvil.

XXII. It is not however only in these marked situations
that the abuse of which I speak takes place. There is hardly,

at present, an application of ornamental work, which is not in some sort liable to blame of the same kind. We have a bad habit of trying to disguise disagreeable necessities by some form of sudden decoration, which is, in all other places, associated with such necessities. I will name only one in- stance, that to which I have alluded before—the roses which conceal the ventilators in the flat roofs of our chapels. Many of those roses are of very beautiful design, borrowed from fine works : all their grace and finish are invisible when they are so placed, but their general form is afterwards associated with the ugly buildings in which they constantly occur ; and all the beautiful roses of the early French and English Gothic, especially such elaborate ones as those of the triforium of Coutances, are in consequence deprived of their pleasurable influence : and this without our having accomplished the smallest good by the use we have made of the dishonored form. Not a single person in the congregation ever receives one ray of pleasure from those roof roses ; they are regarded with mere indifference, or lost in the general impression of harsh emptiness.

XXIII. Must not beauty, then, it will be asked, be sought for in the forms which we associate with our every-day life ? Yes, if you do it consistently, and in places where it can be calmly seen ; but not if you use the beautiful form only as a mask and covering of the proper conditions and uses of things, nor if you thrust it into the places set apart for toil. Put it in the drawing-room, not into the workshop ; put it upon do- mestic furniture, not upon tools of handicraft. All men have sense of what is right in this manner, if they would only use and apply that sense ; every man knows where and how beauty gives him pleasure, if he would only ask for it when it does so, and not allow it to be forced upon him when he does not want it. Ask any one of the passengers over London Bridge at this instant whether he cares about the forms of the bronze leaves on its lamps, and he will tell you, No. Modify these forms of leaves to a less scale, and put them on his milk- jug at breakfast, and ask him whether he likes them, and he will tell you, Yes. People have no need of teaching if they

could only think and speak truth, and ask for what they like
and want, and for nothing else : nor can a right disposition
of beauty be ever arrived at except by this common sense,
and allowance for the circumstances of the time and place.
It does not follow, because bronze leafage is in bad taste on
the lamps of London Bridge, that it would be so on those of
the Ponte della Trinita ; nor, because it would be a folly to
decorate the house fronts of Gracechurch Street, that it would
be equally so to adorn those of some quiet provincial town.
The question of greatest external or internal decoration depends entirely on the conditions of probable repose.   It was
a wise feeling which made the streets of Venice so rich in external ornament, for there is no couch of rest like the gondola.
So, again, there is no subject of street ornament so wisely
chosen as the fountain, where it is a fountain of use ; for it is
just there that perhaps the happiest pause takes place in the
labor of the day, when the pitcher is rested on the edge of it,
and the breath of the bearer is drawn deeply, and the hair
swept from the forehead, and the uprightness of the form
declined against the marble ledge, and the sound of the kind
word or light laugh mixes with the trickle of the falling water,
heard shriller and shriller as the pitcher fills.   What pause is
so sweet as that—so full of the depth of ancient days, so softened with the calm of pastoral solitude ?

XXIV. II. Thus far, then, of the place for beauty. We
were next to inquire into the characters which fitted it peculiarly for architectural appliance, and into the principles of
choice and of arrangement which best regulate the imitation
of natural forms in which it consists.   The full answering of
these questions would be a treatise on the art of design : I in-
tend only to say a few words respecting the two conditions of
that art which are essentially architectural,—Proportion and
Abstraction.   Neither of these qualities is necessary, to the
same extent, in other fields of design.   The sense of proportion
is, by the landscape painter, frequently sacrificed to character
and accident ; the power of abstraction to that of complete
realisation.   The flowers of his foreground must often be un-
measured in their quantity, loose in their arrangement : what

is calculated, either in quantity or disposition, must be artfully concealed. That calculation is by the architect to be prominently exhibited. So the abstraction of few characteristics out of many is shown only in the painter's sketch; in his finished work it is concealed or lost in completion. Architecture, on the contrary, delights in Abstraction and fears to complete her forms. Proportion and Abstraction, then, are the two especial marks of architectural design as distinguished from all other. Sculpture must have them in inferior degrees; leaning, on the one hand, to an architectural manner, when it is usually greatest (becoming, indeed, a part of Architecture), and, on the other, to a pictorial manner, when it is apt to lose its dignity, and sink into mere ingenious carving.

XXV. Now, of Proportion so much has been written, that I believe the only facts which are of practical use have been overwhelmed and kept out of sight by vain accumulations of particular instances and estimates. Proportions are as infinite (and that in all kinds of things, as severally in colors, lines, shades, lights, and forms) as possible airs in music: and it is just as rational an attempt to teach a young architect how to proportion truly and well by calculating for him the proportions of fine works, as it would be to teach him to compose melodies by calculating the mathematical relations of the notes in Beethoven's Adelaïde or Mozart's Requiem. The man who has eye and intellect will invent beautiful proportions, and cannot help it; but he can no more tell *us* how to do it than Wordsworth could tell us how to write a sonnet, or than Scott could have told us how to plan a romance. But there are one or two general laws which can be told: they are of no use, indeed, except as preventives of gross mistake, but they are so far worth telling and remembering; and the more so because, in the discussion of the subtle laws of proportion (which will never be either numbered or known), architects are perpetually forgetting and transgressing the very simplest of its necessities.

XXVI. Of which the first is, that wherever Proportion exists at all, one member of the composition must be either larger than, or in some way supreme over, the rest. There is no proportion between equal things. They can have symmetry only, and symmetry without proportion is not composition. It is necessary to perfect beauty, but it is the least necessary of its elements, nor of course is there any difficulty in obtaining it. Any succession of equal things is agreeable ; but to compose is to arrange unequal things, and the first thing to be done in beginning a composition is to determine which is to be the principal thing. I believe that all that has been written and taught about proportion, put together, is not to the architect worth the single rule, well enforced, "Have one large thing and several smaller things, or one principal thing and several inferior things, and bind them well together." Sometimes there may be a regular gradation, as between the heights of stories in good designs for houses ; sometimes a monarch with a lowly train, as in the spire with its pinnacles : the varieties of arrangement are infinite, but the law is universal—have one thing above the rest, either by size, or office, or interest. Don't put the pinnacles without the spire. What a host of ugly church towers have we in England, with pinnacles at the corners, and none in the middle ! How many buildings like King's College Chapel at Cambridge, looking like tables upside down, with their four legs in the air ! What ! it will be said, have not beasts four legs ? Yes, but legs of different shapes, and with a head between them. So they have a pair of ears : and perhaps a pair of horns : but not at both ends. Knock down a couple of pinnacles at either end in King's College Chapel, and you will have a kind of proportion instantly. So in a cathedral you may have one tower in the centre, and two at the west end ; or two at the west end only, though a worse arrangement : but you must not have two at the west and two at the east end, unless you have some central member to connect them ; and even then, buildings are generally bad which have large balancing features at the extremities, and small connecting ones in the centre, because it is not easy then to make the centre dominant. The bird or moth may indeed have wide wings, because the size of the wing does not give supremacy to the wing. The head and life are the mighty things, and the plumes, however wide, are subordinate. In fine west fronts with a pediment and two towers, the centre is always the principal mass, both in bulk and interest (as having the main gateway), and the towers are subordinated to it, as an animal's horns are to its head. The moment the towers rise so high as to overpower the body and centre, and become themselves the principal masses, they will destroy the proportion, unless they are made unequal, and one of them the leading feature of the cathedral, as at Antwerp and Strasburg. But the purer method is to keep them down in due relation to the centre, and to throw up the pediment into a steep connecting mass, drawing the eye to it by rich tracery. This is nobly done in St. Wulfran of Abbeville, and attempted partly at Rouen, though that west front is made up of so many unfinished and supervening designs that it is impossible to guess the real intention of any one of its builders.

XXVII. This rule of supremacy applies to the smallest as well as to the leading features: it is interestingly seen in the arrangement of all good mouldings. I have given one, on the opposite page, from Rouen cathedral; that of the tracery before distinguished as a type of the noblest manner of Northern Gothic (Chap. II. § XXII.). It is a tracery of three orders, of which the first is divided into a leaf moulding, fig. 4, and *b* in the section, and a plain roll, also seen in fig. 4, *c* in the section ; these two divisions surround the entire window or panelling, and are carried by two-face shafts of corresponding sections. The second and third orders are plain rolls following the line of the tracery ; four divisions of moulding in all : of these four, the leaf moulding is, as seen in the sections, much the largest ; next to it the outer roll ; then, by an exquisite alternation, the innermost roll (*e*), in order that it may not be lost in the recess and the intermediate (*d*), the smallest. Each roll has its own shaft and capital ; and the two smaller, which in effect upon the eye, owing to the retirement of the innermost, are nearly equal, have smaller capitals than the two larger, lifted a little to bring them to the same level. The wall in the trefoiled lights is curved, as from *e* to *f* in the section ; but in the quatrefoil it is flat, only thrown back to the full depth of the recess below so as to get a sharp shadow in-

stead of a soft one, the mouldings falling back to it in nearly
a vertical curve behind the roll *e.* This could not, however,
be managed with the simpler mouldings of the smaller quatrefoil above, whose half section is given from g to g_2 ; but
the architect was evidently fretted by the heavy look of its
circular foils as opposed to the light spring of the arches below : so he threw its cusps obliquely clear from the wall, as
seen in fig. 2, attached to it where they meet the circle, but
with their finials pushed out from the natural level (h, in the
section) to that of the first order (g_2) and supported by stone
props behind, as seen in the profile fig. 2, which I got from
the correspondent panel on the buttress face (fig. 1 being on
its side), and of which the lower cusps, being broken away,
show the remnant of one of their props projecting from the
wall. The oblique curve thus obtained in the profile is of
singular grace. Take it all in all, I have never met with a
more exquisite piece of varied, yet severe, proportioned and
general arrangement (though all the windows of the period
are fine, and especially delightful in the subordinate proportioning of the smaller capitals to the smaller shafts). The
only fault it has is the inevitable misarrangement of the central shafts ; for the enlargement of the inner roll, though
beautiful in the group of four divisions at the side, causes,
in the triple central shaft, the very awkwardness of heavy
lateral members which has just been in most instances condemned. In the windows of the choir, and in most of the
period, this difficulty is avoided by making the fourth order a
fillet which only follows the foliation, while the three outermost are nearly in arithmetical progression of size, and the central triple shaft has of course the largest roll in front. The
moulding of the Palazzo Foscari (Plate VIII., and Plate IV.
fig. 8) is, for so simple a group, the grandest in effect I have
even seen : it is composed of a large roll with two subordi-
nates.

XXVIII. It is of course impossible to enter into details of
instances belonging to so intricate division of our subject, in
the compass of a general essay. I can but rapidly name the
chief conditions of right. Another of these is the connection

of Symmetry with horizontal, and of Proportion with vertical, division. Evidently there is in symmetry a sense not merely of equality, but of balance : now a thing cannot be balanced by another on the top of it, though it may by one at the side of it. Hence, while it is not only allowable, but often necessary, to divide buildings, or parts of them, horizontally into halves, thirds, or other equal parts, all vertical divisions of this kind are utterly wrong ; worst into half, next worst in the regular numbers which more betray the equality. I should have thought this almost the first principle of proportion which a young architect was taught : and yet I remember an important building, recently erected in England, in which the columns are cut in half by the projecting architraves of the central windows; and it is quite usual to see the spires of modern Gothic churches divided by a band of ornament half way up. In all fine spires there are two bands and three parts, as at Salisbury. The ornamented portion of the tower is there cut in half, and allowably, because the spire forms the third mass to which the other two are subordinate : two stories are also equal in Giotto's campanile, but dominant over smaller divisions below, and subordinated to the noble third above. Even this arrangement is difficult to treat ; and it is usually safer to increase or diminish the height of the divisions regularly as they rise, as in the Doge's Palace, whose three divisions are in a bold geometrical progression : or, in towers, to get an alternate proportion between the body, the belfry, and the crown, as in the campanile of St. Mark's. But, at all events, get rid of equality ; leave that to children and their card houses : the laws of nature and the reason of man are alike against it, in arts, as in politics. There is but one thoroughly ugly tower in Italy that I know of, and that is so because it is divided into vertical equal parts : the tower of Pisa.[12]

XXIX. One more principle of Proportion I have to name, equally simple, equally neglected. Proportion is between three terms at *least*. Hence, as the pinnacles are not enough without the spire, so neither the spire without the pinnacles. All men feel this and usually express their feeling by saying that the pinnacles conceal the junction of the spire and tower. This is one reason ; but a more influential one is, that the pinnacles furnish the third term to the spire and tower. So that it is not enough, in order to secure proportion, to divide a building unequally ; it must be divided into at least three parts ; it may be into more (and in details with advantage), but on a large scale I find three is about the best number ol parts in elevation, and five in horizontal extent, with freedom of increase to five in the one case and seven in the other ; but not to more without confusion (in architecture, that is to say ; for in organic structure the numbers cannot be limited). I purpose, in the course of works which are in preparation, to give copious illustrations of this subject, but I will take at present only one instance of vertical proportion, from the flower stem of the common water plantain, *Alisma Plantago.* Fig. 5, Plate XII. is a reduced profile of one side of a plant gathered at random ; it is seen to have five masts, of which, however, the uppermost is a mere shoot, and we can consider only their relations up to the fourth. Their lengths are measured on the line A B, which is the actual length of the lowest mass $a\ b$, A C$=b\ c$, A D$=c\ d$, and A E$=d\ e$. If the reader will take the trouble to measure these lengths and compare them, he will find that, within half a line, the uppermost A E$=\frac{6}{7}$ of A D, A D$=\frac{6}{8}$ of A C, and A C$=\frac{4}{5}$ of A B ; a most subtle diminishing proportion. From each of the joints spring three major and three minor branches, each between each ; but the major branches, at any joint, are placed over the minor branches at the joint below, by the curious arrangement of the joint itself—the stem is bluntly triangular ; fig. 6 shows the section of any joint. The outer darkened triangle is the section of the lower stem ; the inner, left light, of the upper stem ; and the three main branches spring from the ledges left by the recession. Thus the stems diminish in diameter just as they diminish in height. The main branches (falsely placed in the profile over each other to show their relations) have respectively seven, six, five, four, and three arm-bones, like the masts of the stem ; these divisions being proportioned in the same subtle manner. From the joints of these, it seems to be the *plan* of the plant that three major and three minor branches should again spring, bearing the flowers : but, in these infinitely complicated members, vegetative nature admits much variety ; in the plant from which these measures were taken the full complement appeared only at one of the secondary joints.

The leaf of this plant has five ribs on each side, as its flower generally five masts, arranged with the most exquisite grace of curve ; but of lateral proportion I shall rather take illustrations from architecture : the reader will find several in the accounts of the Duomo at Pisa and St. Mark's at Venice, in Chap. V. §§ XIV.—XVI. I give these arrangements merely as illustrations, not as precedents : all beautiful proportions are unique, they are not general formulæ.

XXX. The other condition of architectural treatment which we proposed to notice was the abstraction of imitated form. But there is a peculiar difficulty in touching within these narrow limits on such a subject as this, because the abstraction of which we find examples in existing art, is partly involuntary ; and it is a matter of much nicety to determine where it begins to be purposed. In the progress of national as well as of individual mind, the first attempts at imitation are always abstract and incomplete. Greater completion marks the progress of art, absolute completion usually its decline ; whence absolute completion of imitative form is often supposed to be in itself wrong. But it is not wrong always, only dangerous. Let us endeavor briefly to ascertain wherein its danger consists, and wherein its dignity.

XXXI. I have said that all art is abstract in its beginnings ; that is to say, it expresses only a small number of the qualities of the thing represented. Curved and complex lines are represented by straight and simple ones ; interior markings of forms are few, and much is symbolical and conventional. There is a resemblance between the work of a great nation, in this phase, and the work of childhood and ignorance, which, in the mind of a careless observer, might attach something like ridicule to it. The form of a tree on the Ninevite sculptures is much like that which, some twenty years ago, was familiar upon samplers ; and

the types of the face and figure in early Italian art are susceptible of easy caricature. On the signs which separate the infancy
of magnificent manhood from every other, I do not pause to
insist (they consist entirely in the choice of the symbol and of
the features abstracted); but I pass to the next stage of art, a
condition of strength in which the abstraction which was begun
in incapability is continued in free will. This is the case, however, in pure sculpture and painting, as well as in architecture;
and we have nothing to do but with that greater severity of
manner which fits either to be associated with the more realist
art. I believe it properly consists only in a due expression of
their subordination, an expression varying according to their
place and office. The question is first to be clearly determined
whether the architecture is a frame for the sculpture, or the
sculpture an ornament of the architecture. If the latter, then
the first office of that sculpture is not to represent the things it
imitates, but to gather out of them those arrangements of
form which shall be pleasing to the eye in their intended places.
So soon as agreeable lines and points of shade have been added
to the mouldings which were meagre, or to the lights which
were unrelieved, the architectural work of the imitation is accomplished; and how far it shall be wrought towards completeness or not, will depend upon its place, and upon other various
circumstances. If, in its particular use or position, it is symmetrically arranged, there is, of course, an instant indication of
architectural subjection. But symmetry is not abstraction.
Leaves may be carved in the most regular order, and yet be
meanly imitative; or, on the other hand, they may be thrown
wild and loose, and yet be highly architectural in their separate
treatment. Nothing can be less symmetrical than the group of
leaves which join the two columns in Plate XIII.; yet, since
nothing of the leaf character is given but what is necessary
for the bare suggestion of its image and the attainment of the
lines desired, their treatment is highly abstract. It shows that
the workman only wanted so much of the leaf as he supposed
good for his architecture, and would allow no more; and how
much is to be supposed good, depends, as I have said, much
more on place and circumstance than on general laws. I know

that this is not usually thought, and that many good architects would insist on abstraction in all cases : the question is so wide and so difficult that I express my opinion upon it most diffidently ; but my own feeling is, that a purely abstract manner, like that of our earliest English work, does not afford room for the perfection of beautiful form, and that its severity is wearisome after the eye has been long accustomed to it. I have not done justice to the Salisbury dog-tooth moulding, of which the effect is sketched in fig. 5, Plate X., but I have done more justice to it nevertheless than to the beautiful French one above it ; and I do not think that any candid reader would deny that, piquant and spirited as is that from Salisbury, the Rouen moulding is, in every respect, nobler. It will be observed that its symmetry is more complicated, the leafage being divided into double groups of two lobes each, each lobe of different structure. With exquisite feeling, one of these double groups is alternately omitted on the other side of the moulding (not seen in the Plate, but occupying the cavetto of the section), thus giving a playful lightness to the whole ; and if the reader will allow for a beauty in the flow of the curved outlines (especially on the angle), of which he cannot in the least judge from my rude drawing, he will not, I think, expect easily to find a nobler instance of decoration adapted to the severest mouldings.

Now it will be observed, that there is in its treatment a high degree of abstraction, though not so conventional as that of Salisbury : that is to say, the leaves have little more than their flow and outline represented ; they are hardly undercut, but their edges are connected by a gentle and most studied curve with the stone behind ; they have no serrations, no veinings, no rib or stalk on the angle, only an incision gracefully made towards their extremities, indicative of the central rib and depression. The whole style of the abstraction shows that the architect could, if he had chosen, have carried the imitation much farther, but stayed at this point of his own free will ; and what he has done is also so perfect in its kind, that I feel disposed to accept his authority without question, so far as I can gather it from his works, on the whole subject of abstraction.

XXXII. Happily his opinion is frankly expressed. This moulding is on the lateral buttress, and on a level with the top of the north gate ; it cannot therefore be closely seen except from the wooden stairs of the belfry ; it is not intended to be so seen, but calculated for a distance of, at least, forty to fifty feet from the eye. In the vault of the gate itself, half as near again, there are three rows of mouldings, as I think, by the same designer, at all events part of the same plan. One of them is given in Plate I. fig. 2 *a.* It will be seen that the abstraction is here infinitely less ; the ivy leaves have stalks and associated fruit, and a rib for each lobe, and are so far undercut as to detach their forms from the stone ; while in the vineleaf moulding above, of the same period, from the south gate, serration appears added to other purely imitative characters. Finally, in the animals which form the ornaments of the portion of the gate which is close to the eye, abstraction nearly vanishes into perfect sculpture.

XXXIII. Nearness to the eye, however, is not the only circumstance which influences architectural abstraction. These very animals are not merely better cut because close to the eye ; they are put close to the eye that they may, without indiscretion, be better cut, on the noble principle, first I think, clearly enunciated by Mr. Eastlake, that the closest imitation shall be of the noblest object. Farther, since the wildness and manner of growth of vegetation render a bonâ fide imitation of it impossible in sculpture—since its members must be reduced in number, ordered in direction, and cut away from their roots, even under the most earnestly imitative treatment, —it becomes a point, as I think, of good judgment, to proportion the completeness of execution of parts to the formality of the whole ; and since five or six leaves must stand for a tree, to let also five or six touches stand for a leaf. But since the animal generally admits of perfect outline—since its form is detached, and may be fully represented, its sculpture may be more complete and faithful in all its parts. And this prin ciple will be actually found, I believe, to guide the old work men. If the animal form be in a gargoyle, incomplete, and coming out of a block of stone, or if a head only, as for a boss or other such partial use, its sculpture will be highly **abstract**. But if it be an entire animal, as a lizard, or a bird, **or a** squirrel, peeping among leafage, its sculpture will be much farther carried, and I think, if small, near the eye, and worked in a fine material, may rightly be carried to the utmost possible completion. Surely we cannot wish a less finish bestowed on those which animate the mouldings of the south door of the cathedral of Florence; nor desire that the birds in the capitals of the Doge's palace should be stripped of a single plume.

XXXIV. Under these limitations, then, I think that perfect sculpture may be made a part of the severest architecture; but this perfection was said in the outset to be dangerous. It is so in the highest degree; for the moment the architect allows himself to dwell on the imitated portions, there is a chance of his losing sight of the duty of his ornament, of its business as a part of the composition, and sacrificing its points of shade and effect to the delight of delicate carving. And then he is lost. His architecture has become a mere framework for the setting of delicate sculpture, which had better be all taken down and put into cabinets. It is well, therefore, that the young architect should be taught to think of imitative ornament as of the extreme of grace in language; not to be regarded at first, not to be obtained at the cost of purpose, meaning, force, or conciseness, yet, indeed, a perfection —the least of all perfections, and yet the crowning one of all —one which by itself, and regarded in itself, is an architectural coxcombry, but is yet the sign of the most highly-trained mind and power when it is associated with others. It is a safe manner, as I think, to design all things at first in severe abstraction, and to be prepared, if need were, to carry them out in that form; then to mark the parts where high finish would be admissible, to complete these always with stern reference to their general effect, and then connect them by a graduated scale of abstraction with the rest. And there is one safeguard against danger in this process on which I would finally insist. Never imitate anything but natural forms, and those the noblest, in the completed parts. The degradation of the cinque cento manner of decoration was not owing to its naturalism, to its faithfulness of imitation, but to its imitation of ugly, i.e. unnatural things. So long as it restrained itself to sculpture of animals and flowers, it remained noble. The balcony, on the opposite page, from a house in the Campo St. Benedetto at Venice, shows one of the earliest occurrences of the cinque cento arabesque, and a fragment of the pattern is given in Plate XII. fig. 8. It is but the arresting upon the stone work of a stem or two of the living flowers, which are rarely wanting in the window above (and which, by the by, the French and Italian peasantry often trellis with exquisite taste about their casements). This arabesque, relieved as it is in darkness from the white stone by the stain of time, is surely both beautiful and pure ; and as long as the renaissance ornament remained in such forms it may be beheld with undeserved admiration. But the moment that unnatural objects were associated with these, and armor, and musical instruments, and wild meaningless scrolls and curled shields, and other such fancies, became principal in its subjects, its doom was sealed, and with it that of the architecture of the world.

XXXV. III. Our final inquiry was to be into the use of color as associated with architectural ornament.

I do not feel able to speak with any confidence respecting the touching of *sculpture* with color. I would only note one point, that sculpture is the representation of an idea, while architecture is itself a real thing. The idea may, as I think, be left colorless, and colored by the beholder's mind : but a reality ought to have reality in all its attributes : its color should be as fixed as its form. I cannot, therefore, consider architecture as in any wise perfect without color. Farther, as I have above noticed, I think the colors of architecture should be those of natural stones ; partly because more durable, but also because more perfect and graceful. For to conquer the harshness and deadness of tones laid upon stone or on gesso, needs the management and discretion of a true painter ; and on this co-operation we must not calculate in laying down rules for general practice. If Tintoret or Giorgione are at hand, and ask us for a wall to paint, we will alter our whole design for their sake, and become their servants ; but we must, as architects, expect the aid of the common workman only ; and the laying of color by a mechanical hand, and its toning under a vulgar eye, are far more offensive than rudeness in cutting the stone. The latter is imperfection only ; the former deadness or discordance. At the best, such color is so inferior to the lovely and mellow hues of the natural stone, that it is wise to sacrifice some of the intricacy of design, if by so doing we may employ the nobler material. And if, as we looked to Nature for instruction respecting form, we look to her also to learn the management of color, we shall, perhaps, find that this sacrifice of intricacy is for other causes expedient.

XXXVI. First, then, I think that in making this reference we are to consider our building as a kind of organized creature ; in coloring which we must look to the single and separately organized creatures of Nature, not to her landscape combinations. Our building, if it is well composed, is one thing, and is to be colored as Nature would color one thing— a shell, a flower, or an animal ; not as she colors groups of things.

And the first broad conclusion we shall deduce from observance of natural color in such cases will be, that it never follows form, but is arranged on an entirely separate system. What mysterious connection there may be between the shape of the spots on an animal's skin and its anatomical system, I do not know, nor even if such a connection has in any wise been traced: but to the eye the systems are entirely separate, and in many cases that of color is accidentally variable. The stripes of a zebra do not follow the lines of its body or limbs, still less the spots of a leopard. In the plumage of birds, each feather bears a part of the pattern which is arbitrarily carried over the body, having indeed certain graceful harmonies with the form, diminishing or enlarging in directions which sometimes follow, but also not unfrequently oppose, the directions of its muscular lines. Whatever harmonies there may be, are distinctly like those of two separate musical parts, coinciding here and there only—never discordant, but essentially different. I hold this, then, for the first great principle of architectural color. Let it be visibly independent of form. Never paint a column with vertical lines, but always cross it.[13] Never give separate mouldings separate colors (I know this is heresy, but I never shrink from any conclusions, however contrary to human authority, to which I am led by observance of natural principles); and in sculptured ornaments I do not paint the leaves or figures (I cannot help the Elgin frieze) of one color and their ground of another, but vary both the ground and the figures with the same harmony. Notice how Nature does it in a variegated flower ; not one leaf red and another white, but a point of red and a zone of white, or whatever it may be, to each. In certain places you may run your two systems closer, and here and there let them be parallel for a note or two, but see that the colors and the forms coincide only as two orders of mouldings do ; the same for an instant, but each holding its own course. So single members may sometimes have single colors : as a bird's head is sometimes of one color and its shoulders another, you may make your capital of one color and your shaft another ; but in general the best place for color is on broad surfaces, not on the points of interest in form. An animal is mottled on its breast and back, rarely on its paws or about its eyes ; so put your variegation boldly on the flat wall and broad shaft, but be shy of it in the capital and moulding; in all cases it is a safe rule to simplify color when form is rich, and vice versâ ; and I think it would be well in general to carve all capitals and graceful ornaments in white marble, and so leave them.

XXXVII. Independence then being first secured, what kind of limiting outlines shall we adopt for the system of color itself ?

I am quite sure that any person familiar with natural objects will never be surprised at any appearance of care or finish in them. That is the condition of the universe. But there is cause both for surprise and inquiry whenever we see anything like carelessness or incompletion : that is not a common condition; it must be one appointed for some singular purpose. I believe that such surprise will be forcibly felt by any one who, after studying carefully the lines of some variegated organic

form, will set himself to copy with similar diligence those of
its colors. The boundaries of the forms he will assuredly,
whatever the object, have found drawn with a delicacy and
precision which no human hand can follow. Those of its
colors he will find in many cases, though governed always by
a certain rude symmetry, yet irregular, blotched, imperfect,
liable to all kinds of accidents and awkwardnesses. Look at
the tracery of the lines on a camp shell, and see how oddly and
awkwardly its tents are pitched. It is not indeed always so :
there is occasionally, as in the eye of the peacock's plume, an
apparent precision, but still a precision far inferior to that of
the drawing of the filaments which bear that lovely stain ; and
in the plurality of cases a degree of looseness and variation,
and, still more singularly, of harshness and violence in arrangement, is admitted in color which would be monstrous in form.
Observe the difference in the precision of a fish's scales and of
the spots on them.

XXXVIII. Now, why it should be that color is best seen
under these circumstances I will not here endeavor to determine ; nor whether the lesson we are to learn from it be that
it is God's will that all manner of delights should never be
combined in one thing. But the fact is certain, that color is
always by Him arranged in these simple or rude forms, and as
certain that, therefore, it must be best seen in them, and that
we shall never mend by refining its arrangements. Experience
teaches us the same thing. Infinite nonsense has been written
about the union of perfect color with perfect form. They never
will, never can be united. Color, to be perfect, *must* have a
soft outline or a simple one : it cannot have a refined one ;
and you will never produce a good painted window with good
figure-drawing in it. You will lose perfection of color as you
give perfection of line. Try to put in order and form the
colors of a piece of opal.

XXXIX. I conclude, then, that all arrangements of color,
for its own sake, in graceful forms, are barbarous ; and that,
to paint a color pattern with the lovely lines of a Greek leaf
moulding, is an utterly savage procedure. I cannot find anything in natural color like this : it is not in the bond. I find

it in all natural form—never in natural color. If, then, our architectural color is to be beautiful as its form was, by being imitative, we are limited to these conditions—to simple masses of it, to zones, as in the rainbow and the zebra; cloudings and flamings, as in marble shells and plumage, or spots of various shapes and dimensions. All these conditions are susceptible of various degrees of sharpness and delicacy, and of complication in arrangement. The zone may become a delicate line, and arrange itself in chequers and zig-zags. The flaming may be more or less defined, as on a tulip leaf, and may at last be represented by a triangle of color, and arrange itself in stars or other shapes; the spot may be also graduated into a stain, or defined into a square or circle. The most exquisite harmonies may be composed of these simple elements: some soft and full of flushed and melting spaces of color; others piquant and sparkling, or deep and rich, formed of close groups of the fiery fragments: perfect and lovely proportion may be exhibited in the relation of their quantities, infinite invention in their disposition: but, in all cases, their shape will be effective only as it determines their quantity, and regulates their operation on each other; points or edges of one being introduced between breadths of others, and so on. Triangular and barred forms are therefore convenient, or others the simplest possible; leaving the pleasure of the spectator to be taken in the color, and in that only. Curved outlines, especially if refined, deaden the color, and confuse the mind. Even in figure painting the greatest colorists have either melted their outline away, as often Correggio and Rubens; or purposely made their masses of ungainly shape, as Titian; or placed their brightest hues in costume, where they could get quaint patterns, as Veronese, and especially Angelico, with whom, however, the absolute virtue of color is secondary to grace of line. Hence, he never uses the blended hues of Correggio, like those on the wing of the little Cupid, in the "Venus and Mercury," but always the severest type—the peacock plume. Any of these men would have looked with infinite disgust upon the leafage and scroll-work which form the ground of color in our modern painted windows, and yet all whom I have named were much infected with the love of renaissance designs.   We must also allow for the freedom of the painter's subject, and looseness of his associated lines ; a pattern being severe in a picture, which is over luxurious upon a building.   I believe, therefore, that it is impossible to be over quaint or angular in architectural coloring ; and thus many dispositions which I have had occasion to reprobate in form, are, in color, the best that can be invented.   I have always, for instance, spoken with contempt of the Tudor style, for this reason, that, having surrendered all pretence to spaciousness and breadth,—having divided its surfaces by an infinite number of lines, it yet sacrifices the only characters which can make lines beautiful ; sacrifices all the variety and grace which long atoned for the caprice of the Flamboyant, and adopts, for its leading feature, an entanglement of cross bars and verticals, showing about as much invention or skill of design as the reticulation of the bricklayer's sieve.   Yet this very reticulation would in color be highly beautiful ; and all the heraldry, and other features which, in form, are monstrous, may be delightful as themes of color (so long as there are no fluttering or over-twisted lines in them) ; and this observe, because, when colored, they take the place of a mere pattern, and the resemblance to nature, which could not be found in their sculptured forms, is found in their piquant variegation of other surfaces.   There is a beautiful and bright bit of wall painting behind the Duomo of Verona, composed of coats of arms, whose bearings are balls of gold set in bars of green (altered blue ?) and white, with cardinal's hats in alternate squares.   This is of course, however, fit only for domestic work.   The front of the Doge's palace at Venice is the purest and most chaste model that I can name (but one) of the fit application of color to public buildings.   The sculpture and mouldings are all white ; but the wall surface is chequered with marble blocks of pale rose, the chequers being in no wise harmonized, or fitted to the forms of the windows ; but looking as if the surface had been completed first, and the windows cut out of it. In Plate XII. fig. 2 the reader will see two of the patterns

used in green and white, on the columns of San Michele of
Lucca, every column having a different design. Both are
beautiful, but the upper one certainly the best. Yet in sculpture its lines would have been perfectly barbarous, and those
even of the lower not enough refined.

XL. Restraining ourselves, therefore, to the use of such
simple patterns, so far forth as our color is subordinate either
to architectural structure, or sculptural form, we have yet one
more manner of ornamentation to add to our general means
of effect, monochrome design, the intermediate condition between coloring and carving. The relations of the entire system of architectural decoration may then be thus expressed.

1. Organic form dominant. True, independent sculpture, and
   alto-relievo ; rich capitals, and mouldings ; to be elaborate
   in completion of form, not abstract, and either to be left
   in pure white marble, or most cautiously touched with
   color in points and borders only, in a system *not* concur-
   rent with their forms.

2. Organic form sub-dominant. Basso-relievo or intaglio. To
   be more abstract in proportion to the reduction of depth ;
   to be also more rigid and simple in contour ; to be
   touched with color more boldly and in an increased degree, exactly in proportion to the reduced depth and fulness of form, but still in a system non-concurrent with
   their forms.

3. Organic form abstracted to outline. Monochrome design,
   still farther reduced to simplicity of contour, and therefore admitting for the first time the color to be concur-
   rent with its outlines ; that is to say, as its name imports,
   the entire figure to be detached in one color from a
   ground of another.

4. Organic forms entirely lost. Geometrical patterns or variable cloudings in the most vivid color.

On the opposite side of this scale, ascending from the color
pattern, I would place the various forms of painting which
may be associated with architecture : primarily, and as most

fit for such purpose, the mosaic, highly abstract in treatment
and introducing brilliant color in masses; the Madonna of
Torcello being, as I think, the noblest type of the manner, and
the Baptistery of Parma the richest: next, the purely decorative fresco, like that of the Arena Chapel; finally, the fresco
becoming principal, as in the Vatican and Sistine.   But I cannot, with any safety, follow the principles of abstraction in
this pictorial ornament; since the noblest examples of it
appear to me to owe their architectural applicability to their
archaic manner; and I think that the abstraction and admirable simplicity which render them fit media of the most splendid coloring, cannot be recovered by a voluntary condescen-
sion.   The Byzantines themselves would not, I think, if they
could have drawn the figure better, have used it for a color
decoration; and that use, as peculiar to a condition of childhood, however noble and full of promise, cannot be included
among those modes of adornment which are now legitimate or
even possible.   There is a difficulty in the management of the
painted window for the same reason, which has not yet been
met, and we must conquer that first, before we can venture to
consider the wall as a painted window on a large scale.   Pictorial subject, without such abstraction, becomes necessarily
principal, or, at all events, ceases to be the architect's concern;
its plan must be left to the painter after the completion of the
building, as in the works of Veronese and Giorgione on the
palaces of Venice.

XLI. Pure architectural decoration, then, may be considered as limited to the four kinds above specified; of which
each glides almost imperceptibly into the other.   Thus, the
Elgin frieze is a monochrome in a state of transition to sculpture, retaining, as I think, the half-cast skin too long.   Of
pure monochrome, I have given an example in Plate VI., from
the noble front of St. Michele of Lucca.   It contains forty
such arches, all covered with equally elaborate ornaments, entirely drawn by cutting out their ground to about the depth
of an inch in the flat white marble, and filling the spaces with
pieces of green serpentine; a most elaborate mode of sculpture, requiring excessive care and precision in the fitting of

the edges, and of course double work, the same line needing
to be cut both in the marble and serpentine. The excessive simplicity of the forms will be at once perceived ; the eyes of the
figures of animals, for instance, being indicated only by a
round dot, formed by a little inlet circle of serpentine, about
half an inch over : but, though simple, they admit often much
grace of curvature, as in the neck of the bird seen above the
right hand pillar.[14] The pieces of serpentine have fallen out
in many places, giving the black shadows, as seen under the
horseman's arm and bird's neck, and in the semi-circular line
round the arch, once filled with some pattern. It would have
illustrated my point better to have restored the lost portions,
but I always draw a thing exactly as it is, hating restoration
of any kind ; and I would especially direct the reader's attention to the completion of the forms in the *sculptured* ornament of the marble cornices, as opposed to the abstraction of
the monochrome figures, of the ball and cross patterns between
the arches, and of the triangular ornament round the arch on
the left.

XLII. I have an intense love for these monochrome figures,
owing to their wonderful life and spirit in all the works on
which I found them ; nevertheless, I believe that the excessive degree of abstraction which they imply necessitates our
placing them in the rank of a progressive or imperfect art,
and that a perfect building should rather be composed of the
highest sculpture (organic form dominant and sub-dominant),
associated with pattern colors on the flat or broad surfaces.
And we find, in fact, that the cathedral of Pisa, which is a
higher type than that of Lucca, exactly follows this condition,
the color being put in geometrical patterns on its surfaces,
and animal-forms and lovely leafage used in the sculptured
cornices and pillars. And I think that the grace of the carved
forms is best seen when it is thus boldly opposed to severe
traceries of color, while the color itself is, as we have seen,
always most piquant when it is put into sharp angular arrangements. Thus the sculpture is approved and set off by the
color, and the color seen to the best advantage in its opposition
both to the whiteness and the grace of the carved marble.

XLIII. In the course of this and the preceding chapters, I
have now separately enumerated most of the conditions of
Power and Beauty, which in the outset I stated to be the
grounds of the deepest impressions with which architecture
could affect the human mind ; but I would ask permission to
recapitulate them in order to see if there be any building
which I may offer as an example of the unison, in such manner as is possible, of them all. Glancing back, then, to the
beginning of the third chapter, and introducing in their place
the conditions incidentally determined in the two previous
sections, we shall have the following list of noble characters :

Considerable size, exhibited by simple terminal lines (Chap.
III. § 6). Projection towards the top (§ 7). Breadth of flat
surface (§ 8). Square compartments of that surface (§ 9).
Varied and visible masonry (§ 11). Vigorous depth of shadow
(§ 13), exhibited especially by pierced traceries (§ 18). Varied
proportion in ascent (Chap. IV. § 28). Lateral symmetry (§ 28).
Sculpture most delicate at the base (Chap. I. § 12). Enriched
quantity of ornament at the top (§ 13). Sculpture abstract in
inferior ornaments and mouldings (Chap. IV. § 31), complete
in animal forms (§ 33). Both to be executed in white marble
(§ 40). Vivid color introduced in flat geometrical patterns
(§ 39), and obtained by the use of naturally colored stone (§ 35).

These characteristics occur more or less in different buildings, some in one and some in another. But all together, and
all in their highest possible relative degrees, they exist, as far
as I know, only in one building in the world, the Campanile
of Giotto at Florence. The drawing of the tracery of its
upper story, which heads this chapter, rude as it is, will nevertheless give the reader some better conception of that tower's
magnificence than the thin outlines in which it is usually
portrayed. In its first appeal to the stranger's eye there is
something unpleasing ; a mingling, as it seems to him, of over
severity with over minuteness. But let him give it time, as he
should to all other consummate art. I remember well how, when
a boy, I used to despise that Campanile, and think it meanly
smooth and finished. But I have since lived beside it many a
day, and looked out upon it from my windows by sunlight and

moonlight, and I shall not soon forget how profound and gloomy appeared to me the savageness of the Northern Gothic, when I afterwards stood, for the first time, beneath the front of Salisbury. The contrast is indeed strange, if it could be quickly felt, between the rising of those grey walls out of their quiet swarded space, like dark and barren rocks out of a green lake, with their rude, mouldering, rough-grained shafts, and triple lights, without tracery or other ornament than the martins' nests in the height of them, and that bright, smooth, sunny surface of glowing jasper, those spiral shafts and fairy traceries, so white, so faint, so crystalline, that their slight shapes are hardly traced in darkness on the pallor of the Eastern sky, that serene height of mountain alabaster, colored like a morning cloud, and chased like a sea shell. And if this be, as I believe it, the model and mirror of perfect architecture, is there not something to be learned by looking back to the early life of him who raised it? I said that the Power of human mind had its growth in the Wilderness; much more must the love and the conception of that beauty, whose every line and hue we have seen to be, at the best, a faded image of God's daily work, and an arrested ray of some star of creation, be given chiefly in the places which He has gladdened by planting there the fir tree and the pine. Not within the walls of Florence, but among the far away fields of her lilies, was the child trained who was to raise that headstone of Beauty above the towers of watch and war. Remember all that he became; count the sacred thoughts with which he filled the heart of Italy; ask those who followed him what they learned at his feet; and when you have numbered his labors, and received their testimony, if it seem to you that God had verily poured out upon this His servant no common nor restrained portion of His Spirit, and that he was indeed a king among the children of men, remember also that the legend upon his crown was that of David's :— "I took thee from the sheepcote, and from following the sheep."

CHAPTER V.

THE LAMP OF LIFE.

I. Among the countless analogies by which the nature and relations of the human soul are illustrated in the material creation, none are more striking than the impressions inseparably connected with the active and dormant states of matter. I have elsewhere endeavored to show, that no inconsiderable part of the essential characters of Beauty depended on the expression of vital energy in organic things, or on the subjection to such energy, of things naturally passive and powerless. I need not here repeat, of what was then advanced, more than the statement which I believe will meet with general acceptance, that things in other respects alike, as in their substance, or uses, or outward forms, are noble or ignoble in proportion to the fulness of the life which either they themselves enjoy, or of whose action they bear the evidence, as sea sands are made beautiful by their bearing the seal of the motion of the waters. And this is especially true of all objects which bear upon them the impress of the highest order of creative life, that is to say, of the mind of man : they become noble or ignoble in proportion to the amount of the energy of that mind which has visibly been employed upon them. But most peculiarly and imperatively does the rule hold with respect to the creations of Architecture, which being properly capable of no other life than this, and being not essentially composed of things pleasant in themselves,—as music of sweet sounds, or painting of fair colors, but of inert substance,—depend, for their dignity and pleasurableness in the utmost degree, upon the vivid expression of the intellectual life which has been concerned in their production.

II. Now in all other kind of energies except that of man's mind, there is no question as to what is life, and what is not. Vital sensibility, whether vegetable or animal, may, indeed, be reduced to so great feebleness, as to render its existence a matter of question, but when it is evident at all, it is evident as such : there is no mistaking any imitation or pretence of it for the life itself ; no mechanism nor galvanism can take its place ; nor is any resemblance of it so striking as to involve even hesitation in the judgment ; although many occur which the human imagination takes pleasure in exalting, without for an instant losing sight of the real nature of the dead things it animates ; but rejoicing rather in its own excessive life, which puts gesture into clouds, and joy into waves, and voices into rocks.

III. But when we begin to be concerned with the energies of man, we find ourselves instantly dealing with a double creature. Most part of his being seems to have a fictitious counterpart, which it is at his peril if he do not cast off and deny. Thus he has a true and false (otherwise called a living and dead, or a feigned or unfeigned) faith. He has a true and a false hope, a true and a false charity, and, finally, a true and a false life. His true life is like that of lower organic beings, the independent force by which he moulds and governs external things ; it is a force of assimilation which converts everything around him into food, or into instruments ; and which, however humbly or obediently it may listen to or follow the guidance of superior intelligence, never forfeits its own authority as a judging principle, as a will capable either of obeying or rebelling. His false life is, indeed, but one of the conditions of death or stupor, but it acts, even when it cannot be said to animate, and is not always easily known from the true. It is that life of custom and accident in which many of us pass much of our time in the world ; that life in which we do what we have not purposed, and speak what we do not mean, and assent to what we do not understand ; that life which is overlaid by the weight of things external to it, and is moulded by them, instead of assimilating them ; that, which instead of growing and blossoming under any wholesome dew, is crystallised over with it, as with hoar frost, and becomes to the true life what an arborescence is to a tree, a candied agglomeration of thoughts and habits foreign to it, brittle, obstinate, and icy, which can neither bend nor grow, but must be crushed and broken to bits, if it stand in our way.

All men are liable to be in some degree frost-bitten in this sort ; all are partly encumbered and crusted over with idle matter ; only, if they have real life in them, they are always breaking this bark away in noble rents, until it becomes, like the black strips upon the birch tree, only a witness of their own inward strength.   But, with all the efforts that the best men make, much of their being passes in a kind of dream, in which they indeed move, and play their parts sufficiently, to the eyes of their fellow-dreamers, but have no clear conscious- ness of what is around them, or within them ; blind to the one, insensible to the other, νωθροι.   I would not press the definition into its darker application to the dull heart and heavy ear ; I have to do with it only as it refers to the too fre- quent condition of natural existence, whether of nations or in- dividuals, settling commonly upon them in proportion to their age.   The life of a nation is usually, like the flow of a lava stream, first bright and fierce, then languid and covered, at last advancing only by the tumbling over and over of its frozen blocks.   And that last condition is a sad one to look upon. All the steps are marked most clearly in the arts, and in Archi- tecture more than in any other ; for it, being especially de- pendent, as we have just said, on the warmth of the true life, is also peculiarly sensible of the hemlock cold of the false ; and I do not know anything more oppressive, when the mind is once awakened to its characteristics, than the aspect of a dead architecture.   The feebleness of childhood is full of promise and of interest,—the struggle of imperfect knowledge full of energy and continuity,—but to see impotence and ri- gidity settling upon the form of the developed man ; to see the types which once had the die of thought struck fresh upon them, worn flat by over use ; to see the shell of the living creature in its adult form, when its colors are faded, and its inhabitant perished,—this is a sight more humiliat- ing, more melancholy, than the vanishing of all knowledge, and the return to confessed and helpless infancy.

Nay, it is to be wished that such return were always possi- ble.   There would be hope if we could change palsy into **puerility** ; but I know not how far we *can* become children again, and renew our lost life. The stirring which has taken place in our architectural aims and interests within these few years, is thought by many to be full of promise : I trust it is, but it has a sickly look to me. I cannot tell whether it be indeed a springing of seed or a shaking among bones ; and I do not think the time will be lost which I ask the reader to spend in the inquiry, how far all that we have hitherto ascertained or conjectured to be the best in principle, may be formally practised without the spirit or the vitality which alone could give it influence, value, or delightfulness.

IV. Now, in the first place—and this is rather an important point—it is no sign of deadness in a present art that it borrows or imitates, but only if it borrows without paying interest, or if it imitates without choice. The art of a great nation, which is developed without any acquaintance with nobler examples than its own early efforts furnish, exhibits always the most consistent and comprehensible growth, and perhaps is regarded usually as peculiarly venerable in its self-origination. But there is something to my mind more majestic yet in the life of an architecture like that of the Lombards, rude and infantine in itself, and surrounded by fragments of a nobler art of which it is quick in admiration and ready in imitation, and yet so strong in its own new instincts that it re-constructs and re-arranges every fragment that it copies or borrows into harmony with its own thoughts,—a harmony at first disjointed and awkward, but completed in the end, and fused into perfect organisation ; all the borrowed elements being subordinated to its own primal, unchanged life. I do not know any sensation more exquisite than the discovering of the evidence of this magnificent struggle into independent existence ; the detection of the borrowed thoughts, nay, the finding of the actual blocks and stones carved by other hands and in other ages, wrought into the new walls, with a new expression and purpose given to them, like the blocks of unsubdued rocks (to go back to our former simile) which we find in the heart of the lava current, great witnesses to the power which has fused all but those calcined fragments into the mass of its homogeneous fire.

V. It will be asked, How is imitation to be rendered health, and vital ? Unhappily, while it is easy to enumerate the signs of life, it is impossible to define or to communicate life ; and while every intelligent writer on Art has insisted on the difference between the copying found in an advancing or recedent period, none have been able to communicate, in the slightest degree, the force of vitality to the copyist over whom they might have influence. Yet it is at least interesting, if not profitable, to note that two very distinguishing characters of vital imitation are, its Frankness and its Audacity ; its Frankness is especially singular ; there is never any effort to conceal the degree of the sources of its borrowing. Raffaelle carries off a whole figure from Masaccio, or borrows an entire composition from Perugino, with as much tranquillity and simplicity of innocence as a young Spartan pickpocket ; and the architect of a Romanesque basilica gathered his columns and capitals where he could find them, as an ant picks up sticks. There is at least a presumption, when we find this frank acceptance, that there is a sense within the mind of power capable of transforming and renewing whatever it adopts ; and too conscious, too exalted, to fear the accusation of plagiarism,—too certain that it can prove, and has proved, its independence, to be afraid of expressing its homage to what it admires in the most open and indubitable way ; and the necessary consequence of this sense of power is the other sign I have named—the Audacity of treatment when it finds treatment necessary, the unhesitating and sweeping sacrifice of precedent where precedent becomes inconvenient. For instance, in the characteristic forms of Italian Romanesque, in which the hypaethral portion of the heathen temple was replaced by the towering nave, and where, in consequence, the pediment of the west front became divided into three portions, of which the central one, like the apex of a ridge of sloping strata lifted by a sudden fault, was broken away from and raised above the wings ; there remained at the extremities of the aisles two triangular fragments of pediment, which could not now be filled by any of the modes of decoration adapted for the unbroken space ; and the difficulty became greater

when the central portion of the front was occupied by colum-
nar ranges, which could not, without painful abruptness, terminate short of the extremities of the wings. I know not
what expedient would have been adopted by architects who
had much respect for precedent, under such circumstances,
but it certainly would not have been that of the Pisan,—to
continue the range of columns into the pedimental space,
shortening them to its extremity until the shaft of the last
column vanished altogether, and there remained only its *capital* resting in the angle on its basic plinth. I raise no question at present whether this arrangement be graceful or otherwise ; I allege it only as an instance of boldness almost without
a parallel, casting aside every received principle that stood in
its way, and struggling through every discordance and difficulty to the fulfilment of its own instincts.

VI. Frankness, however, is in itself no excuse for repetition,
nor audacity for innovation, when the one is indolent and the
other unwise. Nobler and surer signs of vitality must be
sought,—signs independent alike of the decorative or original
character of the style, and constant in every style that is de-
terminedly progressive.

Of these, one of the most important I believe to be a certain neglect or contempt of refinement in execution, or, at all
events, a visible subordination of execution to conception,
commonly involuntary, but not unfrequently intentional.
This is a point, however, on which, while I speak confidently,
I must at the same time reservedly and carefully, as there
would otherwise be much chance of my being dangerously
misunderstood. It has been truly observed and well stated
by Lord Lindsay, that the best designers of Italy were also
the most careful in their workmanship ; and that the stability
and finish of their masonry, mosaic, or other work whatsoever,
were always perfect in proportion to the apparent improbabil-
ity of the great designers condescending to the care of details
among us so despised. Not only do I fully admit and re-as-
sert this most important fact, but I would insist upon perfect
and most delicate finish in its right place, as a characteristic
of all the highest schools of architecture, as much as it is

those of painting. But on the other hand, as perfect finish belongs to the perfected art, a progressive finish belongs to progressive art; and I do not think that any more fatal sign of a stupor or numbness settling upon that undeveloped art could possibly be detected, than that it had been *taken aback* by its own execution, and that the workmanship had gone ahead of the design; while, even in my admission of absolute finish in the right place, as an attribute of the perfected school, I must reserve to myself the right of answering in my own way the two very important questions, what *is* finish? and what *is* its right place?

VII. But in illustrating either of these points, we must remember that the correspondence of workmanship with thought is, in existent examples, interfered with by the adoption of the designs of an advanced period by the workmen of a rude one. All the beginnings of Christian architecture are of this kind, and the necessary consequence is of course an increase of the visible interval between the power of realisation and the beauty of the idea. We have at first an imitation, almost savage in its rudeness, of a classical design; as the art advances, the design is modified by a mixture of Gothic grotesqueness, and the execution more complete, until a harmony is established between the two, in which balance they advance to new perfection. Now during the whole period in which the ground is being recovered, there will be found in the living architecture marks not to be mistaken, of intense impatience; a struggle towards something unattained, which causes all minor points of handling to be neglected; and a restless disdain of all qualities which appear either to confess contentment or to require a time and care which might be better spent. And, exactly as a good and earnest student of drawing will not lose time in ruling lines or finishing backgrounds about studies which, while they have answered his immediate purpose, he knows to be imperfect and inferior to what he will do hereafter,—so the vigor of a true school of early architecture, which is either working under the influence of high example or which is itself in a state of rapid development, is very curiously traceable, among other signs, in the contempt of exact symmetry and measurement, which in dead architecture are the most painful necessities.

VIII. In Plate XII. fig. 1 I have given a most singular instance both of rude execution and defied symmetry, in the little pillar and spandril from a panel decoration under the pulpit of St. Mark's at Venice. The imperfection (not merely simplicity, but actual rudeness and ugliness) of the leaf ornament will strike the eye at once : this is general in works of the time, but it is not so common to find a capital which has been so carelessly cut; its imperfect volutes being pushed up one side far higher than on the other, and contracted on that side, an additional drill hole being put in to fill the space ; besides this, the member a, of the mouldings, is a roll where it follows the arch, and a flat fillet at a; the one being slurred into the other at the angle b, and finally stopped short altogether at the other side by the most uncourteous and remorseless interference of the outer moulding : and in spite of all this, the grace, proportion, and feeling of the whole arrangement are so great, that, in its place, it leaves nothing to be desired ; all the science and symmetry in the world could not beat it. In fig. 4 I have endeavored to give some idea of the execution of the subordinate portions of a much higher work, the pulpit of St. Andrea at Pistoja, by Nicolo Pisano. It is covered with figure sculptures, executed with great care and delicacy ; but when the sculptor came to the simple arch mouldings, he did not choose to draw the eye to them by over precision of work or over sharpness of shadow. The section adopted, k, m, is peculiarly simple, and so slight and obtuse in its recessions as never to produce a sharp line ; and it is worked with what at first appears slovenliness, but it is in fact sculptural *sketching* ; exactly correspondent to a painter's light execution of a background : the lines appear and disappear again, are sometimes deep, sometimes shallow, sometimes quite broken off ; and the recession of the cusp joins that of the external arch at n, in the most fearless defiance of all mathematical laws of curvilinear contact.

IX. There is something very delightful in this bold expression of the mind of the great master. I do not say that it is the "perfect work" of patience, but I think that impatience is a glorious character in an advancing school; and I love the Romanesque and early Gothic especially, because they afford so much room for it; accidental carelessness of measurement or of execution being mingled undistinguishably with the purposed departures from symmetrical regularity, and the luxuriousness of perpetually variable fancy, which are eminently characteristic of both styles. How great, how frequent they are, and how brightly the severity of architectural law is relieved by their grace and suddenness, has not, I think, been enough observed; still less, the unequal measurements of even important features professing to be absolutely symmetrical. I am not so familiar with modern practice as to speak with confidence respecting its ordinary precision; but I imagine that the following measures of the western front of the cathedral of Pisa, would be looked upon by present architects as very blundering approximations. That front is divided into seven arched compartments, of which the second, fourth or central, and sixth contain doors; the seven are in a most subtle alternating proportion; the central being the largest, next to it the second and sixth, then the first and seventh, lastly the third and fifth. By this arrangement, of course, these three pairs should be equal; and they are so to the eye, but I found their actual measures to be the following, taken from pillar to pillar, in Italian braccia, palmi (four inches each), and inches:—

	Braccia.	Palmi.	Inches.	Total in Inches.
1. Central door....................... 8		0	0	= 192
2. Northern door ⎱ 6		3	1¼	= 157¼
3. Southern door ⎰ 6		4	3	= 163
4. Extreme northern space ⎱ 5		5	3½	= 143½
5. Extreme southern space ⎰ 6		1	0¼	= 148¼
6. Northern intervals between the doors ⎱ 5		2	1	= 129
7. Southern intervals between the doors ⎰ 5		2	1¼	= 129¼

There is thus a difference, severally, between 2, 3 and 4, 5, of five inches and a half in the one case, and five inches in the other.

X. This, however, may perhaps be partly attributable to

some accommodation of the accidental distortions which evidently took place in the walls of the cathedral during their
building, as much as in those of the campanile. To my mind,
those of the Duomo are far the most wonderful of the two : I
do not believe that a single pillar of its walls is absolutely
vertical : the pavement rises and falls to different heights, or
rather the plinth of the walls sinks into it continually to different depths, the whole west front literally overhangs (I have
not plumbed it ; but the inclination may be seen by the eye,
by bringing it into visual contact with the upright pilasters of
the Campo Santo) : and a most extraordinary distortion in
the masonry of the southern wall shows that this inclination
had begun when the first story was built. The cornice above
the first arcade of that wall touches the tops of eleven out of
its fifteen arches ; but it suddenly leaves the tops of the four
westernmost ; the arches nodding westward and sinking into
the ground, while the cornice rises (or seems to rise), leaving
at any rate, whether by the rise of the one or the fall of the
other, an interval of more than two feet between it and the
top of the western arch, filled by added courses of masonry.
There is another very curious evidence of this struggle of the
architect with his yielding wall in the columns of the main
entrance. (These notices are perhaps somewhat irrelevant to
our immediate subject, but they appear to me highly interesting ; and they, at all events, prove one of the points on which
I would insist,—how much of imperfection and variety in
things professing to be symmetrical the eyes of those eager
builders could endure : they looked to loveliness in detail, to
nobility in the whole, never to petty measurements.) Those
columns of the principal entrance are among the loveliest in
Italy ; cylindrical, and decorated with a rich arabesque of
sculptured foliage, which at the base extends nearly all round
them, up to the black pilaster in which they are lightly engaged : but the shield of foliage, bounded by a severe line,
narrows to their tops, where it covers their frontal segment
only ; thus giving, when laterally seen, a terminal line sloping
boldly outwards, which, as I think, was meant to conceal the
accidental leaning of the western walls, and, by its exagger

ated inclination in the same direction, to throw them by comparison into a seeming vertical.

XI. There is another very curious instance of distortion above the central door of the west front. All the intervals between the seven arches are filled with black marble, each containing in its centre a white parallelogram filled with animal mosaics, and the whole surmounted by a broad white band, which, generally, does not touch the parallelogram below. But the parallelogram on the north of the central arch has been forced into an oblique position, and touches the white band ; and, as if the architect was determined to show that he did not care whether it did or not, the white band suddenly gets thicker at that place, and remains so over the two next arches. And these differences are the more curious because the workmanship of them all is most finished and masterly, and the distorted stones are fitted with as much neatness as if they tallied to a hair's breadth. There is no look of slurring or blundering about it ; it is all coolly filled in, as if the builder had no sense of anything being wrong or extraordinary : I only wish we had a little of his impudence.

XII. Still, the reader will say that all these variations are probably dependent more on the bad foundation than on the architect's feeling. Not so the exquisite delicacies of change in the proportions and dimensions of the apparently symmetrical arcades of the west front. It will be remembered that I said the tower of Pisa was the only ugly tower in Italy, because its tiers were equal, or nearly so, in height ; a fault this, so contrary to the spirit of the builders of the time, that it can be considered only as an unlucky caprice. Perhaps the general aspect of the west front of the cathedral may then have occurred to the reader's mind, as seemingly another contradiction of the rule I had advanced. It would not have been so, however, even had its four upper arcades been actually equal ; as they are subordinated to the great seven-arched lower story, in the manner before noticed respecting the spire of Salisbury, and as is actually the case in the Duomo of Lucca and Tower of Pistoja. But the Pisan front is far more subtly proportioned. Not one of its four arcades is of like height with another. The highest is the third, counting upwards; and they diminish in nearly arithmetical proportion alternately ; in the order 3rd, 1st, 2nd, 4th. The inequalities in their arches are not less remarkable : they at first strike the eye as all equal ; but there is a grace about them which equality never obtained : on closer observation, it is perceived that in the first row of nineteen arches, eighteen are equal, and the central one larger than the rest ; in the second arcade, the nine central arches stand over the nine below, having, like them, the ninth central one largest. But on their flanks, where is the slope of the shoulder-like pediment, the arches vanish, and a wedge-shaped frieze takes their place, tapering outwards, in order to allow the columns to be carried to the extremity of the pediment ; and here, where the heights of the shafts are so far shortened, they are set thicker ; five shafts, or rather four and a capital, above, to four of the arcade below, giving twenty-one intervals instead of nineteen. In the next or third arcade,—which, remember, is the highest,—eight arches, all equal, are given in the space of the nine below, so that there is now a central shaft instead of a central arch, and the span of the arches is increased in porportion to their increased height. Finally, in the uppermost arcade, which is the lowest of all, the arches, the same in number as those below, are narrower than any of the façade ; the whole eight going very nearly above the six below them, while the terminal arches of the lower arcade are surmounted by flanking masses of decorated wall with projecting figures.

XIII. Now I call *that* Living Architecture. There is sensation in every inch of it, and an accommodation to every architectural necessity, with a determined variation in arrangement, which is exactly like the related proportions and provisions in the structure of organic form. I have not space to examine the still lovelier proportioning of the external shafts of the apse of this marvellous building. I prefer, lest the reader should think it a peculiar example, to state the structure of another church, the most graceful and grand piece of Romanesque work, as a fragment, in north Italy, that of San Giovanni Evangelista at Pistoja.

The side of that church has three stories of arcade, diminishing in height in bold geometrical proportion, while the arches, for the most part, increase in number in arithmetical, *i. e.* two in the second arcade, and three in the third, to one in the first. Lest, however, this arrangement should be too formal, of the fourteen arches in the lowest series, that which contains the door is made larger than the rest, and is not in the middle, but the sixth from the West, leaving five on one side and eight on the other. Farther: this lowest arcade is terminated by broad flat pilasters, about half the width of its arches; but the arcade above is continuous; only the two extreme arches at the west end are made larger than all the rest, and instead of coming, as they should, into the space of the lower extreme arch, take in both it and its broad pilaster. Even this, however, was not out of order enough to satisfy the architect's eye; for there were still two arches above to each single one below: so at the east end, where there are more arches, and the eye might be more easily cheated, what does he do but *narrow* the two extreme *lower* arches by half a braccio; while he at the same time slightly enlarged the upper ones, so as to get only seventeen upper to nine lower, instead of eighteen to nine. The eye is thus thoroughly confused, and the whole building thrown into one mass, by the curious variations in the adjustments of the superimposed shafts, not one of which is either exactly in nor positively out of its place; and, to get this managed the more cunningly, there is from an inch to an inch and a half of gradual gain in the space of the four eastern arches, besides the confessed half braccio. Their measures, counting from the east, I found as follows :—

	Braccia.	Palmi.	Inches.
1st	3	0	1
2nd	3	0	2
3rd	3	3	2
4th	3	3	3½

The upper arcade is managed on the same principle; it looks at first as if there were three arches to each under pair; but there are, in reality, only thirty-eight (or thirty-seven,

am not quite certain of this number) to the twenty-seven below ; and the columns get into all manner of relative positions. Even then, the builder was not satisfied, but must
needs carry the irregularity into the spring of the arches,
and actually, while the general effect is of a symmetrical
arcade, there is not one of the arches the same in height as
another ; their tops undulate all along the wall like waves
along a harbor quay, some nearly touching the string course
above, and others falling from it as much as five or six
inches.

XIV. Let us next examine the plan of the west front of St.
Mark's at Venice, which, though in many respects imperfect,
is in its proportions, and as a piece of rich and fantastic color,
as lovely a dream as ever filled human imagination. It may,
perhaps, however, interest the reader to hear one opposite
opinion upon this subject, and after what has been urged in the
preceding pages respecting proportion in general, more especially respecting the wrongness of balanced cathedral towers
and other regular designs, together with my frequent references
to the Doge's palace, and campanile of St. Mark's, as models
of perfection, and my praise of the former especially as projecting above its second arcade, the following extracts from
the journal of Wood the architect, written on his arrival
at Venice, may have a pleasing freshness in them, and may
show that I have not been stating principles altogether trite
or accepted.

" The strange looking church, and the great ugly campanile,
could not be mistaken. The exterior of this church surprises
you by its extreme ugliness, more than by anything else."

" The Ducal Palace is even more ugly than anything I have
previously mentioned. Considered in detail, I can imagine no
alteration to make it tolerable ; but if this lofty wall had been
set back behind the two stories of little arches, it would have
been a very noble production."

After more observations on " a certain justness of proportion," and on the appearance of riches and power in the church,
to which he ascribes a pleasing effect, he goes on : " Some persons are of opinion that irregularity is a necessary part of its

excellence. I am decidedly of a contrary opinion, and am convinced that a regular design of the same sort would be far superior. Let an oblong of good architecture, but not very showy, conduct to a fine cathedral, which should appear between *two lofty towers* and have *two obelisks* in front, and on each side of this cathedral let other squares partially open into the first, and one of these extend down to a harbor or sea shore, and you would have a scene which might challenge any thing in existence."

Why Mr. Wood was unable to enjoy the color of St. Mark's, or perceive the majesty of the Ducal Palace, the reader will see after reading the two following extracts regarding the Caracci and Michael Angelo.

" The pictures here (Bologna) are to my taste far preferable to those of Venice, for if the Venetian school surpass in coloring, and, perhaps, in composition, the Bolognese is decidedly superior in drawing and expression, and the Caraccis *shine here like Gods.*"

"What is it that is so much admired in this artist (M. Angelo) ? Some contend for a grandeur of composition in the lines and disposition of the figures ; this, I confess, I do not comprehend ; yet, while I acknowledge the beauty of certain forms and proportions in architecture, I cannot consistently deny that similar merits may exist in painting, though I am unfortunately unable to appreciate them."

I think these passages very valuable, as showing the effect of a contracted knowledge and false taste in painting upon an architect's understanding of his own art; and especially with what curious notions, or lack of notions, about proportion, that art has been sometimes practised. For Mr. Wood is by no means unintelligent in his observations generally, and his criticisms on classical art are often most valuable. But those who love Titian better than the Caracci, and who see something to admire in Michael Angelo, will, perhaps, be willing to proceed with me to a charitable examination of St. Mark's. For, although the present course of European events affords us some chance of seeing the changes proposed by Mr. Wood carried into execution, we may still esteem ourselves fortunate in having first known how it was left by the builders of the eleventh century.

XV. The entire front is composed of an upper and lower series of arches, enclosing spaces of wall decorated with mosaic, and supported on ranges of shafts of which, in the lower series of arches, there is an upper range superimposed on a lower. Thus we have five vertical divisions of the façade ; *i.e.* two tiers of shafts, and the arched wall they bear, below ; one tier of shafts, and the arched wall they bear, above. In order, however, to bind the two main divisions together, the central lower arch (the main entrance) rises above the level of the gallery and balustrade which crown the lateral arches.

The proportioning of the columns and walls of the lower story is so lovely and so varied, that it would need pages of description before it could be fully understood ; but it may be generally stated thus : The height of the lower shafts, upper shafts, and wall, being severally expressed by a, b, and c, then $a : c :: c : b$ (a being the highest) ; and the diameter of shaft b is generally to the diameter of shaft a as height b is to height a, or something less, allowing for the large plinth which diminishes the apparent height of the upper shaft : and when this is their proportion of width, one shaft above is put above one below, with sometimes another upper shaft interposed : but in the extreme arches a single under shaft bears two upper, proportioned as truly as the boughs of a tree ; that is to say, the diameter of each upper $= \frac{2}{3}$ of lower. There being thus the three terms of proportion gained in the lower story, the upper, while it is only divided into two main members, in order that the whole height may not be divided into an even number, has the third term added in its pinnacles. So far of the vertical division. The lateral is still more subtle. There are seven arches in the lower story ; and, calling the central arch a, and counting to the extremity, they diminish in the alternate order a, c, b, d. The upper story has five arches, and two added pinnacles ; and these diminish in *regular* order, the central being the largest, and the outermost the least. Hence, while one proportion ascends, another descends, like parts in music ; and yet the pyramidal form is secured for the whole and, which was another great point of attention, none of the shafts of the upper arches stand over those of the lower.

XVI. It might have been thought that, by this plan, enough variety had been secured, but the builder was not satisfied even thus : for—and this is the point bearing on the present part of our subject—always calling the central arch *a*, and the lateral ones *b* and *c* in succession, the northern *b* and *c* are considerably wider than the southern *b* and *c*, but the southern *d* is as much wider than the northern *d*, and lower beneath its cornice besides ; and, more than this, I hardly believe that one of the effectively symmetrical members of the façade is actually symmetrical with any other. I regret that I cannot state the actual measures. I gave up the taking them upon the spot, owing to their excessive complexity, and the embarrassment caused by the yielding and subsidence of the arches.

Do not let it be supposed that I imagine the Byzantine workmen to have had these various principles in their minds as they built. I believe they built altogether from feeling, and that it was because they did so, that there is this marvellous life, changefulness, and subtlety running through their every arrangement ; and that we reason upon the lovely building as we should upon some fair growth of the trees of the earth, that know not their own beauty.

XVII. Perhaps, however, a stranger instance than any I have yet given, of the daring variation of pretended symmetry, is found in the front of the Cathedral of Bayeux. It consists of five arches with steep pediments, the outermost filled, the three central with doors ; and they appear, at first, to diminish in regular proportion from the principal one in the centre. The two lateral doors are very curiously managed. The tympana of their arches are filled with bas-reliefs, in four tiers ; in the lowest tier there is in each a little temple or gate containing the principal figure (in that on the right, it is the gate of Hades with Lucifer). This little temple is carried, like a capital, by an isolated shaft which divides the whole arch at about ⅔ of its breadth, the larger portion outmost ; and in that larger portion is the inner entrance door. This exact correspondence, in the treatment of both gates, might lead us to expect a corre-

spondence in dimension. Not at all. The small inner northern
entrance measures, in English feet and inches, 4 ft. 7 in. from
jamb to jamb, and the southern five feet exactly. Five inches
in five feet is a considerable variation. The outer northern
porch measures, from face shaft to face shaft, 13 ft. 11 in., and
the southern, 14 ft. 6 in.; giving a difference of 7 in. on 14½ ft
There are also variations in the pediment decorations not less
extraordinary.

XVIII. I imagine I have given instances enough, though I
could multiply them indefinitely, to prove that these variations
are not mere blunders, nor carelessnesses, but the result of a
fixed scorn, if not dislike, of accuracy in measurements; and, in
most cases, I believe, of a determined resolution to work out
an effective symmetry by variations as subtle as those of Nature. To what lengths this principle was sometimes carried,
we shall see by the very singular management of the towers of
Abbeville. I do not say it is right, still less that it is wrong,
but it is a wonderful proof of the fearlessness of a living architecture ; for, say what we will of it, that Flamboyant of France,
however morbid, was as vivid and intense in its animation as
ever any phase of mortal mind ; and it would have lived till
now, if it had not taken to telling lies. I have before noticed
the general difficulty of managing even lateral division, when
it is into two equal parts, unless there be some third reconcil-
ing member. I shall give, hereafter, more examples of the
modes in which this reconciliation is effected in towers with
double lights : the Abbeville architect put his sword to the
knot perhaps rather too sharply. Vexed by the want of unity
between his two windows he literally laid their heads together,
and so distorted their ogee curves, as to leave only one of the
trefoiled panels above, on the inner side, and three on the
outer side of each arch. The arrangement is given in Plate
XII. fig. 3. Associated with the various undulation of flamboyant curves below, it is in the real tower hardly observed,
while it binds it into one mass in general effect. Granting it,
however, to be ugly and wrong, I like sins of the kind, for the
sake of the courage it requires to commit them. In plate II.
(part of a small chapel attached to the West front of the

Cathedral of St. Lo), the reader will see an instance, from the same architecture, of a violation of its own principles, for the sake of a peculiar meaning. If there be any one feature which the flamboyant architect loved to decorate richly, it was the niche—it was what the capital is to the Corinthian order; yet in the case before us there is an ugly beehive put in the place of the principal niche of the arch. I am not sure if I am right in my interpretation of its meaning, but I have little doubt that two figures below, now broken away, once represented an Annunciation; and on another part of the same cathedral, I find the descent of the Spirit, encompassed by rays of light, represented very nearly in the form of the niche in question; which appears, therefore, to be intended for a representation of this effulgence, while at the same time it was made a canopy for the delicate figures below. Whether this was its meaning or not, it is remarkable as a daring departure from the common habits of the time.

XIX. Far more splendid is a license taken with the niche decoration of the portal of St. Maclou at Rouen. The subject of the tympanum bas-relief is the Last Judgment, and the sculpture of the inferno side is carried out with a degree of power whose fearful grotesqueness I can only describe as a mingling of the minds of Orcagna and Hogarth. The demons are perhaps even more awful than Orcagna's; and, in some of the expressions of debased humanity in its utmost despair, the English painter is at least equalled. Not less wild is the imagination which gives fury and fear even to the placing of the figures. An evil angel, poised on the wing, drives the condemned troops from before the Judgment seat; with his left hand he drags behind him a cloud, which is spreading like a winding-sheet over them all; but they are urged by him so furiously, that they are driven not merely to the extreme limit of that scene, which the sculptor confined elsewhere within the tympanum, but out of the tympanum and *into the niches* of the arch; while the flames that follow them, bent by the blast, as it seems, of the angel's wings, rush into the niches also, and burst up *through their tracery,* the three lowermost niches being represented as all on fire, while, instead of their usual vaulted and ribbed ceiling, there is a demon in the roof of each, with his wings folded over it, grinning down out of the black shadow.

XX. I have, however, given enough instances of vitality shown in mere daring, whether wise, as surely in this last instance, or inexpedient; but, as a single example of the Vitality of Assimilation, the faculty which turns to its purposes all material that is submitted to it, I would refer the reader to the extraordinary columns of the arcade on the south side of the Cathedral of Ferrara. A single arch of it is given in Plate XIII. on the right. Four such columns forming a group, there are interposed two pairs of columns, as seen on the left of the same plate; and then come another four arches. It is a long arcade of, I suppose, not less than forty arches, perhaps of many more; and in the grace and simplicity of its stilted Byzantine curves I hardly know its equal. Its like, in fancy of column, I certainly do not know; there being hardly two correspondent, and the architect having been ready, as it seems, to adopt ideas and resemblances from any sources whatsoever. The vegetation growing up the two columns is fine, though bizarre; the distorted pillars beside it suggest images of less agreeable character; the serpentine arrangements founded on the usual Byzantine double knot are generally graceful; but I was puzzled to account for the excessively ugly type of the pillar, fig. 3, one of a group of four. It so happened, fortunately for me, that there had been a fair in Ferrara; and, when I had finished my sketch of the pillar, I had to get out of the way of some merchants of miscellaneous wares, who were removing their stall. It had been shaded by an awning supported by poles, which, in order that the covering might be raised or lowered according to the height of the sun, were composed of two separate pieces, fitted to each other by a *rack*, in which I beheld the prototype of my ugly pillar. It will not be thought, after what I have above said of the inexpedience of imitating anything but natural form, that I advance this architect's practice as altogether exemplary; yet the humility is instructive, which condescended to such sources for motives of thought, the boldness, which could depart so

11

far from all established types of form, and the life and feeling, which out of an assemblage of such quaint and uncouth
materials, could produce an harmonious piece of ecclesiastical
architecture.

XXI. I have dwelt, however, perhaps, too long upon that
form of vitality which is known almost as much by its errors
as by its atonements for them.   We must briefly note the
operation of it, which is always right, and always necessary,
upon those lesser details, where it can neither be superseded
by precedents, nor repressed by proprieties.

I said, early in this essay, that hand-work might always be
known from machine-work ; observing, however, at the same
time, that it was possible for men to turn themselves into machines, and to reduce their labor to the machine level ; but so
long as men work *as* men, putting their heart into what they
do, and doing their best, it matters not how bad workmen they
may be, there will be that in the handling which is above all
price : it will be plainly seen that some places have been delighted in more than others—that there has been a pause, and
a care about them ; and then there will come careless bits, and
fast bits ; and here the chisel will have struck hard, and there
lightly, and anon timidly ; and if the man's mind as well as
his heart went with his work, all this will be in the right
places, and each part will set off the other ; and the effect of
the whole, as compared with the same design cut by a machine
or a lifeless hand, will be like that of poetry well read and
deeply felt to that of the same verses jangled by rote.   There
are many to whom the difference is imperceptible ; but to
those who love poetry it is everything—they had rather not
hear it at all, than hear it ill read ; and to those who love Architecture, the life and accent of the hand are everything.
They had rather not have ornament at all, than see it ill cut—
deadly cut, that is.   I cannot too often repeat, it is not coarse
cutting, it is not blunt cutting, that is necessarily bad ; but it
is cold cutting—the look of equal trouble everywhere—the
smooth, diffused tranquillity of heartless pains—the regularity
of a plough in a level field.   The chill is more likely, indeed,
to show itself in finished work than in any other—men cool

and tire as they complete : and if completeness is thought to
be vested in polish, and to be attainable by help of sand paper,
we may as well give the work to the engine-lathe at once.   But
right finish is simply the full rendering of the intended impression ; and *high* finish is the rendering of a well intended
and vivid impression ; and it is oftener got by rough than fine
handling.   I am not sure whether it is frequently enough observed that sculpture is not the mere cutting of the *form* of
anything in stone ; it is the cutting of the *effect* of it.   Very
often the true form, in the marble, would not be in the least
like itself.   The sculptor must paint with his chisel : half his
touches are not to realize, but to put power into the form : they
are touches of light and shadow ; and raise a ridge, or sink a
hollow, not to represent an actual ridge or hollow, but to get a
line of light, or a spot of darkness.   In a coarse way, this kind
of execution is very marked in old French woodwork ; the
irises of the eyes of its chimeric monsters being cut boldly
into holes, which, variously placed, and always dark, give all
kinds of strange and startling expressions, averted and askance,
to the fantastic countenances.   Perhaps the highest examples
of this kind of sculpture-painting are the works of Mino da
Fiesole ; their best effects being reached by strange angular,
and seemingly rude, touches of the chisel.   The lips of one of
the children on the tombs in the church of the Badia, appear
only half finished when they are seen close ; yet the expression
is farther carried and more ineffable, than in any piece of marble I have ever seen, especially considering its delicacy, and the
softness of the child-features.   In a sterner kind, that of the
statues in the sacristy of St. Lorenzo equals it, and there again
by incompletion.   I know no example of work in which the
forms are absolutely true and complete where such a result is
attained ; in Greek sculptures is not even attempted.

XXII. It is evident that, for architectural appliances, such
masculine handling, likely as it must be to retain its effective-
ness when higher finish would be injured by time, must always be the most expedient ; and as it is impossible, even
were it desirable that the highest finish should be given to
the quantity of work which covers a large building, it will be

understood how precious the intelligence must become, which renders incompletion itself a means of additional expression; and how great must be the difference, when the touches are rude and few, between those of a careless and those of a regardful mind. It is not easy to retain anything of their character in a copy; yet the reader will find one or two illustrative points in the examples, given in Plate XIV., from the bas-reliefs of the north of Rouen Cathedral. There are three square pedestals under the three main niches on each side of it, and one in the centre; each of these being on two sides decorated with five quatrefoiled panels. There are thus seventy quatrefoils in the lower ornament of the gate alone, without counting those of the outer course round it, and of the pedestals outside: each quatrefoil is filled with a bas-relief, the whole reaching to something above a man's height. A modern architect would, of course, have made all the five quatrefoils of each pedestal-side equal: not so the Mediæval. The general form being apparently a quatrefoil composed of semicircles on the sides of a square, it will be found on examination that none of the arcs are semicircles, and none of the basic figures squares. The latter are rhomboids, having their acute or obtuse angles uppermost according to their larger or smaller size; and the arcs upon their sides slide into such places as they can get in the angles of the enclosing parallelogram, leaving intervals, at each of the four angles, of various shapes, which are filled each by an animal. The size of the whole panel being thus varied, the two lowest of the five are tall, the next two short, and the uppermost a little higher than the lowest; while in the course of bas-reliefs which surrounds the gate, calling either of the two lowest (which are equal), a, and either of the next two b, and the fifth and sixth c and d, then d (the largest): $c :: c : a :: a : b$. It is wonderful how much of the grace of the whole depends on these variations.

XXIII. Each of the angles, it was said, is filled by an animal. There are thus $70 \times 4 = 280$ animals, all different, in the mere fillings of the intervals of the bas-reliefs. Three of these intervals, with their beasts, actual size, the curves being traced upon the stone, I have given in Plate XIV.

I say nothing of their general design, or of the lines of the wings and scales, which are perhaps, unless in those of the central dragon, not much above the usual commonplaces of good ornamental work ; but there is an evidence in the features of thoughtfulness and fancy which is not common, at least now-a-days. The upper creature on the left is biting something, the form of which is hardly traceable in the defaced stone—but biting he is ; and the reader cannot but recognise in the peculiarly reverted eye the expression which is never seen, as I think, but in the eye of a dog gnawing something in jest, and preparing to start away with it : the meaning of the glance, so far as it can be marked by the mere incision of the chisel, will be felt by comparing it with the eye of the couchant figure on the right, in its gloomy and angry brooding. The plan of this head, and the nod of the cap over its brow, are fine ; but there is a little touch above the hand especially well meant : the fellow is vexed and puzzled in his malice ; and his hand is pressed hard on his cheek bone, and the flesh of the cheek is *wrinkled* under the eye by the pressure. The whole, indeed, looks wretchedly coarse, when it is seen on a scale in which it is naturally compared with delicate figure etchings ; but considering it as a mere filling of an interstice on the outside of a cathedral gate, and as one of more than three hundred (for in my estimate I did not include the outer pedestals), it proves very noble vitality in the art of the time.

XXIV. I believe the right question to ask, respecting all ornament, is simply this : Was it done with enjoyment—was the carver happy while he was about it ? It may be the hardest work possible, and the harder because so much pleasure was taken in it ; but it must have been happy too, or it will not be living. How much of the stone mason's toil this condition would exclude I hardly venture to consider, but the condition is absolute. There is a Gothic church lately built near Rouen, vile enough, indeed, in its general composition, but excessively rich in detail ; many of the details are designed with taste, and all evidently by a man who has studied old work closely. But it is all as dead as leaves in December :

there is not one tender touch, not one warm stroke, on the whole façade. The men who did it hated it, and were thankful when it was done. And so long as they do so they are merely loading your walls with shapes of clay: the garlands of everlastings in Père la Chaise are more cheerful ornaments. You cannot get the feeling by paying for it—money will not buy life. I am not sure even that you can get it by watching or waiting for it. It is true that here and there a workman may be found who has it in him, but he does not rest contented in the inferior work—he struggles forward into an Academician ; and from the mass of available handicraftsmen the power is gone—how recoverable I know not : this only I know, that all expense devoted to sculptural ornament, in the present condition of that power, comes literally under the head of Sacrifice for the sacrifice's sake, or worse. I believe the only manner of rich ornament that is open to us is the geometrical color-mosaic, and that much might result from our strenuously taking up this mode of design. But, at all events, one thing we have in our power—the doing without machine ornament and cast-iron work. All the stamped metals, and artificial stones, and imitation woods and bronzes, over the invention of which we hear daily exultation—all the short, and cheap, and easy ways of doing that whose difficulty is its honor —are just so many new obstacles in our already encumbered road. They will not make one of us happier or wiser—they will extend neither the pride of judgment nor the privilege of enjoyment. They will only make us shallower in our understandings, colder in our hearts, and feebler in our wits. And most justly. For we are not sent into this world to do any thing into which we cannot put our hearts. We have certain work to do for our bread, and that is to be done strenuously ; other work to do for our delight, and that is to be done heartily : neither is to be done by halves or shifts, but with a will ; and what is not worth this effort is not to be done at all. Perhaps all that we have to do is meant for nothing more than an exercise of the heart and of the will, and is useless in itself ; but, at all events, the little use it has may well be spared if it is not worth putting our hands and our strength to. It does

not become our immortality to take an ease inconsistent with
its authority, nor to suffer any instruments with which it can
dispense, to come between it and the things it rules : and he
who would form the creations of his own mind by any other
instrument than his own hand, would, also, if he might, give
grinding organs to Heaven's angels, to make their music easier.
There is dreaming enough, and earthiness enough, and sensuality enough in human existence without our turning the few
glowing moments of it into mechanism ; and since our life
must at the best be but a vapor that appears for a little time
and then vanishes away, let it at least appear as a cloud in the
height of Heaven, not as the thick darkness that broods over
the blast of the Furnace, and rolling of the Wheel.

CHAPTER VI.

THE LAMP OF MEMORY.

I. Among the hours of his life to which the writer looks
back with peculiar gratitude, as having been marked by more
than ordinary fulness of joy or clearness of teaching, is one
passed, now some years ago, near time of sunset, among the
broken masses of pine forest which skirt the course of the
Ain, above the village of Champagnole, in the Jura. It is a
spot which has all the solemnity, with none of the savageness,
of the Alps ; where there is a sense of a great power beginning to be manifested in the earth, and of a deep and majestic
concord in the rise of the long low lines of piny hills ; the
first utterance of those mighty mountain symphonies, soon to
be more loudly lifted and wildly broken along the battlements
of the Alps. But their strength is as yet restrained ; and the
far-reaching ridges of pastoral mountain succeed each other,
like the long and sighing swell which moves over quiet waters
from some far-off stormy sea. And there is a deep tenderness
pervading that vast monotony. The destructive forces and
the stern expression of the central ranges are alike withdrawn.
No frost-ploughed, dust-encumbered paths of ancient glacier

fret the soft Jura pastures ; no splintered heaps of ruin break
the fair ranks of her forests ; no pale, defiled, or furious rivers
rend their rude and changeful ways among her rocks. Pa-
tiently, eddy by eddy, the clear green streams wind along their
well-known beds ; and under the dark quietness of the undis-
turbed pines, there spring up, year by year, such company of
joyful flowers as I know not the like of among all the blessings of the earth. It was Spring time, too ; and all were coming forth in clusters crowded for very love ; there was room
enough for all, but they crushed their leaves into all manner
of strange shapes only to be nearer each other. There was
the wood anemone, star after star, closing every now and then
into nebulæ : and there was the oxalis, troop by troop like
virginal processions of the Mois de Marie, the dark vertical
clefts in the limestone choked up with them as with heavy
snow, and touched with ivy on the edges—ivy as light and
lovely as the vine ; and ever and anon, a blue gush of violets,
and cowslip bells in sunny places ; and in the more open
ground, the vetch, and comfrey, and mezereon, and the small
sapphire buds of the Polygala Alpina, and the wild strawberry,
just a blossom or two, all showered amidst the golden softness
of deep, warm, amber-colored moss. I came out presently on
the edge of the ravine ; the solemn murmur of its waters rose
suddenly from beneath, mixed with the singing of the thrushes
among the pine boughs ; and, on the opposite side of the
valley, walled all along as it was by grey cliffs of limestone,
there was a hawk sailing slowly off their brow, touching them
nearly with his wings, and with the shadows of the pines
flickering upon his plumage from above ; but with a fall of a
hundred fathoms under his breast, and the curling pools of the
green river gliding and glittering dizzily beneath him, their
foam globes moving with him as he flew. It would be difficult to conceive a scene less dependent upon any other interest
than that of its own secluded and serious beauty ; but the
writer well remembers the sudden blankness and chill which
were cast upon it when he endeavored, in order more strictly
to arrive at the sources of its impressiveness, to imagine it, for
a moment, a scene in some aboriginal forest of the New Con-

tinent. The flowers in an instant lost their light, the river its
music [15] ; the hills became oppressively desolate ; a heaviness
in the boughs of the darkened forest showed how much of
their former power had been dependent upon a life which was
not theirs, how much of the glory of the imperishable, or continually renewed, creation is reflected from things more precious in their memories than it, in its renewing.   Those ever
springing flowers and ever flowing streams had been dyed by
the deep colors of human endurance, valor, and virtue ; and
the crests of the sable hills that rose against the evening sky
received a deeper worship, because their far shadows fell east-
ward over the iron wall of Joux and the four-square keep of
Granson.

II. It is as the centralisation and protectress of this sacred
influence, that Architecture is to be regarded by us with the
most serious thought. We may live without her, and worship
without her, but we cannot remember without her.   How cold
is all history how lifeless all imagery, compared to that which
the living nation writes, and the uncorrupted marble bears !
how many pages of doubtful record might we not often spare,
for a few stones left one upon another !   The ambition of the
old Babel builders was well directed for this world : there are
but two strong conquerors of the forgetfulness of men, Poetry
and Architecture ; and the latter in some sort includes the
former, and is mightier in its reality ; it is well to have, not
only what men have thought and felt, but what their hands
have handled, and their strength wrought, and their eyes
beheld, all the days of their life.   The age of Homer is surrounded with darkness, his very personality with doubt.   Not
so that of Pericles : and the day is coming when we shall confess, that we have learned more of Greece out of the crumbled
fragments of her sculpture than even from her sweet singers
or soldier historians.   And if indeed there be any profit in our
knowledge of the past, or any joy in the thought of being remembered hereafter, which can give strength to present exertion, or patience to present endurance, there are two duties
respecting national architecture whose importance it is impossible to overrate ; the first, to render the architecture of the

day historical ; and, the second, to preserve, as the most pre-cious of inheritances, that of past ages.

III. It is in the first of these two directions that Memory may truly be said to be the Sixth Lamp of Architecture ; for it is in becoming memorial or monumental that a true perfec-tion is attained by civil and domestic buildings ; and this partly as they are, with such a view, built in a more stable manner, and partly as their decorations are consequently animated by a metaphorical or historical meaning.

As regards domestic buildings, there must always be a cer-tain limitation to views of this kind in the power, as well as in the hearts, of men ; still I cannot but think it an evil sign of a people when their houses are built to last for one generation only.   There is a sanctity in a good man's house which cannot be renewed in every tenement that rises on its ruins : and I believe that good men would generally feel this ; and that having spent their lives happily and honorably, they would be grieved at the close of them to think that the place of their earthly abode, which had seen, and seemed almost to sympa-thise in all their honor, their gladness, or their suffering,—that this, with all the record it bare of them, and all of material things that they had loved and ruled over, and set the stamp of themselves upon—was to be swept away, as soon as there was room made for them in the grave ; that no respect was to be shown to it, no affection felt for it, no good to be drawn from it by their children ; that though there was a monument in the church, there was no warm monument in the heart and house to them ; that all that they ever treasured was despised, and the places that had sheltered and comforted them were dragged down to the dust.   I say that a good man would fear this ; and that, far more, a good son, a noble descendant, would fear doing it to his father's house.   I say that if men lived like men indeed, their houses would be temples—temples which we should hardly dare to injure, and in which it would make us holy to be permitted to live ; and there must be a strange dis-solution of natural affection, a strange unthankfulness for all that homes have given and parents taught, a strange conscious-ness that we have been unfaithful to our fathers' honor, or that

our own lives are not such as would make our dwellings sacred
to our children, when each man would fain build to himself,
and build for the little revolution of his own life only. And I
look upon those pitiful concretions of lime and clay which
spring up in mildewed forwardness out of the kneaded fields
about our capital—upon those thin, tottering, foundationless
shells of splintered wood and imitated stone—upon those
gloomy rows of formalised minuteness, alike without difference
and without fellowship, as solitary as similar—not merely with
the careless disgust of an offended eye, not merely with sorrow for a desecrated landscape, but with a painful foreboding
that the roots of our national greatness must be deeply can-
kered when they are thus loosely struck in their native ground ;
that those comfortless and unhonored dwellings are the signs
of a great and spreading spirit of popular discontent; that
they mark the time when every man's aim is to be in some
more elevated sphere than his natural one, and every man's
past life is his habitual scorn ; when men build in the hope of
leaving the places they have built, and live in the hope of forgetting the years that they have lived ; when the comfort, the
peace, the religion of home have ceased to be felt; and the
crowded tenements of a struggling and restless population dif-
fer only from the tents of the Arab or the Gipsy by their less
healthy openness to the air of heaven, and less happy choice of
their spot of earth ; by their sacrifice of liberty without the
gain of rest, and of stability without the luxury of change.

IV. This is no slight, no consequenceless evil : it is ominous, infectious, and fecund of other fault and misfortune.
When men do not love their hearths, nor reverence their
thresholds, it is a sign that they have dishonored both, and that
they have never acknowledged the true universality of that
Christian worship which was indeed to supersede the idolatry,
but not the piety, of the pagan. Our God is a household
God, as well as a heavenly one ; He has an altar in every
man's dwelling ; let men look to it when they rend it lightly
and pour out its ashes. It is not a question of mere ocular
delight, it is no question of intellectual pride, or of cultivated
and critical fancy, how, and with what aspect of durability

and of completeness, the domestic buildings of a nation shall be raised. It is one of those moral duties, not with more impunity to be neglected because the perception of them depends on a finely toned and balanced conscientiousness, to build our dwellings with care, and patience, and fondness, and diligent completion, and with a view to their duration at least for such a period as, in the ordinary course of national revolutions, might be supposed likely to extend to the entire alteration of the direction of local interests. This at the least; but it would be better if, in every possible instance, men built their own houses on a scale commensurate rather with their condition at the commencement, than their attainments at the termination, of their worldly career; and built them to stand as long as human work at its strongest can be hoped to stand; recording to their children what they have been, and from what, if so it had been permitted them, they had risen. And when houses are thus built, we may have that true domestic architecture, the beginning of all other, which does not disdain to treat with respect and thoughtfulness the small habitation as well as the large, and which invests with the dignity of contented manhood the narrowness of worldly circumstance.

V. I look to this spirit of honorable, proud, peaceful self-possession, this abiding wisdom of contented life, as probably one of the chief sources of great intellectual power in all ages, and beyond dispute as the very primal source of the great architecture of old Italy and France. To this day, the interest of their fairest cities depends, not on the isolated richness of palaces, but on the cherished and exquisite decoration of even the smallest tenements of their proud periods. The most elaborate piece of architecture in Venice is a small house at the head of the Grand Canal, consisting of a ground floor with two stories above, three windows in the first, and two in the second. Many of the most exquisite buildings are on the narrower canals, and of no larger dimensions. One of the most interesting pieces of fifteenth century architecture in North Italy, is a small house in a back street, behind the market-place of Vicenza; it bears date 1481, and the motto,

Il. n'est. rose. sans. épine ; it has also only a ground floor and two stories, with three windows in each, separated by rich flower-work, and with balconies, supported, the central one by an eagle with open wings, the lateral ones by winged griffins standing on cornucopiæ. The idea that a house must be large in order to be well built, is altogether of modern growth, and is parallel with the idea, that no picture can be historical, except of a size admitting figures larger than life.

VI. I would have, then, our ordinary dwelling-houses built to last, and built to be lovely ; as rich and full of pleasantness as may be, within and without; with what degree of likeness to each other in style and manner, I will say presently, under another head ; but, at all events, with such differences as might suit and express each man's character and occupation, and partly his history. This right over the house, I conceive, belongs to its first builder, and is to be respected by his children ; and it would be well that blank stones should be left in places, to be inscribed with a summary of his life and of its experience, raising thus the habitation into a kind of monument, and developing, into more systematic instructiveness, that good custom which was of old universal, and which still remains among some of the Swiss and Germans, of acknowledging the grace of God's permission to build and possess a quiet resting-place, in such sweet words as may well close our speaking of these things. I have taken them from the front of a cottage lately built among the green pastures which descend from the village of Grindelwald to the lower glacier :—

> " Mit herzlichem Vertrauen
> Hat Johannes Mooter und Maria Rubi
> Dieses Haus bauen lassen.
> Der liebe Gott woll uns bewahren
> Vor allem Unglück und Gefahren,
> Und es in Segen lassen stehn
> Auf der Reise durch diese Jammerzeit
> Nach dem himmlischen Paradiese,
> Wo alle Frommen wohnen,
> Da wird Gott sie belohnen
> Mit der Friedenskrone
> Zu alle Ewigkeit."

VII. In public buildings the historical purpose should be still more definite. It is one of the advantages of Gothic architecture,—I use the word Gothic in the most extended sense as broadly opposed to classical,—that it admits of a richness of record altogether unlimited. Its minute and multitudinous sculptural decorations afford means of expressing, either symbolically or literally, all that need be known of national feeling or achievement. More decoration will, indeed, be usually required than can take so elevated a character ; and much, even in the most thoughtful periods, has been left to the freedom of fancy, or suffered to consist of mere repetitions of some national bearing or symbol. It is, however, generally unwise, even in mere surface ornament, to surrender the power and privilege of variety which the spirit of Gothic architecture admits ; much more in important features—capitals of columns or bosses, and string-courses, as of course in all confessed bas-reliefs. Better the rudest work that tells a story or records a fact, than the richest without meaning. There should not be a single ornament put upon great civic buildings, without some intellectual intention. Actual representation of history has in modern times been checked by a difficulty, mean indeed, but steadfast : that of unmanageable costume ; nevertheless, by a sufficiently bold imaginative treatment, and frank use of symbols, all such obstacles may be vanquished ; not perhaps in the degree necessary to produce sculpture in itself satisfactory, but at all events so as to enable it to become a grand and expressive element of architectural composition. Take, for example, the management of the capitals of the ducal palace at Venice. History, as such, was indeed entrusted to the painters of its interior, but every capital of its arcades was filled with meaning. The large one, the corner stone of the whole, next the entrance, was devoted to the symbolisation of Abstract Justice ; above it is a sculpture of the Judgment of Solomon, remarkable for a beautiful subjection in its treatment to its decorative purpose. The figures, if the subject had been entirely composed of them, would have awkwardly interrupted the line of the angle, and diminished its apparent strength ; and therefore in the midst of them, entirely without

relation to them, and indeed actually between the executioner
and interceding mother, there rises the ribbed trunk of a massy
tree, which supports and continues the shaft of the angle, and
whose leaves above overshadow and enrich the whole. The
capital below bears among its leafage a throned figure of Justice, Trajan doing justice to the widow, Aristotle " che die
legge," and one or two other subjects now unintelligible from
decay. The capitals next in order represent the virtues and
vices in succession, as preservative or destructive of national
peace and power, concluding with Faith, with the inscription
"Fides optima in Deo est." A figure is seen on the opposite
side of the capital, worshipping the sun. After these, one or
two capitals are fancifully decorated with birds (Plate V.), and
then come a series representing, first the various fruits, then
the national costumes, and then the animals of the various
countries subject to Venetian rule.

VIII. Now, not to speak of any more important public
building, let us imagine our own India House adorned in this
way, by historical or symbolical sculpture : massively built in
the first place ; then chased with bas-reliefs of our Indian bat-
tles, and fretted with carvings of Oriental foliage, or inlaid with
Oriental stones ; and the more important members of its decoration composed of groups of Indian life and landscape, and
prominently expressing the phantasms of Hindoo worship in
their subjection to the Cross. Would not one such work be
better than a thousand histories ? If, however, we have not
the invention necessary for such efforts, or if, which is probably one of the most noble excuses we can offer for our deficiency in such matters, we have less pleasure in talking about
ourselves, even in marble, than the Continental nations, at least
we have no excuse for any want of care in the points which in-
sure the building's endurance. And as this question is one of
great interest in its relations to the choice of various modes of
decoration, it will be necessary to enter into it at some length.

IX. The benevolent regards and purposes of men in masses
seldom can be supposed to extend beyond their own generation. They may look to posterity as an audience, may hope
for its attention, and labor for its praise : they may trust to

its recognition of unacknowledged merit, and demand its jus tice for contemporary wrong. But all this is mere selfishness, and does not involve the slightest regard to, or consideration of, the interest of those by whose numbers we would fain swell the circle of our flatterers, and by whose authority we would gladly support our presently disputed claims. The idea of self-denial for the sake of posterity, of practising present economy for the sake of debtors yet unborn, of planting forests that our descendants may live under their shade, or of raising cities for future nations to inhabit, never, I suppose, efficiently takes place among publicly recognised motives of exertion. Yet these are not the less our duties; nor is our part fitly sustained upon the earth, unless the range of our intended and deliberate usefulness include not only the companions, but the successors, of our pilgrimage. God has lent us the earth for our life; it is a great entail. It belongs as much to those who are to come after us, and whose names are already written in the book of creation, as to us; and we have no right, by anything that we do or neglect, to involve them in unnecessary penalties, or deprive them of benefits which it was in our power to bequeath. And this the more, because it is one of the appointed conditions of the labor of men that, in proportion to the time between the seed-sowing and the harvest, is the fulness of the fruit; and that generally, therefore, the farther off we place our aim, and the less we desire to be ourselves the witnesses of what we have labored for, the more wide and rich will be the measure of our success. Men cannot benefit those that are with them as they can benefit those who come after them; and of all the pulpits from which human voice is ever sent forth, there is none from which it reaches so far as from the grave.

X. Nor is there, indeed, any present loss, in such respect, for futurity. Every human action gains in honor, in grace, in all true magnificence, by its regard to things that are to come. It is the far sight, the quiet and confident patience, that, above all other attributes, separate man from man, and near him to his Maker; and there is no action nor art, whose majesty we may not measure by this test. Therefore, when we build, let us think that we build for ever. Let it not be for present delight, nor for present use alone ; let it be such work as our descendants will thank us for, and let us think, as we lay stone on stone, that a time is to come when those stones will be held sacred because our hands have touched them, and that men will say as they look upon the labor and wrought substance of them, "See! this our fathers did for us." For, indeed, the greatest glory of a building is not in its stones, or in its gold. Its glory is in its Age, and in that deep sense of voicefulness, of stern watching, of mysterious sympathy, nay, even of approval or condemnation, which we feel in walls that have long been washed by the passing waves of humanity. It is in their lasting witness against men, in their quiet contrast with the transitional character of all things, in the strength which, through the lapse of seasons and times, and the decline and birth of dynasties, and the changing of the face of the earth, and of the limits of the sea, maintains its sculptured shapeliness for a time insuperable, connects forgotten and following ages with each other, and half constitutes the identity, as it concentrates the sympathy, of nations ; it is in that golden stain of time, that we are to look for the real light, and color, and preciousness of architecture ; and it is not until a building has assumed this character, till it has been entrusted with the fame, and hallowed by the deeds of men, till its walls have been witnesses of suffering, and its pillars rise out of the shadows of death, that its existence, more lasting as it is than that of the natural objects of the world around it, can be gifted with even so much as these possess of language and of life.

XI. For that period, then, we must build ; not, indeed, refusing to ourselves the delight of present completion, nor hesitating to follow such portions of character as may depend upon delicacy of execution to the highest perfection of which they are capable, even although we may know that in the course of years such details must perish ; but taking care that for work of this kind we sacrifice no enduring quality, and that the building shall not depend for its impressiveness upon anything that is perishable. This would, indeed, be the law of good composition under any circumstances, the arrangement of the larger masses being always a matter of greater importance than the treatment of the smaller ; but in architecture there is much in that very treatment which is skilful or otherwise in proportion to its just regard to the probable effects of time : and (which is still more to be considered) there is a beauty in those effects themselves, which nothing else can replace, and which it is our wisdom to consult and to desire. For though, hitherto, we have been speaking of the sentiment of age only, there is an actual beauty in the marks of it, such and so great as to have become not unfrequently the subject of especial choice among certain schools of art, and to have impressed upon those schools the character usually and loosely expressed by the term " picturesque." It is of some importance to our present purpose to determine the true meaning of this expression, as it is now generally used ; for there is a principle to be developed from that use which, while it has occultly been the ground of much that is true and just in our judgment of art, has never been so far understood as to become definitely serviceable. Probably no word in the language (exclusive of theological expressions), has been the subject of so frequent or so prolonged dispute ; yet none remained more vague in their acceptance, and it seems to me to be a matter of no small interest to investigate the essence of that idea which all feel, and (to appearance) with respect to similar things, and yet which every attempt to define has, as I believe, ended either in mere enumeration of the effects and objects to which the term has been attached, or else in attempts at abstraction more palpably nugatory than any which have disgraced metaphysical investigation on other subjects. A recent critic on Art, for instance, has gravely advanced the theory that the essence of the picturesque consists in the expression of "universal decay." It would be curious to see the result of an attempt to illustrate this idea of the picturesque, in a painting of dead flowers and decayed fruit, and equally curious to trace the steps of any reasoning which, on such a theory, should account for the picturesqueness of an ass colt as opposed to a horse foal. But there is much excuse for even the most utter failure in reasonings of this kind, since the subject is, indeed, one of the most obscure of all that may legitimately be submitted to human reason ; and the idea is itself so varied in the minds of different men, according to their subjects of study, that no definition can be expected to embrace more than a certain number of its infinitely multiplied forms.

XII. That peculiar character, however, which separates the picturesque from the characters of subject belonging to the higher walks of art (and this is all that is necessary for our present purpose to define), may be shortly and ·decisively expressed. Picturesqueness, in this sense, is *Parasitical Sublimity*. Of course all sublimity, as well as all beauty, is, in the simple etymological sense, picturesque, that is to say, fit to become the subject of a picture ; and all sublimity is, even in the peculiar sense which I am endeavoring to develope, picturesque, as opposed to beauty ; that is to say, there is more picturesqueness in the subject of Michael Angelo than of Perugino, in proportion to the prevalence of the sublime element over the beautiful. But that character, of which the extreme pursuit is generally admitted to be degrading to art, is *parasitical* sublimity ; *i.e.*, a sublimity dependent on the accidents, or on the least essential characters, of the objects to which it belongs ; and the picturesque is *developed distinctively exactly in proportion to the distance from the centre of thought of those points of character in which the sublimity is found.* Two ideas, therefore, are essential to picturesqueness,—the first, that of sublimity (for pure beauty is not picturesque at all, and becomes so only as the sublime element mixes with it), and the second, the subordinate or parasitical position of that sublimity. Of course, therefore, whatever characters of line or shade or expression are productive of sublimity, will become productive of picturesqueness ; what these characters are I shall endeavor hereafter to show at length ; but, among those which are generally acknowledged, I may name angular and broken lines, vigorous oppositions of light and shadow, and grave, deep, or boldly contrasted color ; and all these are in a still higher degree effective, when, by resemblance or association, they remind us of objects on which a true and essential sublimity exists, as of rocks or mountains, or stormy clouds or waves. Now if these characters, or any others of a higher and more abstract sublimity, be found in the very heart and substance of what we contemplate, as the sublimity of Michael Angelo depends on the expression of mental character in his figures far more than even on the noble lines of their arrangement, the art which represents such characters cannot be properly called picturesque : but, if they be found in the accidental or external qualities, the distinctive picturesque will be the result.

XIII. Thus, in the treatment of the features of the human face by Francia or Angelico, the shadows are employed only to make the contours of the features thoroughly felt ; and to those features themselves the mind of the observer is exclusively directed (that is to say, to the essential characters of the thing represented). All power and all sublimity rest on these ; the shadows are used only for the sake of the features. On the contrary, by Rembrandt, Salvator, or Caravaggio, the features are used *for the sake of the shadows ;* and the attention is directed, and the power of the painter addressed to characters of accidental light and shade cast across or around those features. In the case of Rembrandt there is often an essential sublimity in invention and expression besides, and always a high degree of it in the light and shade itself ; but it is for the most part parasitical or engrafted sublimity as regards the subject of the painting, and, just so far, picturesque.

XIV. Again, in the management of the sculptures of the Parthenon, shadow is frequently employed as a dark field on which the forms are drawn. This is visibly the case in the metopes, and must have been nearly as much so in the pediment. But the use of that shadow is entirely to show the confines of the figures ; and it is to *their lines,* and not to the shapes of the shadows behind them, that the art and the eye are addressed. The figures themselves are conceived as much as possible in full light, aided by bright reflections ; they are drawn exactly as, on vases, white figures on a dark ground : and the sculptors have dispensed with, or even struggled to avoid, all shadows which were not absolutely necessary to the explaining of the form. On the contrary, in Gothic sculpture, the shadow becomes itself a subject of thought. It is considered as a dark color, to be arranged in certain agreeable masses ; the figures are very frequently made even subordinate to the placing of its divisions : and their costume is enriched at the expense of the forms underneath, in order to increase the complexity and variety of the points of shade. There are thus, both in sculpture and painting, two, in some sort, opposite schools, of which the one follows for its subject the essential forms of things, and the other the accidental lights and shades upon them. There are various degrees of their contrariety : middle steps, as in the works of Correggio, and all degrees of nobility and of degradation in the several manners : but the one is always recognised as the pure, and the other as the picturesque school. Portions of picturesque treatment will be found in Greek work, and of pure and unpicturesque in Gothic ; and in both there are countless instances, as preeminently in the works of Michael Angelo, in which shadows become valuable as media of expression, and therefore take rank among essential characteristics. Into these multitudinous distinctions and exceptions I cannot now enter, desiring only to prove the broad applicability of the general definition.

XV. Again, the distinction will be found to exist, not only between forms and shades as subjects of choice, but between essential and inessential forms. One of the chief distinctions between the dramatic and picturesque schools of sculpture is found in the treatment of the hair. By the artists of the time of Pericles it was considered as an excrescence,[16] indicated by few and rude lines, and subordinated in every particular to the principality of the features and person. How completely this was an artistical, not a national idea, it is unnecessary to prove. We need but remember the employment of the Lacedæmonians, reported by the Persian spy on the evening before the battle of Thermopylæ, or glance at any Homeric description of ideal form, to see how purely *sculpturesque* was the law which reduced the markings of the hair, lest, under the necessary disadvantages of material, they should interfere with the distinctness of the personal forms. On the contrary, in later sculpture, the hair receives almost the principal care of the workman ; and while the features and limbs are clumsily and bluntly executed, the hair is curled and twisted, cut into bold and shadowy projections, and arranged in masses elaborately ornamental : there is true sublimity in the lines and the chiaroscuro of these masses, but it is, as regards the creature represented, parasitical, and therefore picturesque. In the same sense we may understand the application of the term to modern animal painting, distinguished as it has been by peculiar attention to the colors, lustre, and texture of skin ; nor is it in art alone that the definition will hold. In animals themselves, when their sublimity depends upon their muscular forms or motions, or necessary and principal attributes, as perhaps more than all others in the horse, we do not call them picturesque, but consider them as peculiarly fit to be associated with pure historical subject. Exactly in proportion as their character of sublimity passes into excrescences ;—into mane and beard as in the lion, into horns as in the stag, into shaggy hide as in the instance above given of the ass colt, into variegation as in the zebra, or into plumage, —they become picturesque, and are so in art exactly in proportion to the prominence of these excrescential characters. It may often be most expedient that they should be prominent ; often there is in them the highest degree of majesty, as in those of the leopard and boar ; and in the hands of men like Tintoret and Rubens, such attributes become means of deepening the very highest and most ideal impressions. But the picturesque direction of their thoughts is always distinctly recognizable, as clinging to the surface, to the less essential character, and as developing out of this a sublimity different from that of the creature itself ; a sublimity which is, in a sort, common to all the objects of creation, and the same in its constituent elements, whether it be sought in the clefts and folds of shaggy hair, or in the chasms and rents of rocks, or in the hanging of thickets or hill sides, or in the alternations of gaiety and gloom in the variegation of the shell, the plume, or the cloud.

XVI. Now, to return to our immediate subject, it so happens that, in architecture, the superinduced and accidental beauty is most commonly inconsistent with the preservation of original character, and the picturesque is therefore sought in ruin, and supposed to consist in decay. Whereas, even when so sought, it consists in the mere sublimity of the rents, or fractures, or stains, or vegetation, which assimilate the architecture with the work of Nature, and bestow upon it those circumstances of color and form which are universally beloved by the eye of man. So far as this is done, to the extinction of the true characters of the architecture, it is picturesque, and the artist who looks to the stem of the ivy instead of the shaft of the pillar, is carrying out in more daring freedom the debased sculptor's choice of the hair instead of the countenance. But so far as it can be rendered consistent with the inherent character, the picturesque or extraneous sublimity of architecture has just this of nobler function in it than that of any other object whatsoever, that it is an exponent of age, of that in which, as has been said, the greatest glory of a building consists ; and, therefore, the external signs of this glory, having power and purpose greater than any belonging to their mere sensible beauty, may be considered as taking rank among pure and essential characters ; so essential to my mind, that I think a building cannot be considered as in its prime until four or five centuries have passed over it ; and that the entire choice and arrangement of its details should have reference to their appearance after that period, so that none should be admitted which would suffer material injury either by the weather-staining, or the mechanical degradation which the lapse of such a period would necessitate.

XVII. It is not my purpose to enter into any of the questions which the application of this principle involves. They are of too great interest and complexity to be even touched upon within my present limits, but this is broadly to be noticed, that those styles of architecture which are picturesque in the sense above explained with respect to sculpture, that is to say, whose decoration depends on the arrangement of points of shade rather than on purity of outline, do not suffer, but commonly gain in richness of effect when their details are partly worn away ; hence such styles, pre-eminently that of French Gothic, should always be adopted when the materials to be employed are liable to degradation, as brick, sandstone, or soft limestone ; and styles in any degree dependent on purity of line, as the Italian Gothic, must be practised altogether in hard and undecomposing materials, granite serpentine, or crystalline marbles. There can be no doubt that the nature of the accessible materials influenced the formation of both styles ; and it should still more authoritatively determine our choice of either.

XVIII. It does not belong to my present plan to consider at length the second head of duty of which I have above spoken ; the preservation of the architecture we possess : but a few words may be forgiven, as especially necessary in modern times. Neither by the public, nor by those who have the care of public monuments, is the true meaning of the word *restoration* understood. It means the most total destruction which a building can suffer : a destruction out of which no remnants can be gathered ; a destruction accompanied with false description of the thing destroyed. Do not let us deceive ourselves in this important matter ; it is *impossible*, as impossible as to raise the dead, to restore anything that has ever been great or beautiful in architecture. That which I have above insisted upon as the life of the whole, that spirit which is given only by the hand and eye of the workman, never can be recalled. Another spirit may be given by another time, and it is then a new building ; but the spirit of the dead workman cannot be summoned up, and commanded to direct other hands, and other thoughts. And as for direct and simple copying, it is palpably impossible. What copying can there be of surfaces that have been worn half an inch down ? The whole finish of the work was in the half inch that is gone ; if you attempt to restore that finish, you do it conjecturally ; if you copy what is left, granting fidelity to be possible (and what care, or watchfulness, or cost can secure it ?), how is the new work better than the old ? There was yet in the old

some life, some mysterious suggestion of what it had been,
and of what it had lost ; some sweetness in the gentle lines
which rain and sun had wrought. There can be none in the
brute hardness of the new carving. Look at the animals which
I have given in Plate 14, as an instance of living work, and
suppose the markings of the scales and hair once worn away,
or the wrinkles of the brows, and who shall ever restore
them ? The first step to restoration (I have seen it, and that
again and again, seen it on the Baptistery of Pisa, seen it on
the Casa d' Oro at Venice, seen it on the Cathedral of Lisieux),
is to dash the old work to pieces ; the second is usually to
put up the cheapest and basest imitation which can escape detection, but in all cases, however careful, and however labored,
an imitation still, a cold model of such parts as *can* be modelled,
with conjectural supplements ; and my experience has as yet
furnished me with only one instance, that of the Palais de
Justice at Rouen, in which even this, the utmost degree of
fidelity which is possible, has been attained or even attempted.

XIX. Do not let us talk then of restoration. The thing is
a Lie from beginning to end. You may make a model of a
building as you may of a corpse, and your model may have
the shell of the old walls within it as your cast might have the
skeleton, with what advantage I neither see nor care ; but the
old building is destroyed, and that more totally and mercilessly
than if it had sunk into a heap of dust, or melted into a mass
of clay : more has been gleaned out of desolated Nineveh than
ever will be out of re-built Milan. But, it is said, there may
come a necessity for restoration ! Granted. Look the necessity full in the face, and understand it on its own terms. It is
a necessity for destruction. Accept it as such, pull the building down, throw its stones into neglected corners, make ballast
of them, or mortar, if you will ; but do it honestly, and do not
set up a Lie in their place. And look that necessity in the face
before it comes, and you may prevent it. The principle of
modern times (a principle which I believe, at least in France,
to be *systematically acted on by the masons*, in order to find
themselves work, as the abbey of St. Ouen was pulled down by
the magistrates of the town by way of giving work to some

vagrants,) is to neglect buildings first, and restore them afterwards. Take proper care of your monuments, and you will
not need to restore them. A few sheets of lead put in time
upon the roof, a few dead leaves and sticks swept in time out
of a water-course, will · save both roof and walls from ruin.
Watch an old building with an anxious care ; guard it as best
you may, and at *any* cost from every influence of dilapidation.
Count its stones as you would jewels of a crown ; set watches
about it as if at the gates of a besieged city ; bind it together
with iron where it loosens ; stay it with timber where it de-
clines ; do not care about the unsightliness of the aid ; better
a crutch than a lost limb ; and do this tenderly, and reverently,
and continually, and many a generation will still be born and
pass away beneath its shadow. Its evil day must come at last ;
but let it come declaredly and openly, and let no dishonoring
and false substitute deprive it of the funeral offices of memory.

XX. Of more wanton or ignorant ravage it is vain to speak ;
my words will not reach those who commit them, and yet, be
it heard or not, I must not leave the truth unstated, that it is
again no question of expediency or feeling whether we shall
preserve the buildings of past times or not. *We have no right
whatever to touch them.* They are not ours. They belong
partly to those who built them, and partly to all the generations of mankind who are to follow us. The dead have still
their right in them : that which they labored for, the praise of
achievement or the expression of religious feeling, or whatsoever else it might be which in those buildings they intended to
be permanent, we have no right to obliterate. What we have
ourselves built, we are at liberty to throw down ; but what
other men gave their strength, and wealth, and life to accom-
plish, their right over does not pass away with their death ;
still less is the right to the use of what they have left vested
in us only. It belongs to all their successors. It may hereafter be a subject of sorrow, or a cause of injury, to millions, that we have consulted our present convenience by casting down such buildings as we choose to dispense with. That
sorrow, that loss we have no right to inflict. Did the cathedral of Avranches belong to the mob who destroyed it, any

more than it did to us, who walk in sorrow to and fro over its
foundation? Neither does any building whatever belong to
those mobs who do violence to it. For a mob it is, and must
be always; it matters not whether enraged, or in deliberate
folly; whether countless, or sitting in committees; the people
who destroy anything causelessly are a mob, and Architecture
is always destroyed causelessly. A fair building is necessarily
worth the ground it stands upon, and will be so until central
Africa and America shall have become as populous as Middle-
sex; nor is any cause whatever valid as a ground for its destruction. If ever valid, certainly not now when the place
both of the past and future is too much usurped in our minds
by the restless and discontented present. The very quietness
of nature is gradually withdrawn from us; thousands who
once in their necessarily prolonged travel were subjected to
an influence, from the silent sky and slumbering fields, more
effectual than known or confessed, now bear with them even
there the ceaseless fever of their life; and along the iron veins
that traverse the frame of our country, beat and flow the fiery
pulses of its exertions, hotter and faster every hour. All
vitality is concentrated through those throbbing arteries into
the central cities; the country is passed over like a green sea
by narrow bridges, and we are thrown back in continually
closer crowds upon the city gates. The only influence which
can in any wise *there* take the place of that of the woods and
fields, is the power of ancient Architecture. Do not part with
it for the sake of the formal square, or of the fenced and
planted walk, nor of the goodly street nor opened quay. The
pride of a city is not in these. Leave them to the crowd;
but remember that there will surely be some within the circuit of the disquieted walls who would ask for some other
spots than these wherein to walk; for some other forms to
meet their sight familiarly: like him who sat so often where
the sun struck from the west, to watch the lines of the dome
of Florence drawn on the deep sky, or like those, his Hosts,
who could bear daily to behold, from their palace chambers,
the places where their fathers lay at rest, at the meeting of
the dark streets of Verona.

CHAPTER VII.

THE LAMP OF OBEDIENCE.

I. It has been my endeavor to show in the preceding pages how every form of noble architecture is in some sort the embodiment of the Polity, Life, History, and Religious Faith of nations. Once or twice in doing this, I have named a principle to which I would now assign a definite place among those which direct that embodiment ; the last place, not only as that to which its own humility would incline, but rather as belonging to it in the aspect of the crowning grace of all the rest ; that principle, I mean, to which Polity owes its stability, Life its happiness, Faith its acceptance, Creation its continuance,—Obedience.

Nor is it the least among the sources of more serious satisfaction which I have found in the pursuit of a subject that at first appeared to bear but slightly on the grave interests of mankind, that the conditions of material perfection which it leads me in conclusion to consider, furnish a strange proof how false is the conception, how frantic the pursuit, of that treacherous phantom which men call Liberty ; most treacherous, indeed, of all phantoms ; for the feeblest ray of reason might surely show us, that not only its attainment, but its being, was impossible. There is no such thing in the universe. There can never be. The stars have it not ; the earth has it not ; the sea has it not ; and we men have the mockery and semblance of it only for our heaviest punishment.

In one of the noblest poems[17] for its imagery and its music belonging to the recent school of our literature, the writer has sought in the aspect of inanimate nature the expression of that Liberty which, having once loved, he had seen among men in its true dyes of darkness. But with what strange fallacy of interpretation ! since in one noble line of his invocation he has contradicted the assumptions of the rest, and acknowledged the presence of a subjection, surely not less severe because eternal? How could he otherwise? since it

there be any one principle more widely than another confessed by every utterance, or more sternly than another im-
printed on every atom, of the visible creation, that principle is
not Liberty, but Law.

II. The enthusiast would reply that by Liberty he meant
the Law of Liberty. Then why use the single and misunderstood word ? If by liberty you mean chastisement of the pas-
sions, discipline of the intellect, subjection of the will ; if you
mean the fear of inflicting, the shame of committing a wrong ;
if you mean respect for all who are in authority, and consideration for all who are in dependence ; veneration for the
good, mercy to the evil, sympathy with the weak ; if you mean
watchfulness over all thoughts, temperance in all pleasures,
and perseverance in all toils ; if you mean, in a word, that
Service which is defined in the liturgy of the English church
to be perfect Freedom, why do you name this by the same
word by which the luxurious mean license, and the reckless
mean change ; by which the rogue means rapine, and the fool
equality, by which the proud mean anarchy, and the malignant
mean violence ? Call it by any name rather than this, but its
best and truest is, Obedience. Obedience is, indeed, founded
on a kind of freedom, else its would become mere subjugation,
but that freedom is only granted that obedience may be more
perfect ; and thus, while a measure of license is necessary to
exhibit the individual energies of things, the fairness and
pleasantness and perfection of them all consist in their Restraint. Compare a river that has burst its banks with one
that is bound by them, and the clouds that are scattered over
the face of the whole heaven with those that are marshalled
into ranks and orders by its winds. So that though restraint,
utter and unrelaxing, can never be comely, this is not because
it is in itself an evil, but only because, when too great, it over-
powers the nature of the thing restrained, and so counteracts
the other laws of which that nature is itself composed. And
the balance wherein consists the fairness of creation is between the laws of life and being in the things governed and
the laws of general sway to which they are subjected ; and the
suspension or infringement of either kind of law, or, literally

disorder, is equivalent to, and synonymous with, disease, while the increase of both honor and beauty is habitually on the side of restraint (or the action of superior law) rather than of character (or the action of inherent law). The noblest word in the catalogue of social virtue is "Loyalty," and the sweetest which men have learned in the pastures of the wilderness is "Fold."

III. Nor is this all; but we may observe, that exactly in proportion to the majesty of things in the scale of being, is the completeness of their obedience to the laws that are set over them. Gravitation is less quietly, less instantly obeyed by a grain of dust than it is by the sun and moon ; and the ocean falls and flows under influences which the lake and river do not recognize. So also in estimating the dignity of any action or occupation of men, there is perhaps no better test than the question "are its laws strait?" For their severity will probably be commensurate with the greatness of the numbers whose labor it concentrates or whose interest it concerns.

This severity must be singular, therefore, in the case of that art, above all others, whose productions are the most vast and the most common ; which requires for its practice the co-operation of bodies of men, and for its perfection the perseverance of successive generations. And taking into account also what we have before so often observed of Architecture, her continual influence over the emotions of daily life, and her realism, as opposed to the two sister arts which are in comparison but the picturing of stories and of dreams, we might beforehand expect that we should find her healthy state and action dependent on far more severe laws than theirs ; that the license which they extend to the workings of individual mind would be withdrawn by her ; and that, in assertion of the relations which she holds with all that is universally important to man, she would set forth, by her own majestic subjection, some likeness of that on which man's social happiness and power depend. We might, therefore, without the light of experience, conclude, that Architecture never could flourish except when it was subjected to a national law as strict and as minutely authoritative as the laws which regulate religion, policy, and social relations; nay, even more authoritative than these, because both capable of more enforcement, as over more passive matter; and needing more enforcement, as the purest type not of one law nor of another, but of the common authority of all. But in this matter experience speaks more loudly than reason. If there be any one condition which, in watching the progress of architecture, we see distinct and general; if, amidst the counter evidence of success attending opposite accidents of character and circumstance, any one conclusion may be constantly and indisputably drawn, it is this; that the architecture of a nation is great only when it is as universal and as established as its language; and when provincial differences of style are nothing more than so many dialects. Other necessities are matters of doubt: nations have been alike successful in their architecture in times of poverty and of wealth; in times of war and of peace; in times of barbarism and of refinement; under governments the most liberal or the most arbitrary; but this one condition has been constant, this one requirement clear in all places and at all times, that the work shall be that of a *school*, that no individual caprice shall dispense with, or materially vary, accepted types and customary decorations; and that from the cottage to the palace, and from the chapel to the basilica, and from the garden fence to the fortress wall, every member and feature of the architecture of the nation shall be as commonly current, as frankly accepted, as its language or its coin.

IV. A day never passes without our hearing our English architects called upon to be original, and to invent a new style: about as sensible and necessary an exhortation as to ask of a man who has never had rags enough on his back to keep out cold, to invent a new mode of cutting a coat. Give him a whole coat first, and let him concern himself about the fashion of it afterwards. We want no new style of architecture. Who wants a new style of painting or sculpture? But we want *some* style. It is of marvellously little importance, if we have a code of laws and they be good laws, whether they be new or old, foreign or native, Roman or Saxon, or Norman or English laws. But it is of considerable importance that we should have a code of laws of one kind or another, and that code accepted and enforced from one side of the island to another, and not one law made ground of judgment at York and another in Exeter. And in like manner it does not matter one marble splinter whether we have an old or new architecture, but it matters everything whether we have an architecture truly so called or not; that is, whether an architecture whose laws might be taught at our schools from Cornwall to Northumberland, as we teach English spelling and English grammar, or an architecture which is to be invented fresh every time we build a workhouse or a parish school. There seems to me to be a wonderful misunderstanding among the majority of architects at the present day as to the very nature and meaning of Originality, and of all wherein it consists. Originality in expression does not depend on invention of new words; nor originality in poetry on invention of new measures; nor, in painting, on invention of new colors, or new modes of using them. The chords of music, the harmonies of color, the general principles of the arrangement of sculptural masses, have been determined long ago, and, in all probability, cannot be added to any more than they can be altered. Granting that they may be, such additions or alterations are much more the work of time and of multitudes than of individual inventors. We may have one Van Eyck, who will be known as the introducer of a new style once in ten centuries, but he himself will trace his invention to some accidental bye-play or pursuit; and the use of that invention will depend altogether on the popular necessities or instincts of the period. Originality depends on nothing of the kind. A man who has the gift, will take up any style that is going, the style of his day, and will work in that, and be great in that, and make everything that he does in it look as fresh as if every thought of it had just come down from heaven. I do not say that he will not take liberties with his materials, or with his rules : I do not say that strange changes will not sometimes be wrought by his efforts, or his fancies, in both. But those changes will be instructive, natural, facile, though sometimes marvellous; they

will never be sought after as things necessary to his dignity
or to his independence ; and those liberties will be like the
liberties that a great speaker takes with the language, not a
defiance of its rules for the sake of singularity ; but inevitable,
uncalculated, and brilliant consequences of an effort to express
what the language, without such infraction, could not. There
may be times when, as I have above described, the life of an
art is manifested in its changes, and in its refusal of ancient
limitations : so there are in the life of an insect ; and there is
great interest in the state of both the art and the insect at
those periods when, by their natural progress and constitu-
tional power, such changes are about to be wrought. But as
that would be both an uncomfortable and foolish caterpillar
which, instead of being contented with a caterpillar's life and
feeding on caterpillar's food, was always striving to turn itself
into a chrysalis ; and as that would be an unhappy chrysalis
which should lie awake at night and roll restlessly in its
cocoon, in efforts to turn itself prematurely into a moth ; so
will that art be unhappy and unprosperous which, instead of
supporting itself on the food, and contenting itself with the
customs which have been enough for the support and guidance of other arts before it and like it, is struggling and fret-
ting under the natural limitations of its existence, and striving
to become something other than it is. And though it is the
nobility of the highest creatures to look forward to, and partly
to understand the changes which are appointed for them, preparing for them beforehand ; and if, as is usual with *appointed*
changes, they be into a higher state, even desiring them, and
rejoicing in the hope of them, yet it is the strength of every
creature, be it changeful or not, to rest for the time being,
contented with the conditions of its existence, and striving
only to bring about the changes which it desires, by fulfilling
to the uttermost the duties for which its present state is
appointed and continued.

V. Neither originality, therefore, nor change, good though
both may be, and this is commonly a most merciful and enthusiastic supposition with respect to either, are ever to be
sought in themselves, or can ever be healthily obtained by any

struggle or rebellion against common laws. We want neither the one nor the other. The forms of architecture already known are good enough for us, and for far better than any of us : and it will be time enough to think of changing them for better when we can use them as they are. But there are some things which we not only want, but cannot do without ; and which all the struggling and raving in the world, nay more, which all the real talent and resolution in England, will never enable us to do without : and these are Obedience, Unity, Fellowship, and Order. And all our schools of design, and committees of tastes ; all our academies and lectures, and journalisms, and essays ; all the sacrifices which we are beginning to make, all the truth which there is in our English nature, all the power of our English will, and the life of our English intellect, will in this matter be as useless as efforts and emotions in a dream, unless we are contented to submit architecture and all art, like other things, to English law.

VI. I say architecture and all art ; for I believe architecture must be the beginning of arts, and that the others must follow her in their time and order ; and I think the prosperity of our schools of painting and sculpture, in which no one will deny the life, though many the health, depends upon that of our architecture. I think that all will languish until that takes the lead, and (this I do not *think*, but I proclaim, as confidently as I would assert the necessity, for the safety of society, of an understood and strongly administered legal government) our architecture *will* languish, and that in the very dust, until the first principle of common sense be manfully obeyed, and an universal system of form and workmanship be everywhere adopted and enforced. It may be said that this is impossible. It may be so—I fear it is so : I have nothing to do with the possibility or impossibility of it ; I simply know and assert the necessity of it. If it be impossible, English art is impossible. Give it up at once. You are wasting time, and money, and energy upon it, and though you exhaust centuries and treasuries, and break hearts for it, you will never raise it above the merest dilettanteism. Think not of it. It is a dangerous vanity, a mere gulph in which genius after genius will be swallowed up, and it will not close. And so it will continue to be, unless the one bold and broad step be taken at the beginning. We shall not manufacture art out of pottery and printed stuffs ; we shall not reason out art by our philosophy ; we shall not stumble upon art by our experiments, not create it by our fancies : I do not say that we can even build it out of brick and stone ; but there is a chance for us in these, and there is none else ; and that chance rests on the bare possibility of obtaining the consent, both of architects and of the public, to choose a style, and to use it universally.

VII. How surely its principles ought at first to be limited, we may easily determine by the consideration of the necessary modes of teaching any other branch of general knowledge. When we begin to teach children writing, we force them to absolute copyism, and require absolute accuracy in the formation of the letters ; as they obtain command of the received modes of literal expression, we cannot prevent their falling into such variations as are consistent with their feeling, their circumstances, or their characters. So, when a boy is first taught to write Latin, an authority is required of him for every expression he uses ; as he becomes master of the language he may take a license, and feel his right to do so without any authority, and yet write better Latin than when he borrowed every separate expression. In the same way our architects would have to be taught to write the accepted style. We must first determine what buildings are to be considered Augustan in their authority ; their modes of construction and laws of proportion are to be studied with the most penetrating care ; then the different forms and uses of their decorations are to be classed and catalogued, as a German grammarian classes the powers of prepositions ; and under this absolute, irrefragable authority, we are to begin to work ; admitting not so much as an alteration in the depth of a cavetto, or the breadth of a fillet. Then, when our sight is once accustomed to the grammatical forms and arrangements, and our thoughts familiar with the expression of them all ; when we can speak this dead language naturally, and apply it to whatever ideas we have to render, that is to say, to every practical purpose of life ; then, and not till then, a license might be permitted ; and individual authority allowed to change or to add to the received forms, always within certain limits ; the decorations, especially, might be made subjects of variable fancy, and enriched with ideas either original or taken from other schools.   And thus in process of time and by a great national movement, it might come to pass, that a new style should arise, as language itself changes ; we might perhaps come to speak Italian instead of Latin, or to speak modern instead of old English ; but this would be a matter of entire indifference, and a matter, besides, which no determination or desire could either hasten or prevent.   That alone which it is in our power to obtain, and which it is our duty to desire, is an unanimous style of some kind, and such comprehension and practice of it as would enable us to adapt its features to the peculiar character of every several building, large or small, domestic, civil, or ecclesiastical.   I have said that it was immaterial what style was adopted, so far as regards the room for originality which its developement would admit : it is not so, however, when we take into consideration the far more important questions of the facility of adaptation to general purposes, and of the sympathy with which this or that style would be popularly regarded.   The choice of Classical or Gothic, again using the latter term in its broadest sense, may be questionable when it regards some single and considerable public building ; but I cannot conceive it questionable, for an instant, when it regards modern uses in general : I cannot conceive any architect insane enough to project the vulgarization of Greek architecture.   Neither can it be rationally questionable whether we should adopt early or late, original or derivative Gothic : if the latter were chosen, it must be either some impotent and ugly degradation, like our own Tudor, or else a style whose grammatical laws it would be nearly impossible to limit or arrange, like the French Flamboyant.   We are equally precluded from adopting styles essentially infantine or barbarous, however Herculean their infancy, or majestic their outlawry, such as our own Norman, or the Lombard Romanesque. The choice would lie I think between four styles :—1. The Pisan Romanesque ; 2. The early Gothic of the Western Italian Republics, advanced as far and as fast as our art would enable us to the Gothic of Giotto ; 3. The Venetian Gothic in its purest developement ; 4. The English earliest decorated. The most natural, perhaps the safest choice, would be of the last, well fenced from chance of again stiffening into the perpendicular ; and perhaps enriched by some mingling of decorative elements from the exquisite decorated Gothic of France, of which, in such cases, it would be needful to accept some well known examples, as the North door of Rouen and the church of St. Urbain at Troyes, for final and limiting authorities on the side of decoration.

VIII. It is almost impossible for us to conceive, in our present state of doubt and ignorance, the sudden dawn of intelligence and fancy, the rapidly increasing sense of power and facility, and, in its *proper sense*, of Freedom, which such wholesome restraint would instantly cause throughout the whole circle of the arts. Freed from the agitation and embarrassment of that liberty of choice which is the cause of half the discomforts of the world ; freed from the accompanying necessity of studying all past, present, or even possible styles ; and enabled, by concentration of individual, and co-operation of multitudinous energy, to penetrate into the uttermost secrets of the adopted style, the architect would find his whole understanding enlarged, his practical knowledge certain and ready to hand, and his imagination playful and vigorous, as a child's would be within a walled garden, who would sit down and shudder if he were left free in a fenceless plain. How many and how bright would be the results in every direction of interest, not to the arts merely, but to national happiness and virtue, it would be as difficult to preconceive as it would seem extravagant to state : but the first, perhaps the least, of them would be an increased sense of fellowship among ourselves, a cementing of every patriotic bond of union, a proud and happy recognition of our affection for and sympathy with each other, and our willingness in all things to submit ourselves to every law that would advance the interest of the community ; a barrier, also, the best conceivable, to the unhappy rivalry of the upper and middle classes, in houses, furniture, and establishments ; and even a check to much of what is as vain as it is painful in the oppositions of religious parties respecting matters of ritual.   These, I say, would be the first consequences.   Economy increased tenfold, as it would be by the simplicity of practice; domestic comforts uninterfered with by the caprice and mistakes of architects ignorant of the capacities of the styles they use, and all the symmetry and sightliness of our harmonized streets and public buildings, are things of slighter account in the catalogue of benefits. But it would be mere enthusiasm to endeavor to trace them farther.   I have suffered myself too long to indulge in the speculative statement of requirements which perhaps we have more immediate and more serious work than to supply, and of feelings which it may be only contingently in our power to recover.   I should be unjustly thought unaware of the difficulty of what I have proposed, or of the unimportance of the whole subject as compared with many which are brought home to our interests and fixed upon our consideration by the wild course of the present century.   But of difficulty and of importance it is for others to judge.   I have limited myself to the simple statement of what, if we desire to have architecture, we MUST primarily endeavor to feel and do : but then it may not be desirable for us to have architecture at all.   There are many who feel it to be so ; many who sacrifice much to that end ; and I am sorry to see their energies wasted and their lives disquieted in vain.   I have stated, therefore, the only ways in which that end is attainable, without venturing even to express an opinion as to its real desirableness.   I have an opinion, and the zeal with which I have spoken may sometimes have betrayed it, but I hold to it with no confidence.   I know too well the undue importance which the study that every man follows must assume in his own eyes, to trust my own impressions of the dignity of that of Architecture ; and yet I think I cannot be utterly mistaken in regarding it as at least useful in the sense of a National employment.   I am confirmed in this impression by what I see passing among the states of Europe at this instant. All the horror, distress, and tumult which oppress the foreign nations, are traceable, among the other secondary causes through which God is working out His will upon them, to the simple one of their not having enough to do. I am not blind to the distress among their operatives ; nor do I deny the nearer and visibly active causes of the movement : the recklessness of villany in the leaders of revolt, the absence of common moral principle in the upper classes, and of common courage and honesty in the heads of governments. But these causes themselves are ultimately traceable to a deeper and simpler one : the recklessness of the demagogue, the immorality of the middle class, and the effeminacy and treachery of the noble, are traceable in all these nations to the commonest and most fruitful cause of calamity in households—idleness. We think too much in our benevolent efforts, more multiplied and more vain day by day, of bettering men by giving them advice and instruction. There are few who will take either : the chief thing they need is occupation. I do not mean work in the sense of bread,—I mean work in the sense of mental interest ; for those who either are placed above the necessity of labor for their bread, or who will not work although they should. There is a vast quantity of idle energy among European nations at this time, which ought to go into handicrafts ; there are multitudes of idle semi-gentlemen who ought to be shoemakers and carpenters ; but since they will not be these so long as they can help it, the business of the philanthropist is to find them some other employment than disturbing governments. It is of no use to tell them they are fools, and that they will only make themselves miserable in the end as well as others : if they have nothing else to do, they will do mischief ; and the man who will not work, and who has no means of intellectual pleasure, is as sure to become an instrument of evil as if he had sold himself bodily to Satan. I have myself seen enough of the daily life of the young educated men of France and Italy, to account for, as it deserves, the deepest national suffering and degradation ; and though, for the most part, our commerce

and our natural habits of industry preserve us from a similar paralysis, yet it would be wise to consider whether the
forms of employment which we chiefly adopt or promote, are
as well calculated as they might be to improve and elevate
us.

We have just spent, for instance, a hundred and fifty millions, with which we have paid men for digging ground from
one place and depositing it in another. We have formed a
large class of men, the railway navvies, especially reckless, unmanageable, and dangerous. We have maintained besides
(let us state the benefits as fairly as possible) a number of iron
founders in an unhealthy and painful employment ; we have
developed (this is at least good) a very large amount of mechanical ingenuity ; and we have, in fine, attained the power
of going fast from one place to another. Meantime we have
had no mental interest or concern ourselves in the operations
we have set on foot, but have been left to the usual vanities
and cares of our existence. Suppose, on the other hand, that
we had employed the same sums in building beautiful houses
and churches. We should have maintained the same number
of men, not in driving wheelbarrows, but in a distinctly technical, if not intellectual, employment, and those who were
more intelligent among them would have been especially
happy in that employment, as having room in it for the developement of their fancy, and being directed by it to that observation of beauty which, associated with the pursuit of natural science, at present forms the enjoyment of many of the
more intelligent manufacturing operatives. Of mechanical ingenuity, there is, I imagine, at least as much required to build
a cathedral as to cut a tunnel or contrive a locomotive : we
should, therefore, have developed as much science, while the
artistical element of intellect would have been added to the
gain. Meantime we should ourselves have been made happier
and wiser by the interest we should have taken in the work
with which we were personally concerned ; and when all was
done, instead of the very doubtful advantage of the power of
going fast from place to place, we should have had the certain
advantage of increased pleasure in stopping at home.

IX. There are many other less capacious, but more constant, channels of expenditure, quite as disputable in their
beneficial tendency ; and we are, perhaps, hardly enough in
the habit of inquiring, with respect to any particular form of
luxury or any customary appliance of life, whether the kind
of employment it gives to the operative or the dependant be
as healthy and fitting an employment as we might otherwise
provide for him. It is not enough to find men absolute sub-
sistence ; we should think of the manner of life which our
demands necessitate ; and endeavor, as far as may be, to
make all our needs such as may, in the supply of them, raise,
as well as feed, the poor. It is far better to give work which
is above the men, than to educate the men to be above their
work. It may be doubted, for instance, whether the habits
of luxury, which necessitate a large train of men servants, be
a wholesome form of expenditure ; and more, whether the
pursuits which have a tendency to enlarge the class of the
jockey and the groom be a philanthropic form of mental occupation. So again, consider the large number of men whose
lives are employed by civilized nations in cutting facets upon
jewels. There is much dexterity of hand, patience, and ingenuity thus bestowed, which are simply burned out in the blaze
of the tiara, without, so far as I see, bestowing any pleasure
upon those who wear or who behold, at all compensatory for
the loss of life and mental power which are involved in the
employment of the workman. He would be far more healthily
and happily sustained by being set to carve stone ; certain
qualities of his mind, for which there is no room in his present
occupation, would develope themselves in the nobler ; and I
believe that most women would, in the end, prefer the pleasure of having built a church, or contributed to the adornment
of a cathedral, to the pride of bearing a certain quantity of
adamant on their foreheads.

X. I could pursue this subject willingly, but I have some
strange notions about it which it is perhaps wiser not loosely
to set down. I content myself with finally reasserting, what
has been throughout the burden of the preceding pages, that
whatever rank, or whatever importance, may be attributed or

attached to their immediate subject, there is at least some value in the analogies with which its pursuit has presented us, and some instruction in the frequent reference of its commonest necessities to the mighty laws, in the sense and scope of which all men are Builders, whom every hour sees laying the stubble or the stone.

I have paused, not once nor twice, as I wrote, and often have checked the course of what might otherwise have been importunate persuasion, as the thought has crossed me, how soon all Architecture may be vain, except that which is not made with hands. There is something ominous in the light which has enabled us to look back with disdain upon the ages among whose lovely vestiges we have been wandering. I could smile when I hear the hopeful exultation of many, at the new reach of worldly science, and vigor of worldly effort ; as if we were again at the beginning of days. There is thunder on the horizon as well as dawn. The sun was risen upon the earth when Lot entered into Zoar.

NOTES.

NOTE 1.

Page 21.

" *With the idolatrous Egyptian.*"

THE probability is indeed slight in comparison, but it *is* a probability nevertheless, and one which is daily on the increase. I trust that I may not be thought to underrate the danger of such sympathy, though I speak lightly of the chance of it. I have confidence in the central religious body of the English and Scottish people, as being not only untainted with Romanism, but immoveably adverse to it: and, however strangely and swiftly the heresy of the Protestant and victory of the Papist may seem to be extending among us, I feel assured that there are barriers in the living faith of this nation which neither can overpass. Yet this confidence is only in the ultimate faithfulness of a few, not in the security of the nation from the sin and the punishment of partial apostasy. Both have, indeed, in some sort, been committed and suffered already ; and, in expressing my belief of the close connection of the distress and burden which the mass of the people at present sustain, with the encouragement which, in various directions, has been given to the Papist, do not let me be called superstitious or irrational. No man was ever more inclined than I, both by natural disposition and by many ties of early association, to a sympathy with the principles and forms of the Romanist Church ; and there is much in its discipline which conscientiously, as well as sympathetically, I could love and advocate. But, in confessing this strength of affectionate prejudice, surely I vindicate more respect for my firmly expressed belief, that the entire doctrine and system of that Church is in the fullest sense anti-Christian ; that its lying and idolatrous Power is the darkest plague that ever held commission to hurt the Earth ; that all those yearnings for unity and fellowship, and common obedience, which have been the root of our late heresies, are as false in their grounds as fatal in their termination ; that we never can have the remotest fellowship with the utterers of that fearful Falsehood, and live ; that we have nothing to look to from them but treacherous hostility ; and that, exactly in proportion to the sternness of our separation from them, will be not only the spiritual but the temporal blessings granted by God to this country. How close has been the correspondence hitherto between the degree of resistance to Romanism marked in our national acts, and the honor with which those acts have been crowned, has been sufficiently proved in a short essay by a writer whose investigations into the influence of Religion upon the fate of Nations have been singularly earnest and successful—a writer with whom I faithfully and firmly believe that England will never be prosperous again, and that the honor of her arms will be tarnished, and her commerce blighted, and her national character degraded, until the Romanist is expelled from the place which has impiously been conceded to him among her legislators. "Whatever be the lot of those to whom error is an inheritance, woe be to the man and the people to whom it is an adoption. If England, free above all other nations, sustained amidst the trials which have covered Europe, before her eyes, with burning and slaughter, and enlightened by the fullest knowledge of divine truth, shall refuse fidelity to the compact by which those matchless privileges have been given, her condemnation will not linger. She has already made one step full of danger. She has committed the capital error of mistaking that for a purely political question which was a purely religious one. Her foot already hangs over the edge of the precipice. It must be retracted, or the empire is but a name. In the clouds and darkness which seem to be deepening on all human policy—in the gathering tumults of Europe, and the feverish discontents at home—it may be even difficult to discern where the power yet lives to erect the fallen majesty of the constitution once more. But there are mighty means in sincerity ; and if no miracle was ever wrought for the faithless and despairing, the country that will help itself will never be left destitute of the help of Heaven " (Historical Essays, by the Rev. Dr. Croly, 1842). The first of these essays, "England the Fortress of Christianity," I most earnestly recommend to the meditation of those who doubt that a special punishment is inflicted by the Deity upon all national crime, and perhaps, of all such crime most instantly upon the betrayal on the part of England of the truth and faith with which she has been entrusted.

NOTE II.

Page 25.

" Not the gift, but the giving."

MUCH attention has lately been directed to the subject of religious art, and we are now in possession of all kinds of interpretations and classifications of it, and of the leading facts of its history. But the greatest question of all connected with it remains entirely unanswered,

What good did it do to real religion ? There is no subject into which I should so much rejoice to see a serious and conscientious inquiry instituted as this ; an inquiry neither undertaken in artistical enthusiasm nor in monkish sympathy, but dogged, merciless and fearless. I love the religious art of Italy as well as most men, but there is a wide difference between loving it as a manifestation of individual feeling, and looking to it as an instrument of popular benefit. I have not knowledge enough to form even the shadow of an opinion on this latter point, and I should be most grateful to any one who would put it in my power to do so. There are, as it seems to me, three distinct questions to be considered : the first, What has been the effect of external splendor on the genuineness and earnestness of Christian worship ? the second, What the use of pictorial or sculptural representation in the communication of Christian historical knowledge, or excitement of affectionate imagination ? the third, What the influence of the practice of religious art on the life of the artist ?

In answering these inquiries, we should have to consider separately every collateral influence and circumstance ; and, by a most subtle analysis, to eliminate the real effect of art from the effects of the abuses with which it was associated. This could be done only by a Christian ; not a man who would fall in love with a sweet color or sweet expression, but who would look for true faith and consistent life as the object of all. It never has been done yet, and the question remains a subject of vain and endless contention between parties of opposite prejudices and temperaments.

Note III.

Page 26.

" To the concealment of what is really good or great."

I HAVE often been surprised at the supposition that Romanism, in its present condition, could either patronise art or profit by it. The noble painted windows of St. Maclou at Rouen, and many other churches in France, are entirely blocked up behind the altars by the erection of huge gilded wooden sunbeams, with interspersed cherubs.

Note IV.

Page 33.

" With different pattern of traceries in each."

I HAVE certainly not examined the seven hundred and four traceries (four to each niche) so as to be sure that none are alike ; but they have the aspect of continual variation, and even the roses of the pendants of the small groined niche roofs are all of different patterns.

Note V.

Page 43.

" Its flamboyant traceries of the last and most degraded forms."

THEY are noticed by Mr. Whewell as forming the figure of the fleur-de lis, always a mark, when in tracery bars, of the most debased flamboyant. It occurs in the central tower of Bayeux, very richly in the buttresses of St. Gervais at Falaise, and in the small niches of some of the domestic buildings at Rouen. Nor is it only the tower of St. Ouen which is overrated. Its nave is a base imitation, in the flamboyant period, of an early Gothic arrangement; the niches on its piers are barbarisms; there is a huge square shaft run through the ceiling of the aisles to support the nave piers, the ugliest excrescence I ever saw on a Gothic building; the traceries of the nave are the most insipid and faded flamboyant; those of the transept clerestory present a singularly distorted condition of perpendicular; even the elaborate door of the south transept is, for its fine period, extravagant and almost grotesque in its foliation and pendants. There is nothing truly fine in the church but the choir, the light triforium, and tall clerestory, the circle of Eastern chapels, the details of sculpture, and the general lightness of proportion; these merits being seen to the utmost advantage by the freedom of the body of the church from all incumbrance.

Note VI.

Page 43.

COMPARE Iliad Σ. l. 219 with Odyssey Ω. l. 5—10.

Note VII.

Page 44.

" Does not admit iron as a constructive material."

EXCEPT in Chaucer's noble temple of Mars.

> " And dounward from an hill under a bent,
> Ther stood the temple of Mars, armipotent,
> Wrought all of burned stele, of which th' entree
> Was longe and streite, and gastly for to see.
> And thereout came a rage and swiche a vise,
> That it made all the gates for to rise.
> The northern light in at the dore shone,
> For window on the wall ne was ther none,
> Thurgh which men mighten any light discerne
> The dore was all of athamant eterne,

Yclenched overthwart and ende long
With yren tough, and for to make it strong,
Every piler the temple to sustene
Was tonne-gret, of yren bright and shene."

The Knighte's Tale.

There is, by the bye, an exquisite piece of architectural *color* just before:

" And northward, in a turret on the wall
  Of alabaster white, and red corall,
  An oratorie riche for to see,
  In worship of Diane of Chastitee."

NOTE VIII.

Page 44.

" *The Builders of Salisbury.*"

" THIS way of tying walls together with iron, instead of making them
of that substance and form, that they shall naturally poise themselves
upon their buttment, is against the rules of good architecture, not only
because iron is corruptible by rust, but because it is fallacious, having
unequal veins in the metal, some places of the same bar being three
times stronger than others, and yet all sound to appearance." Survey
of Salisbury Cathedral in 1668, by Sir C. Wren. For my own part, I
think it better work to bind a tower with iron, than to support a false
dome by a brick pyramid.

NOTE IX.

Page 60.

PLATE III.

IN this plate, figures 4, 5, and 6, are glazed windows, but fig. 2 is the
open light of a belfry tower, and figures 1 and 3 are in triforia, the latter also occurring filled, on the central tower of Coutances.

NOTE X.

Page 94.

" *Ornaments of the transept towers of Rouen.*"

THE reader cannot but observe agreeableness, as a mere arrangement of
shade, which especially belongs to the " sacred trefoil." I do not think
that the element of foliation has been enough insisted upon in its inti-
mate relations with the power of Gothic work. If I were asked what

was the most distinctive feature of its perfect style, I should say the Trefoil. It is the very soul of it ; and I think the loveliest Gothic is always formed upon simple and bold tracings of it, taking place between the blank lancet arch on the one hand, and the overcharged cinque-foiled arch on the other.

NOTE XI.

Page 95.

" *And levelled cusps of stone.*"

THE plate represents one of the lateral windows of the third story of the Palazzo Foscari. It was drawn from the opposite side of the Grand Canal, and the lines of its traceries are therefore given as they appear in somewhat distant effect. It shows only segments of the characteristic quatrefoils of the central windows. I found by measurement their construction exceedingly simple. Four circles are drawn in contact within the large circle. Two tangential lines are then drawn to each opposite pair, enclosing the four circles in a hollow cross. An inner circle struck through the intersections of the circles by the tangents, truncates the cusps.

NOTE XII.

Page 124.

" *Into vertical equal parts.*"

NOT absolutely so. There are variations partly accidental (or at least compelled by the architect's effort to recover the vertical), between the sides of the stories ; and the upper and lower story are taller than the rest. There is, however, an apparent equality between five out of the eight tiers.

NOTE XIII.

Page 133.

" *Never paint a column with vertical lines.*"

IT should be observed, however, that any pattern which gives opponent lines in its parts, may be arranged on lines parallel with the main structure. Thus, rows of diamonds, like spots on a snake's back, or the bones on a sturgeon, are exquisitely applied both to vertical and spiral columns. The loveliest instances of such decoration that I know, are the pillars of the cloister of St. John Lateran, lately illustrated by Mr. Digby Wyatt, in his most valuable and faithful work on antique mosaic.

NOTE XIV.

Page 139.

ON the cover of this volume the reader will find some figure outlines of the same period and character, from the floor of San Miniato at Florence. I have to thank its designer, Mr. W. Harry Rogers, for his intelligent arrangement of them, and graceful adaptation of the connecting arabesque. (Stamp on cloth cover of *London* edition.)

NOTE XV.

Page 169.

" The flowers lost their light, the river its music."

YET not all their light, nor all their music. Compare Modern Painters, vol. ii. sec. 1. chap. iv. § 8.

NOTE XVI.

Page 181.

" By the artists of the time of Pericles."

THIS subordination was first remarked to me by a friend, whose profound knowledge of Greek art will not, I trust, be reserved always for the advantage of his friends only : Mr. C. Newton, of the British Museum.

NOTE XVII.

Page 188.

" In one of the noblest poems."

COLERIDGE'S Ode to France :

> " Ye Clouds ! that far above me float and pause,
>   Whose pathless march no mortal may control !
>   Ye Ocean-Waves ! that wheresoe'er ye roll,
> Yield homage only to eternal laws !
> Ye Woods ! that listen to the night-birds singing,
>   Midway the smooth and perilous slope reclined,
> Save when your own imperious branches swinging,
>   Have made a solemn music of the wind !
> Where, like a man beloved of God,
> Through glooms, which never woodman trod,
>   How oft, pursuing fancies holy,
> My moonlight way o'er flowering weeds I wound,
>   Inspired, beyond the guess of folly,

By each rude shape and wild unconquerable sound!
O ye loud Waves! and O ye Forests high!
   And O ye Clouds that far above me soared!
Thou rising Sun! thou blue rejoicing Sky!
   Yea, everything that is and will be free!
   Bear witness for me, wheresoe'er ye be,
   With what deep worship I have still adored
     The spirit of divinest Liberty."

Noble verse, but erring thought : contrast George Herbert :—

" Slight those who say amidst their sickly healths,
   Thou livest by rule.   What doth not so but man
   Houses are built by rule and Commonwealths.
   Entice the trusty sun, if that you can,
   From his ecliptic line ; beckon the sky.
   Who lives by rule then, keeps good company.

" Who keeps no guard upon himself is slack,
   And rots to nothing at the next great thaw ;
   Man is a shop of rules : a well-truss'd pack
   Whose every parcel underwrites a law.
   Lose not thyself, nor give thy humors way ;
   God gave them to thee under lock and key.